THUTMOSE III AND HATSHEPSUT
PHARAOHS OF EGYPT

THUTMOSE III AND HATSHEPSUT

PHARAOHS OF EGYPT

THEIR LIVES AND AFTERLIVES

AIDAN DODSON

The American University in Cairo Press
Cairo New York

First published in 2025 by
The American University in Cairo Press
113 Sharia Kasr el Aini, Cairo, Egypt
420 Lexington Avenue, Suite 1644, New York, NY 10170
www.aucpress.com

ISBN 978 1 649 03159 4

Library of Congress Cataloging-in-Publication Data

Names: Dodson, Aidan, 1962, author.
Title: Thutmose III & Hatshepsut, pharaohs of Egypt: their lives and afterlives / Aidan Dodson.
Identifiers: LCCN 2024020271 | ISBN 9781649031594 (hardback) | ISBN 9781649031600 (pdf)
Subjects: LCSH: Thutmose III, King of Egypt. | Hatshepsut, King of Egypt. | Egypt--Kings and rulers--Biography. | Egypt--History--Eighteenth dynasty, ca. 1570-1320 B.C.
Classification: LCC DT87.2 .D63 2025 | DDC 932/.014--dc23/eng/20240531

1 2 3 4 5 29 28 27 26 25

Designed by Sally Boylan

To the memory of
Martin Rodney Davies
(1935–2023)
‘nḫ rn.f ḏt ḥn‘ nḥḥ

Contents

Preface

Thutmose III and Hatshepsut are generally held to be two of Egypt's greatest rulers, and are among the best-known figures in ancient Egyptian history. Their recorded exploits and perceived modes of interaction have provided a fertile basis for modern researchers and writers, especially in light of Hatshepsut's status as one of the handful of female pharaohs. This latter aspect has regularly led to "gendered" assessments of her role, through either modern feminist interpretations or older gender stereotyping which placed Hatshepsut at the head of a "peace" party, and Thutmose at the head of one of "war."

Hatshepsut is often paired with Cleopatra VII as a female ruler of Egypt. However, the latter never took full pharaonic titles, although on occasion affecting a Horus name. In contrast, Hatshepsut was a fully fledged pharaoh, with a full five-fold titulary. As such, she was one of the only four securely attested female kings of Egypt, the others being Sobekneferu of the Twelfth Dynasty, Neferneferuaten of the Amarna Period of the Eighteenth Dynasty, and Tawosret of the end of the Nineteenth Dynasty.

Thutmose III and Hatshepsut also provide one of the very few undoubted examples in Egyptian history of two co-equal rulers acting together. Although many examples of such coregencies have been posited by Egyptologists, and often accepted as "facts" in reconstructions of Egyptian history, in reality the vast majority are based on nothing more than circumstantial evidence, often in support of a broader historical/chronological thesis. The case of Thutmose III and Hatshepsut is one of that few where we have two kings unequivocally shown acting together on monuments and sharing a dating system. As such their example provides an important lens for exploring alleged partnerships.

More broadly, the period during which Thutmose III and Hatshepsut ruled Egypt marked in many ways the point at which many features that typified the New Kingdom were baselined. Examples of this can be seen in the iconography of kingship, especially that of the warrior-pharaoh, and also in the funerary monuments of Thutmose III and Hatshepsut. These provided the prototypes of both form and decoration of royal tombs and memorial temples for the coming centuries.

Following the pattern established by previous volumes in this series, the objective of this book is to set the lives of Thutmose III and Hatshepsut in their historical and historiographical context—both ancient and modern. In doing so, it will trace what we know about their careers and the ways in which they were perceived by their own posterity, and investigate their memorial temples and tombs. Finally, it will explore how they were rediscovered and variously interpreted by modern scholarship and the wider audience. It may be noted that the period is being viewed from the perspective of another protagonist—Hatshepsut's close associate, Senenmut—in another volume in this Lives and Afterlives series, by Dr. Campbell Price.

As is always the case when writing the history of "early-literate" civilizations such as Egypt, while the broad picture may seem reasonably clear, many details can often be no more than "working hypotheses." These may be based on the most skeletal of data, meaning that there is frequently scope for radical revision should additional material become available—or where old material is subjected to reinterpretation. The posthumous fate of Hatshepsut has been subject to such revisions during the past century, and there remains scope for more. Thus, I will, as always, attempt to tease out the raw data, and highlight instances where alternative views exist.

As always in ventures such as this, I am indebted in various ways to friends and colleagues, especially for the provision of images and information, including Rachel Barclay, Dylan Bickerstaffe, Lesley Hammam, Salima Ikram, Jadwiga Iwaszczuk, Piers Litherland, Maiken Mosleth King, Adam Lowe, Gary Parks, Bill Petty, Campbell Price, Heike Schmidt, and the late Stephanie Roberts. For proofreading, I must thank Alison Ball, Victoria Baylis-Jones, Gemma Burgham, Vanessa Foott, Anne Hilton, Cindie Lovelace, Sid and Mary Kitchel, and of course my wife Dyan, who also provided a number of excellent photographs. I am also extremely grateful to my manuscript's academic reviewers for their highly useful corrections and comments. Any residual errors or infelicities remain my responsibility.

I dedicate this book to the memory of my dear friend Martin Davies, who died full of years while it was being written. Martin was a fine photographer, and like many of my books this one includes fruits of his lens—in particular, images taken in the tomb of Thutmose III long before the days of Perspex panels and fluorescent lamps.

Abbreviations and Conventions

Berlin	Ägyptisches Museum und Papyrussammlung, Berlin, Germany
BM	British Museum, London, UK
Bologna	Museo Civico Archeologico, Bologna, Italy
Bournemouth	Bournemouth Natural Science Society, Bournemouth, UK
Cairo	Egyptian/Grand Egyptian Museum, Cairo, Egypt
Dundee	The McManus: Dundee's Art Gallery and Museum, UK
Durham	Oriental Museum, University of Durham, UK
EES	Egypt Exploration Society
EK	El-Kab tomb number
Fitzwilliam	Fitzwilliam Museum, Cambridge, UK
Florence	Museo Archeologico Nazionale di Firenze, Florence, Italy
Khartoum	Sudan National Museum, Khartoum, Sudan
KV	Kings Valley tomb number
Louvre	Musée du Louvre, Paris, France
MFA	Museum of Fine Arts, Boston, USA
MMA	Metropolitan Museum of Art, New York, USA
NMEC	National Museum of Egyptian Civilization, Cairo-Fustat, Egypt
RMO	Rijksmuseum van Oudheden, Leiden, Netherlands
ROM	Royal Ontario Museum, Toronto, Canada
TT	Theban Tomb number
Vatican	Museo Gregoriano Egiziano, Vatican City
Vienna	Kunsthistorisches Museum, Vienna, Austria
*	biography of individual available in Bierbrier 2019

Ancient Egyptian dates are given in terms of the king's regnal year, and the months and days of the three Egyptian seasons (*3ḫt, prt,* and *šmw*). So "Year 23, IV *prt* 5" means "23rd regnal year, 4th month of the *prt*-season, day 5."

Introduction

The beginning of the sixteenth century BC found the northern portion of Egypt ruled by kings of Palestinian origin—the "Hyksos" Fifteenth Dynasty—with a rump native regime in the south (Sixteenth/Seventeenth Dynasties). The latter was threatened not only by their northern neighbors, but also from the south, by the rulers of Nubia. Both antagonists would invade the remaining Egyptian-held territory at least once during this period. However, by the first decades of the following century, Egypt had converted almost the whole of Nubia into an Egyptian province, and her armies were operating in northern Syria, ranging as far as the upper reaches of the great river Euphrates.

This transformation had been the work of a series of kings ruling from Thebes (Luxor), scions of the Sixteenth/Seventeenth Dynasty line who had maintained Egyptian rule in the area in the face of threats from both north and south. While a significant number of monuments of these kings survive (fig. 1 left), the succession only becomes fully clear toward the end of the dynasty, starting from a King Senakhtenre Ahmose (the Elder)[1] (fig. 1 right). His successor was Seqenenre Taa, depicted by later tradition as initiating hostilities against the Hyksos, and who certainly died by violence (fig. 1 bottom).[2]

Three stelae from the reign of the next king, Wadjkheperre Kamose, record the next phase of the conflict (fig. 2).[3] These relate that, in his Year 3, Kamose decided to resume hostilities against the Hyksos, which seem to have been discontinued following the death of Taa. By then, the Thebans were in control of the section of Egypt between Ashmunein in Middle Egypt and Aswan. While Kamose's army was pushing further north to the area of Sheikh Fadl, some eighty kilometers south of the Fayyum, a Hyksos messenger was captured. He was carrying a letter from the Fifteenth Dynasty King Apepy to the king of Nubia, which called upon the latter to come to Apepy's aid by attacking the Egyptians from the south while their main forces were engaged in the Delta. It is evident that Kamose had not previously feared assault from the direction of Nubia but, thus warned, he was able to take steps to protect himself against such an eventuality. Indeed, there is evidence to suggest that, as part of his response, Kamose launched a southern offensive, conceivably as far as Buhen.

It appears that Kamose died before the next northern campaigning season and, owing to the youth of the new king, Nebpehtyre Ahmose I, no further progress seems to have been made toward the expulsion of the Hyksos for the subsequent decade. Ultimately,

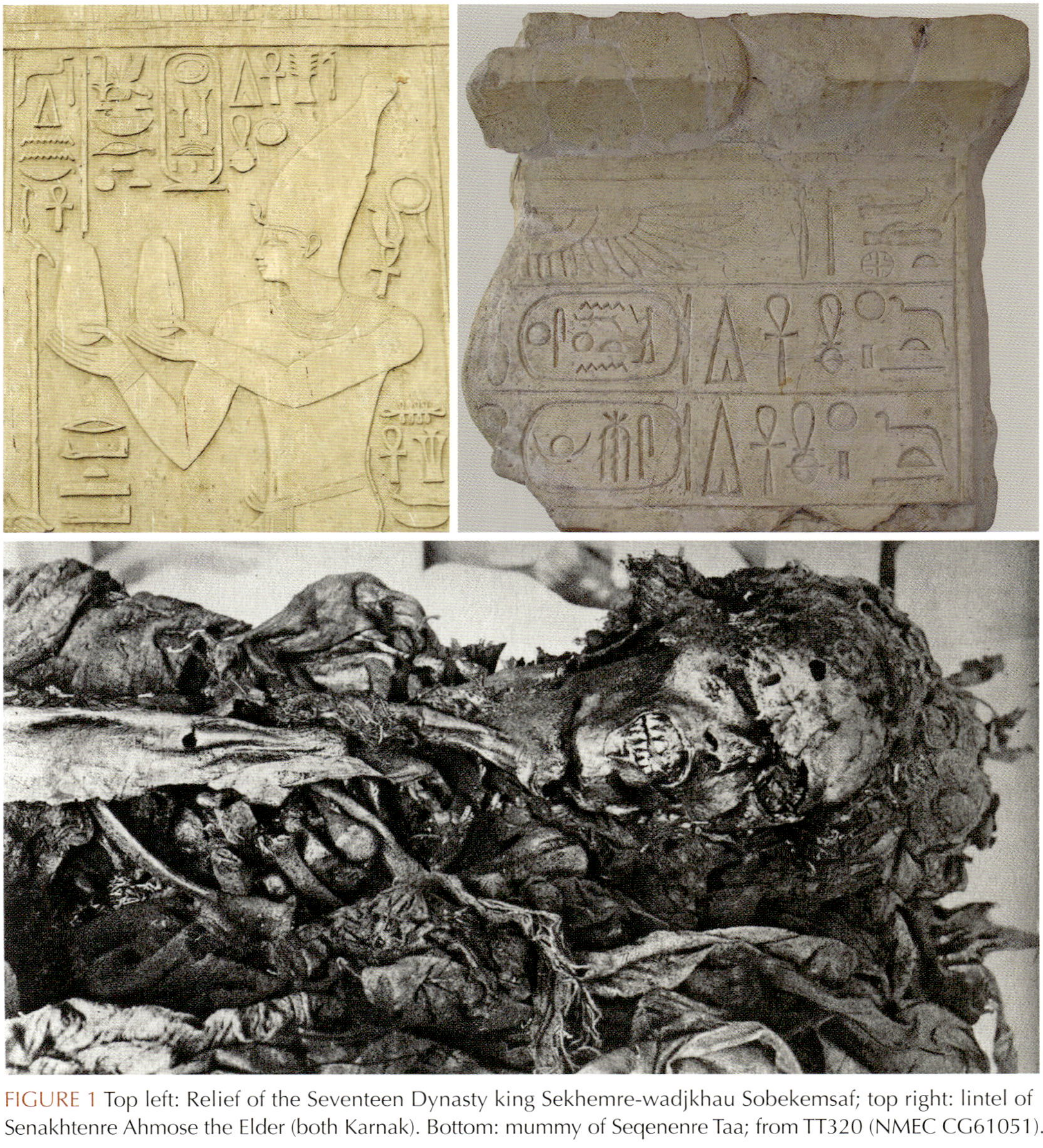

FIGURE 1 Top left: Relief of the Seventeen Dynasty king Sekhemre-wadjkhau Sobekemsaf; top right: lintel of Senakhtenre Ahmose the Elder (both Karnak). Bottom: mummy of Seqenenre Taa; from TT320 (NMEC CG61051).

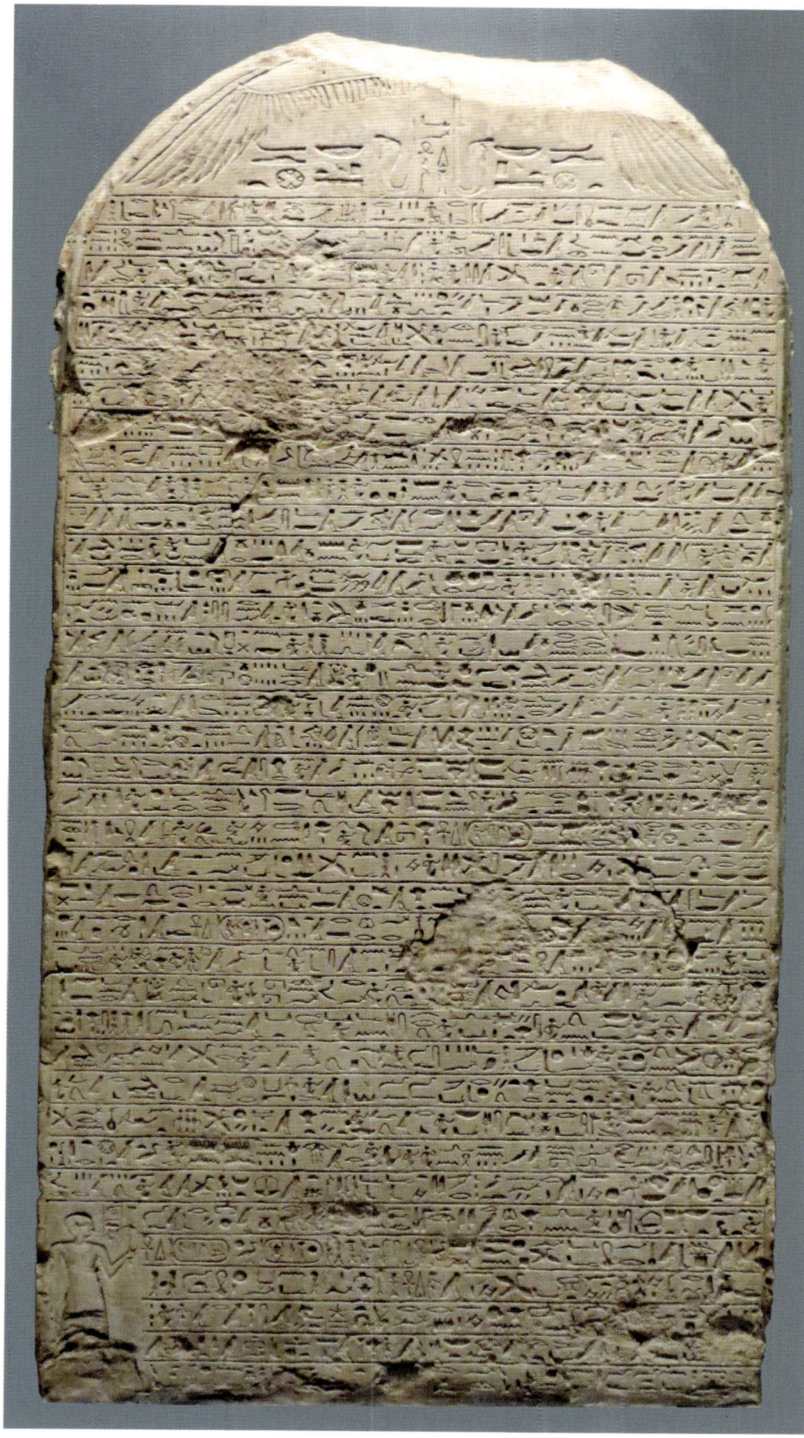

FIGURE 2 Stela of Kamose (K2), relating his campaign against the Hyksos; from Karnak (Luxor Museum J43).

FIGURE 3 Relief of Amenhotep I, Karnak.

however, operations began once more, the Thebans managing to take Heliopolis before pressing on into the Delta to finally settle scores with the Hyksos at their capital, Avaris (Tell el-Daba).[4] The siege of the city was fairly drawn out, interrupted by the need to put down insurrections in already liberated territory, the Hyksos city finally falling somewhere between Years 12 and 15. This was followed up by a six-year siege of the southwest Palestinian fortress of Sharuhen, whose surrender marked the end of Hyksos power.

Having freed Egypt of foreign rule, Ahmose I turned his attention to Nubia. As noted above, Kamose may have managed to regain at least some of the area, but now Egyptian forces reasserted rule over the region south of the Second Cataract, enabling the establishment of a new civil administration headed by a viceroy. The king's absence in Nubia may have encouraged rebellions by former Hyksos allies in Middle Egypt but, at length, and having dealt with these distractions, Ahmose I seems to have returned to Palestine to undertake a further campaign to extend the area of Egyptian power into Syria, possibly as far north as the Euphrates.

Ahmose I was succeeded after a quarter-century reign by his son, Djeserkare Amenhotep I (fig. 3), whose reign, of twenty-one years, saw the consolidation of the achievements of his father. Military activity "to extend the borders of Egypt" is recorded in Nubia, as recorded in the autobiographical text of Ahmose-son-of-Ibana, on the walls of his tomb-chapel at El-Kab (EK5).[5] This text is an important source for the military history of the early Eighteenth Dynasty. A campaign into Libya is mentioned in the autobiographical text of Ahmose-Pennekhbet, found in another tomb-chapel at El-Kab (EK2), also a key source for the period.[6] The reign also saw major building work at Karnak, although most of Amenhotep I's structures would be subsequently dismantled to make way for buildings of later kings. By Amenhotep's death, much of the groundwork for the achievements of the succeeding kings had been laid, and the humiliations of the Hyksos era largely exorcised.

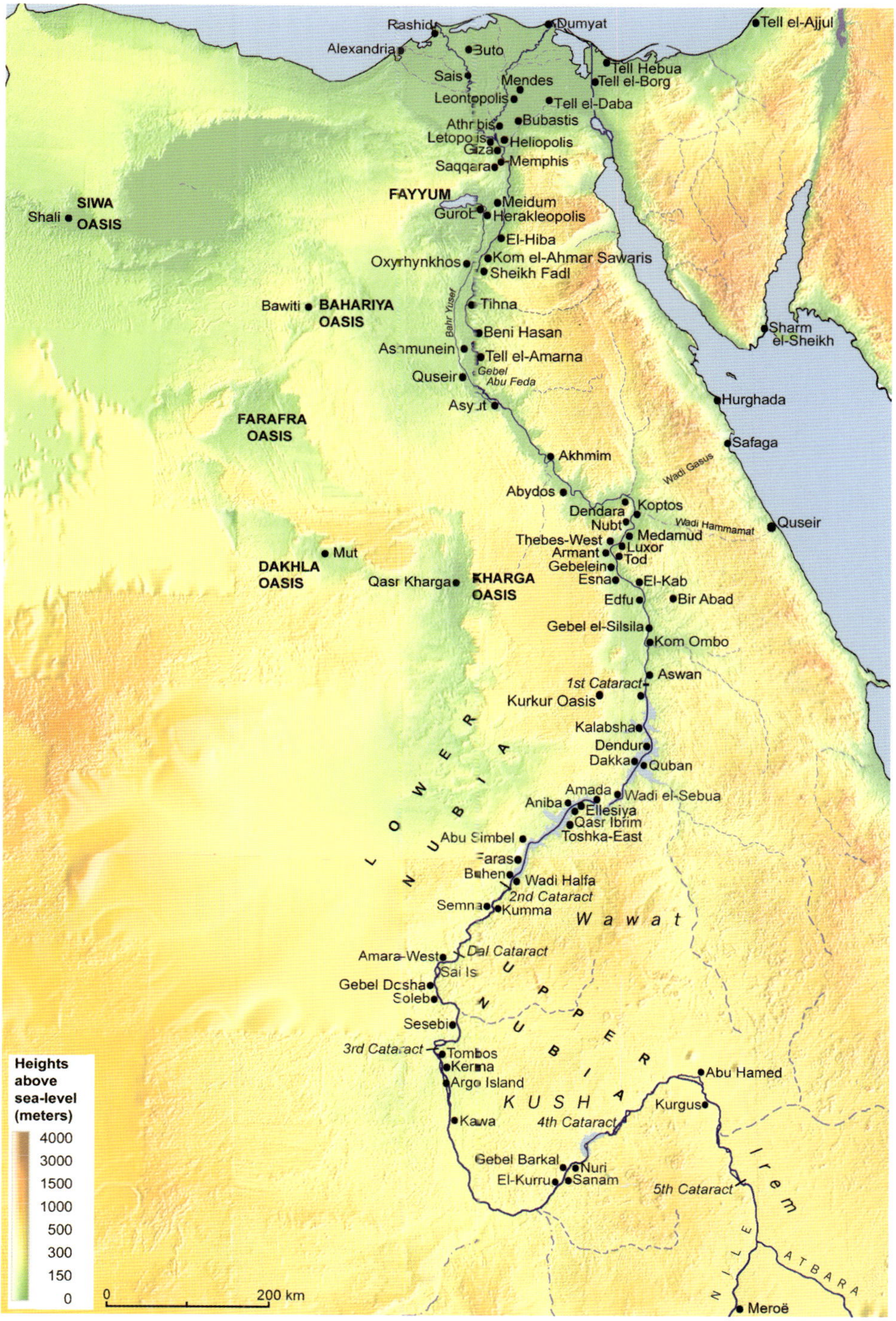

FIGURE 4 Egypt and Nubia.

1 The House of Thutmose

Thutmose I

Amenhotep I was succeeded by a man named Thutmose (, *ḏḥwty-ms(w)*). Like the name Ahmose/Ahmes ("The Moon Is Born"), which was common during the late Second Intermediate Period and early New Kingdom, that of the new monarch invoked a lunar deity. Thoth (*ḏḥwty*) also had a wide range of other "responsibilities," acting as the scribe of the gods, patron of earthly scribes and wisdom, and playing a role in the protection of the dead. Probably as a result of its royal use, the name continued to be employed into Greco-Roman times.

The paternity of Thutmose I remains unknown, although it is certain that his mother was named Seniseneb (fig. 5). During her son's reign she is found with the title of King's Mother, but not that of King's Wife, which one would have expected had she been the widow of Amenhotep I or any earlier king. Indeed, there is no evidence that Amenhotep I had any spouse other than his Great Wife Meryetamun, nor that he had any children.

One of Thutmose's wives, Ahmes, had the title of King's Sister (fig. 6), and this has led to suggestions that she might have been a sibling of Amenhotep I. If so, Amenhotep might then, in default of any children of his own, have appointed a brother-in-law as his successor. However, Ahmes is never called "King's Daughter," referring to Ahmose I, which would normally be found alongside "King's Sister" if she were indeed a royal sibling. This would argue against such a solution, leaving the only conclusion seemingly that the monarch of whom Ahmes was a "King's Sister" was Thutmose himself.

This need not, however, necessarily mean that Thutmose and Ahmes were biological siblings. It could simply be a statement of equivalency of status with her husband: close female relations (including wives) could be referred to as "sisters" (cf. pages 19, 177), and

FIGURE 5 Painted relief of Thutmose I and his mother Seniseneb; Upper Shrine of Anubis, temple of Hatshepsut at Deir el-Bahari.

during the Twenty-fifth Dynasty, we find the God's Wife of Amun Amenirdis I called "King's Sister" of the contemporary King Shabaka, who seems not to have been her actual sibling.[1]

Where a king lacked a direct heir, it seems that it was possible for him to nominate a successor (see page 26), as occurred when the childless Horemheb appointed the future Rameses I to roles that marked him out as the man to become next king.[2] This seems likely to have been the case with Thutmose, but as well as the option that he was a commoner, unrelated to the royal family, it has been suggested that he was a son of Prince Ahmose-sipairi. The latter was an individual particularly prominent among the "Lords of the West"—members of the Seventeenth/early Eighteenth Dynasty royal family, who became patrons of the Theban necropolis during the Rameside Period.[3] While Ahmose-sipairi is often regarded as someone who died as a child, this is by no means certain,[4] and making him the father of Thutmose would neatly solve the problem of his status and the king's parentage.[5] As for Ahmose-sipairi's own ancestry, he is perhaps most likely to have been a son of Taa.

FIGURE 6 Thutmose I, Queen Ahmes, and Princess Neferubity; Main Sanctuary of Amun, temple of Hatshepsut at Deir el-Bahari.

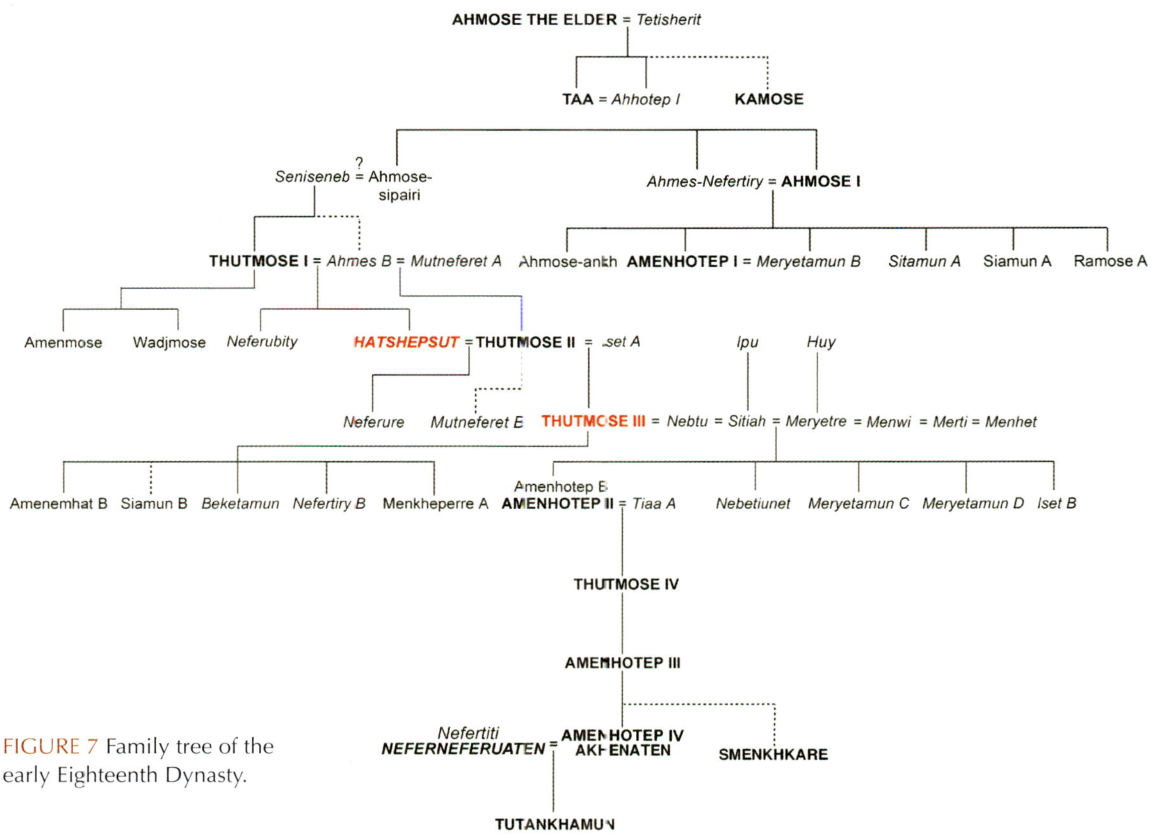

FIGURE 7 Family tree of the early Eighteenth Dynasty.

The royal children

A number of children are known to have been born to Thutmose I, not just by Ahmes, but also with Mutneferet (A), the latter being securely attested as King's Mother of Thutmose II (on the statue shown in fig. 8, left). A colossus that ultimately depicted Thutmose II, in front of Pylon VIII at Karnak (figs. 13 right, 47 top), incorporates a figure of a Mutneferet with the titles of King's Daughter and King's Sister, who has often been equated with the king's mother. However, the lack of the King's Mother title would suggest that this is *not* his mother, but either a sibling or a daughter, perhaps most likely the latter, since the statue's final form was the work of Thutmose III.

FIGURE 8 Statues of two royal mothers. Left: Mutneferet A, mother of Thutmose II, from the chapel of Wadjmose at Thebes-West (Cairo CG572); right: Iset A, mother of Thutmose III, from Karnak (CG42072).

FIGURE 9 Princes Amenmose and Wadjmose, as depicted in the tomb-chapel of Paheri at El-Kab (EK3); inset: naos of Amenmose (Louvre E8074).

There were three sons, the eldest two being Amenmose and Wadjmose, neither of whose maternity is known. As usual with royal sons, they were allocated tutors from among the nobility, including Paheri of El-Kab, in whose tomb-chapel (EK3) they are both depicted (fig. 9). Amenmose appears to have held the rank of general in his father's Year 4, at which time he had, for a prince, the unusual distinction of having his name in a cartouche, suggesting that at this point he was heir to the throne (fig. 9, inset).[6] He is also named, with other members of the royal family, at Kurgus, deep in Upper Nubia (see pages 12–13). The third son, Thutmose, born of Mutneferet, would later become king. With Ahmes, Thutmose had two daughters. One, Neferubity, seems to have died young, and is depicted with her parents in scenes in the memorial temple of her full sister, Hatshepsut (fig. 6).

FIGURE 10 Statue of Sitre-In, nurse of Hatshepsut; from Deir el-Bahari (Cairo JE56264).

The latter, the future female pharaoh, bore a name (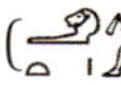), *ḥ3t-špswt*, meaning "Foremost of Noble Women," that was a not uncommon one. Its use extended from the Middle Kingdom down to at least the late Third Intermediate Period, and earlier bearers included a Thirteenth Dynasty princess, buried at Dahshur-South.[7]

Royal nurses were important figures during the Eighteenth Dynasty,[8] and on occasion were granted impressive memorials by their former charges. Hatshepsut's nurse, Sitre-In, was no exception, being memorialized in her former ward's Deir el-Bahari temple by a life-sized sandstone statue of her with Hatshepsut on her lap (fig. 10).[9] She was also granted burial, alongside a temple singer named Ty, in a tomb (KV60) just outside Hatshepsut's own in the Valley of the Kings (figs. 91, 92 top; on this tomb, see further pages 201–202, below).

Kingship

The coronation decree of Thutmose I, dated Year 1, III *prt* 21, and preserved in two copies from Nubia,[10] gives his prenomen of Aakheperkare and the rest of his five-fold titulary. The king's particular interest in continuing the reconquest of the region, supported by the long-serving viceroy Turi (in office from Ahmose I to Thutmose III), is shown by Thutmose I's inscriptions at Tombos, at the Third Cataract, dated to II *3ḫt* 15 of his Year 2, which claim an overwhelming victory.[11] The king ultimately reached Kurgus, between the Fourth and Fifth Cataracts, on the Abu Hamed Reach of the Nile. It would stand as the furthest-ever extension of formal Egyptian power into Nubia. There, on the white quartz outcrop of Hagr el-Marwa, he left a rock-cut stela, with a number of subsidiary texts (fig. 11).[12] The main inscription threatens the local inhabitants with drought, barren cattle, and a lack of heirs should they damage the stela. The carving would later be duplicated on the same rock by his grandson Thutmose III. The subsidiary texts include the names of Queen Ahmes, Princes Amenmose and Wadjmose, and a princess whose name is lost, but as it was placed in a cartouche (unlike those of the princes), might have been that of Hatshepsut.

FIGURE 11 The Hagr el-Marwa at Kurgus, seen from the east, and the inscriptions at the southern end of this face. The right-hand tableau was inscribed under Thutmose I, with the central near-duplicate dating to the reign of Thutmose III. The names at the bottom left include the names of Prince Amenmose, while his brother Wadjmose is named some nine meters to the right, as is a Prince Amenemhat, perhaps the son of Thutmose III. Further texts, at the southern end of the west face, include mentions of Queen Ahmes, officials, and a princess, most probably Hatshepsut. The cartouches at the bottom right belong to Rameses II.

Whether this means that these members of the royal family came with Thutmose to this remote location is unclear. But there is little doubt that the king relished taking Egyptian power well beyond any point reached by a predecessor, and it may indeed have been that his family—perhaps including Hatshepsut—were with him in his triumph. Thutmose I arrived back at Aswan in I *šmw* of Year 3, passing through the newly cleared First Cataract canal of Senwosret III on Day 22,[13] after more than a year away from Egypt.

The Tombos inscription speaks of the king's dominions extending as far as the Euphrates ("the inverted water which goes north in going upstream"—the reverse of the Egyptian Nile), although contemporary texts seem to imply that it was only after he had finished with Nubia that Thutmose I set out for Syria-Palestine, fighting successfully in the northern region of Mitanni (figs. 63, 64 top left).[14] A solution may be that by the time that the Tombos inscription had actually been carved, the conquest of

FIGURE 12 Pylon IV and the obelisks of Thutmose I (right) and Hatshepsut (left).

northern Syria had taken place. According to Thutmose III (see below, page 87), a stela was erected by Thutmose I on the west bank of the Euphrates to mark his achievement.

Thutmose I undertook extensive building work at Karnak, including the completion of projects begun by Amenhotep I. Overall direction of the king's works was in the hands of Ineni, who had begun service under Amenhotep I, and would continue in office into the early reign of Thutmose III. Ineni's autobiographical text in his tomb-chapel (TT81) is an important source of data for the period.[15] Work at Karnak included enclosing the whole of the existing temple complex within a new wall, accessed from the west via what is now Pylon V (fig. 42).[16] Another, larger, pylon (IV) was then added further to the west, fronted by a pair of obelisks (fig. 12). The space between the pylons was converted into a columned hall (initially known as the Iunyt Hall), and an outer enclosure wall added.

The length of the reign of Thutmose I remains unclear. A substantial period of rule has often been assumed, but the king's highest certain date remains his Year 3 return from Nubia.[17] A fragment from Karnak may attest retrospectively to Years 8 and 9 of Thutmose I's reign,[18] but beyond this there is only an entry in the work of the third century BC historian Manetho, which gives around thirteen years to kings who may represent Thutmose I on his list (see page 164). The burial arrangements of Thutmose I and his immediate predecessors present a number of problems, which will be discussed in chapter five.

The Reign of Thutmose II

The autobiographical text of Ineni makes it clear that Thutmose I was directly followed on the throne by Aakheperenre Thutmose II (fig. 13). The new king's senior wife was his half-sister Hatshepsut (fig. 14).[19] As Thutmose II's queen, Hatshepsut's principal titles were:

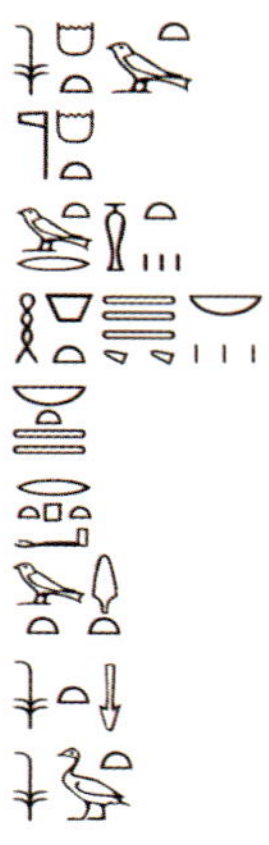

ḥmt-nsw-wrt	King's Great Wife
ḥmt-nṯr	God's Wife
wrt-ḥswt	Great of Praises
ḥnwt-tꜣw-nbw	Mistress of All Lands
nbt-tꜣwy	Lady of the Two Lands
irt-pꜥt	Noblewoman
wrt-imꜣt	Great of Scepter/Charm
snt-nsw	King's Sister
sꜣt-nsw	King's Daughter

With the exception of the final two, which implicitly related her to Thutmose I and II, these titles were typical for the chief wife of a king of the period. That of God's Wife stands out as a new development of the Eighteenth Dynasty, and one that was not necessarily specific to being the wife of a king, although first attested as a (probably posthumous) title of Queen Ahhotep I, wife of Taa and mother of Ahmose I.

Although the king was a "god," and thus potentially the individual to whom the title referred, from later expansions of the God's Wife title, it is clear that the "god"

FIGURE 13 Left: statue of Thutmose II, from Elephantine (Elephantine Museum 1200); right: colossus in front of Pylon VIII at Karnak, in its final form representing Thutmose II. However, it was "perfected" *(snfr)* by Thutmose III, and was probably made for Hatshepsut, and subsequently altered to represent her husband.

in question was Amun, and that the title marked out its holder as a representative of the royal family in the clergy of the god. Later, the title would have equivalent status with that of the high priest (and later still would subsume his role), but it is unclear whether this was yet formally the case during the Eighteenth Dynasty. Thutmose II and Hatshepsut had a daughter, Neferure, but no known sons. However, by a lesser wife, Iset (fig. 8 right), the king had a son, Thutmose III. The dates of the children's births are unknown, as are their parents' dates of marriage.

As far as events of the reign of Thutmose II are concerned, little is known. However, II *3ḫt* 8 in Year 1 saw a report of a Nubian rebellion,[20] an army being sent that successfully suppressed the rebels. A campaign against *š3sw*-nomads in Palestine is also attested, in the autobiographical text[21] of Ahmose-Pennekhbet. How long the reign lasted remains a matter for debate, past estimates ranging between three and thirteen years, with the modern consensus at the lower end of the range.[22]

Architectural elements naming Thutmose II are to be found in various parts of Egypt. At Karnak, blocks reused in later buildings attest to a number of projects, including a "festival court," which probably included a pylon in front of Pylon IV (fig. 42). Now dubbed the "Dismantled Pylon," this would have been demolished when Amenhotep III built his Pylon III, the filling of which included parts of the Thutmose II structure. A pair of obelisks were also manufactured (probably originally placed in the festival court).

Thutmose II died prematurely,[23] leaving two young children, Neferure and Thutmose. As their dates of birth are unknown, and with the uncertainty regarding the length of Thutmose II's reign, their ages at his death are also obscure. As a junior wife, Iset possibly married the king only after his accession, making the junior Thutmose little more

FIGURE 14 Jar bearing the name and titles of Hatshepsut as queen (Durham N1380).

than a toddler when his father died. However, it is likely that Hatshepsut and Thutmose II married during the reign of their father, Thutmose I, making Neferure perhaps a few years older than her half-brother. It seems likely that it was Thutmose II who appointed an elderly official, Senimen (TT252),[24] as Neferure's Steward and Tutor (fig. 15); he continued to exercise those roles after Thutmose II's death.[25]

As with his immediate predecessors, the burial arrangements of Thutmose II present problems (pages 23–24, 150). What was later labeled as his mummy[26] was eventually placed alongside other New Kingdom royal mummies in a tomb (TT320) south of Deir el-Bahari, probably during the tenth century BC (cf. page 159).

FIGURE 15 Rock-cut statue of Senimen and Princess Neferure, above his tomb (TT252) at Sheikh Abd el-Qurna.

2 The Boy-King and the Regent

The new king, Thutmose III, was a child at his coronation, on I *šmw* 4, and accordingly in need of a regency. That this was undertaken by the queen dowager Hatshepsut is set out clearly in the autobiographical text of Ineni (pages 14–15), who relates that on the death of Thutmose II,

> his son took his place as king of the Two Lands . . . and his sister, the God's Wife Hatshepsut, governed the land; the Two Lands were under her direction . . . (she being) the prow rope of Upper Egypt, the mooring post of the southerners, the excellent stern rope of Lower Egypt, a lady of command, with excellent plans, who satisfies the Two Banks when she speaks.

The vesting of a regency in the widow of the late king has been a common practice in many countries. Although we do not have such explicit statements of such a role in earlier times, it seems clear that, among others, Merneith, the mother of Den, and Ankhenespepy II, the mother of Pepy II, undertook this function for their sons back in the First and Sixth Dynasties, while Tawosret would fulfill it for Siptah four centuries later.[1]

The names bestowed on the young king were as follows:

Horus		*k3-nḫt ḫʿ-m-w3st*	Strong bull, appearing in Thebes
Nebti		*w3ḥ-nswyt*	Enduring in kingship
Golden Falcon	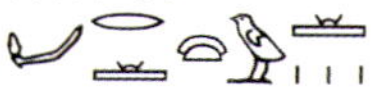	*ḏsr-ḫʿw*	Sacred of appearances
Prenomen	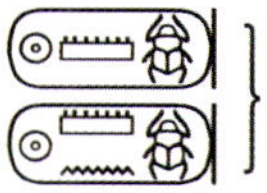	*mn-ḫpr-rʿ*	Established manifestation of Re
Nomen		*ḏḥwty-ms(w)*	Thoth is born

FIGURE 16 The temple dedicated to Dedwen and Senwosret III within the fortress of Semna, as seen from the east, in 1962. The lower image shows the decoration of the west exterior wall of the temple, showing Thutmose III in the center, kneeling before Dedwen, with the goddess Wadjet behind him. Behind her is Thutmose III's text dedicating the temple, but the two columns (A and B) on the far left (one truncated by a later alteration to the wall, and both later erased) making the regent Hatshepsut also responsible for building the temple. A figure of the queen (possibly later reworked to show her as a king) originally occupied the far right end of the wall (at C), but this was also later erased, as was the label text above.

FIGURE 17 Relief of Thutmose II and Hatshepsut, from the external north wall of their limestone bark shrine at Karnak (Luxor Museum).

FIGURE 18 Hatshepsut as regent, with Princess Neferure, as depicted on another element of the bark shrine complex at Karnak.

They followed the pattern of those of Thutmose I and II, which had introduced the element *k3-nḫt* at the beginning of the Horus name into royal titularies. This would continue as a standard feature for some seven centuries until the radical simplification of royal titularies early in the eighth century BC.[2] One variation was the dropping of the *n*-sign as a phonetic complement to the *mn*-sign.

Alongside the formal position of Thutmose III as the formal ruler of Egypt, Hatshepsut's position as the person actually directing affairs is soon made clear iconographically.[3] For example, while the foundation of his temple to the deified king Senwosret III and the god Dedwen at Semna is decreed in the king's name, in a coda to the main text it is stated that Hatshepsut, with the titles of God's Wife and King's Great Wife, "made (the temple) as her monument to her father Dedwen,"[4] thus adding her as a further dedicator (fig. 16).[5] An actual figure of the queen appeared at the opposite end of the wall, as well as in a series of structures erected to the east of Thutmose I's pylons at Karnak.[6]

These included a new bark shrine, of fine limestone, at the heart of the temple. This would turn out to be the first of three such structures that would replace each other in turn over the coming decades. Its decoration features Thutmose II and Hatshepsut, depicted on equal terms (fig. 17), while another structure from the same project focuses its decoration on Hatshepsut and her daughter, Neferure (fig. 18).

The Karnak project[7] also incorporated a pair of obelisks (now largely destroyed), their commissioning by Hatshepsut being recorded in a graffito at Aswan (fig. 19).[8] This

FIGURE 19 Graffito at Aswan, recording the commissioning of a pair of obelisks by Regent Hatshepsut.

is particularly interesting in that the author of this inscription was Senenmut—an individual who would loom large over the career of Hatshepsut.

> Coming (by) the Nobleman and Mayor, the great one who fills the heart of the God's Wife, the one who pacifies the Mistress of the Two Lands by his words, the Chancellor of the King, the Great Steward of the King's Daughter Neferure, may she live, Senenmut, order to begin(?) work on the two big obelisks of millions of years. It happened as it was ordered concerning everything, it happened because of the might of Her Person.

Also likely to be related to the Karnak project is the construction, by Senenmut, of a shrine at the sandstone quarries of Gebel Silsila (fig. 20). As well as his involvement in the royal building project, as mentioned in the graffito, he was the steward of Princess Neferure, his linked role as her tutor made explicit in many of the statues that would be made of him over the coming years (figs. 21, 38 top right).[9] Senimen, who had previously held the role (page 18), was presumably now dead, as may also have been the retired army officer Ahmose-Pennekhbet, who had acted as a tutor to the princess. Senenmut was also Steward of the God's Wife—initially Hatshepsut herself, later Neferure.

A man of apparently humble origins, the son of a certain Ramose and Hatneferet, Senenmut would accrue a range of some ninety further titles over the coming years. Perhaps the most important were those of Great Steward of the King, (Great) Steward of Amun—making him the senior administrator at Karnak, Overseer of Works of Amun—and Overseer of Works at Djeser-djeseru (Deir el-Bahari). The question of the precise nature of his relationship with Hatshepsut will be considered later (pages 47–53).

It is clear that Hatshepsut, as regent, planned to be buried in a tomb in the Wadi Sikkat Taqa el-Zeide in the southwestern part of the Theban necropolis (figs. 87, 88).[10] This area would continue to house royal family tombs down to the time of Amenhotep III.[11] It is likely that Hatshepsut's tomb (see pages 117–21) had been begun when she was the wife of Thutmose II. However, it is probable that the quartzite sarcophagus found within (fig. 89) was commissioned during the regency. Such an item is without

FIGURE 20 The sandstone quarries of Gebel Silsila-West, with shrines 14 (Nehesy), 15 (Hapuseneb), 16 (Senenmut), and 17 (Useramun).

parallel earlier in the dynasty, and is likely to be a manifestation of Hatshepsut's growing status and ambitions.

It seems likely that the tomb of Thutmose II himself was constructed in the same area. Tomb C4 in the adjacent Wadi Gabbanet el-Qurud (under excavation at the time of writing),[12] has a similar, but slightly more elaborate, plan to that of Hatshepsut, with its innermost chamber (of the same size as that of the tomb of Hatshepsut) decorated with the Book of *Amduat*, surmounted by a dado of *kheker* motifs, as in the tomb of Thutmose III (figs. 107, 108, 136). This is something almost exclusive to kingly burials

FIGURE 21 Senenmut with Neferure on his lap (a. BM EA174; b. NMEC CG42116; c. Cairo CG42115; d. Cairo CG42114; e. Berlin ÄM2296).

(pages 126, 147, figs. 92, 108). In addition, the tomb contained fragments bearing the name of either Thutmose I or Thutmose II (the decisive hieroglyph being missing), with others naming Hatshepsut as queen, and fragments of pottery stamped with the prenomina of Hatshepsut as king and of Thutmose III. The state of the tomb suggests that it may have been evacuated following collapse soon after the original burial in the tomb took place.

The idea that C4 may have been the tomb of Thutmose II is reinforced by the fact that it lies on the extended axis of that king's mortuary temple at Medinet Habu (see fig. 87),[13] which is consistent with the way in which the axes of the memorial temples of Thutmose III and Amenhotep II intersect the Valley of the Kings close to the sites of these pharaohs' tombs (pages 143–44, with fig. 105). A mummy labeled as that of Thutmose II was found in the TT320 cache.[14]

3 Coregents

Late in the seventh year after the death of Thutmose II a momentous change occurred: "The crowns of the God's Wife were removed and [Hatshepsut] wore the insignia of Re, the Southern Crown and the Northern one being united on her head."[1] In doing so, Hatshepsut also laid down her queenly titles in favor of the five-fold titulary of a king:[2]

Horus		*wsrt-kꜣw*	Powerful of *kas*
Nebti	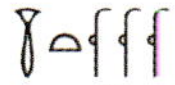	*wꜣḏt-rnpwt*	Flourishing of years
Golden Falcon		*nṯrt-ḫꜥw*	Divine of appearances
Prenomen		*mꜣꜥt-kꜣ-rꜥ*	True *ka* of Re
Nomen	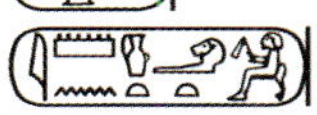	*ḥ3t-špswt-ḫnmt-imn*	Foremost of noble women, united with Amun

As clearly inappropriate to a woman, the element *k3-nḫt* ("strong bull") was not employed in Hatshepsut's Horus name, although in a text in her Chapelle Rouge (pages 54–57) she was happy to compare herself to a wild bull.[3] As with most pre-Rameside titularies, all but one of the components were original. The exception was the Golden Falcon name, which was the feminine form of the Horus and Nebti name of the long-lived Pepy II at the beginning of the Sixth Dynasty. An innovation was the all-but-constant use of an epithet (in this case *ḫnmt-ỉmn*—"United with Amun") within the nomen. Although epithets had been incorporated into the cartouche names of Thutmose I and Thutmose II, it had been on an irregular basis (as would also be the case with Thutmose III): they would not be a regular feature of cartouche names until the time of Amenhotep II, and then not a constant until Rameses II. They then remained a standard feature, like the *k3-nḫt* element in the Horus name, until the early eighth century.

Concerning the question of why Hatshepsut decided to elevate herself to kingship, there is no data available to us. However, it would seem reasonable to assume that it was a result of Hatshepsut's desire to continue to rule Egypt beyond the point at which Thutmose III would come of age, thus terminating the regency. A "late-regency" monument showing Hatshepsut and Neferure in leading roles, accompanied by the "resurrection" of Thutmose II (in some cases replacing existing images of Thutmose III), have been used to suggest that an option other than full coregency may have been considered for a short period, with a new kind of regime, centered on Hatshepsut and her daughter, deriving their legitimacy from their late husband and father, with Thutmose III sidelined, if not in danger of deposition. Alternatively, it may have represented a conscious "testing of the water" toward elevation to kingship. However, against this interpretation is the fact that when Hatshepsut did actually become king, the legitimization of her accession did not rely on her affinity with Thutmose II, but on her being the offspring of Thutmose I.

The Making of a Female King

Insofar as can be gauged from indications going back at least to the Middle Kingdom, the legitimacy of a new king has been inferred from various sources to have been derived from three elements. First, the individual should be the physical son of a paramount deity (in the New Kingdom, Amun), who had become incarnate in their mortal father at the moment of conception. The new king was thus simultaneously the child of the god and of the previous king. Second, an heir should be presented to an assembly of notables and their status as prospective king proclaimed. Third, on the death of the old king, the heir should carry out the funeral, as Horus buried Osiris, fulfilling the divine archetype of Egyptian royalty.

In the legitimizing propaganda that followed her assumption of kingship, Hatshepsut made use of all three of these modes. The first two are writ large in the memorial temple that she created at Deir el-Bahari (for which see pages 129–41). These began with an extensive "divine birth" sequence (figs. 22, 101) of a kind first found on the causeway of the pyramid complex of Senwosret III at Dahshur,[4] and with a possible precursor known from the late Fifth Dynasty complex of Isesi.[5] That this sequence was a standard one is shown by the survival of a complete version for Amenhotep III in the Luxor temple,[6] fragments from one for Rameses II (originally from his memorial temple),[7] and one for Taharqa in Temple A in the Mut complex at Karnak.[8] It is likely that this composition was originally present in many New Kingdom memorial temples, but the almost complete destruction of most of them (cf. pages 142–43) makes it difficult to be certain.

The sequence begins with Amun announcing the coming of the female king, and Thoth being commanded to seek an appropriate mother for Hatshepsut. After this, Amun comes to Queen Ahmes in the form of Thutmose I. They then sit together on a couch, which is supported by the goddesses Neith and Selqet. Amun then holds an *'nḫ-sign* to her nose—emblematic of sexual intercourse—and instructs Khnum to construct Hatshepsut's body and *ka* out of clay. Thoth next informs Ahmes of the identity of her unborn child, the queen being led to the birth room by Khnum and Heket, accompanied by twelve deities to aid the birth. Hatshepsut is born, held by her mother, and then suckled by deities. In parallel with this, Thutmose I is depicted presenting the child to the court, with the following speech (fig. 23).

> She is my daughter, Hatshepsut-Khnemetamun, may she live! I have appointed her to my place, so that she is upon my throne. Indeed, it is she who shall sit on the noble throne; she shall command the people from every throne of the palace; she shall lead you, and you shall proclaim her word; you shall be united at her command. He who shall praise her shall live, he who shall speak evil against Her Person shall die. As for everybody who shall say the complete name of Her Person, he shall enter immediately into the king's room, as it was done in the name of My Person . . . .[9]

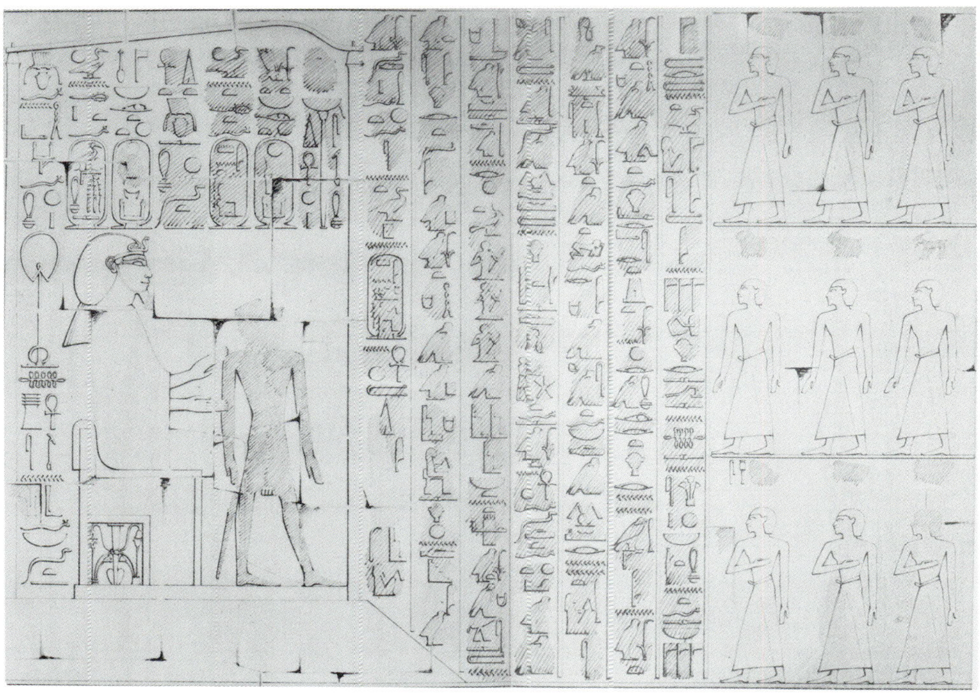

FIGURE 23 Hatshepsut presented to the court by Thutmose I, Deir el-Bahari.

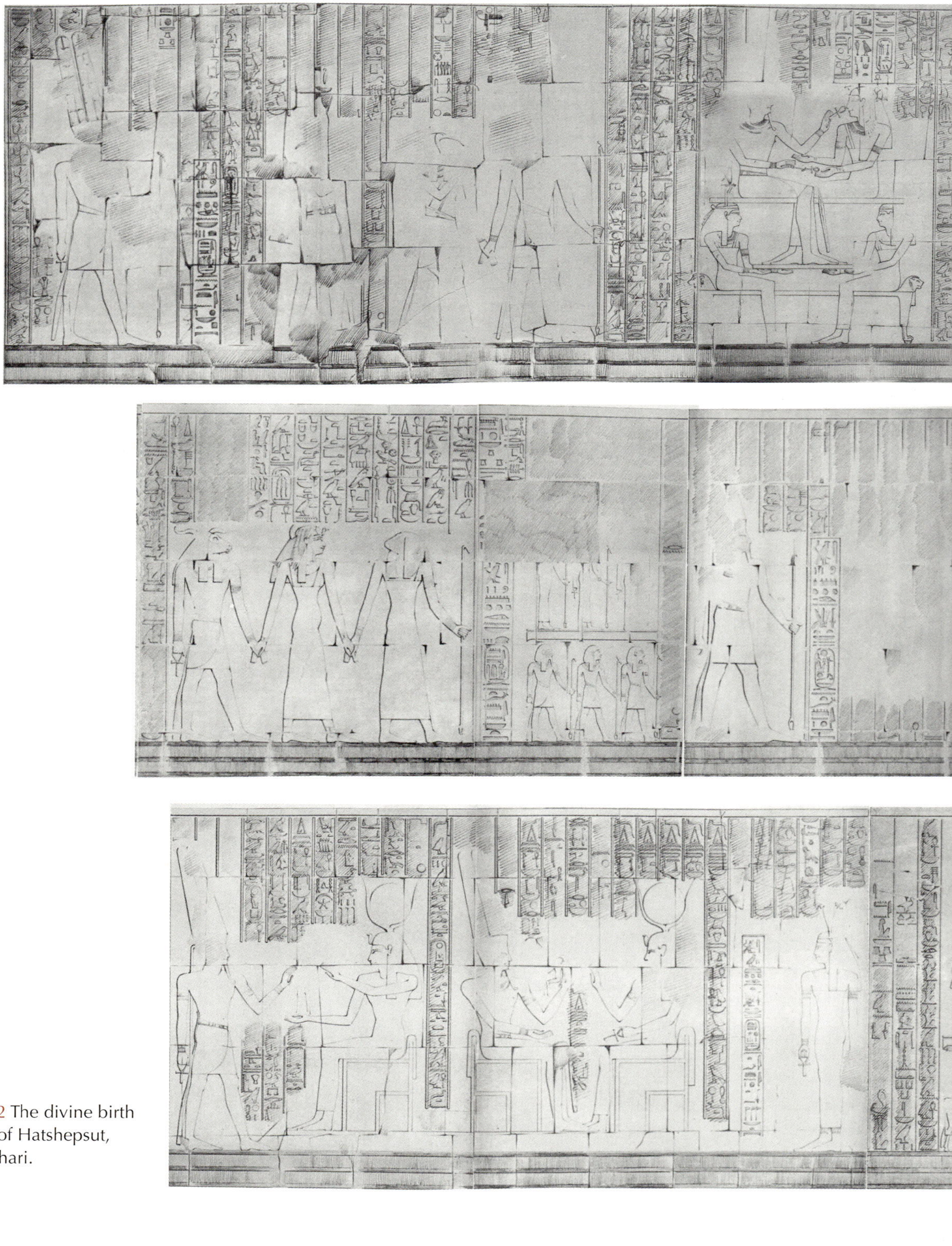

FIGURE 22 The divine birth sequence of Hatshepsut, Deir el-Bahari.

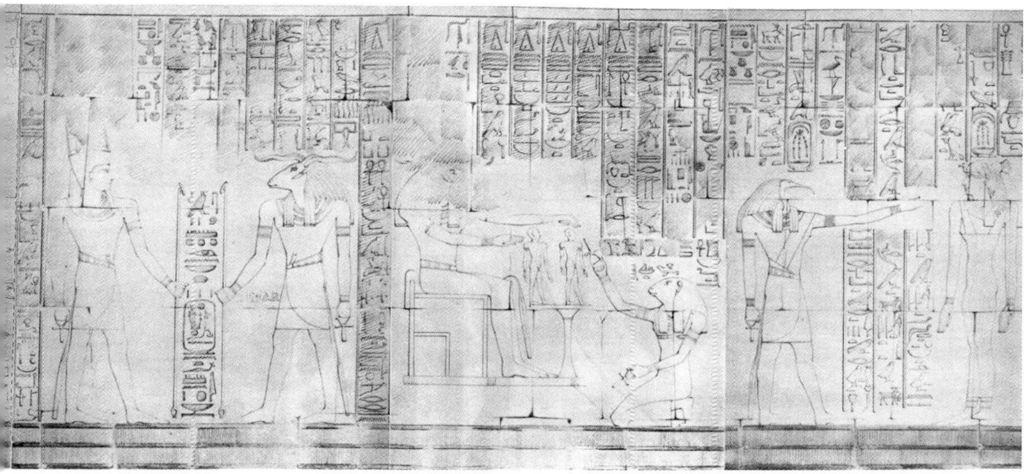

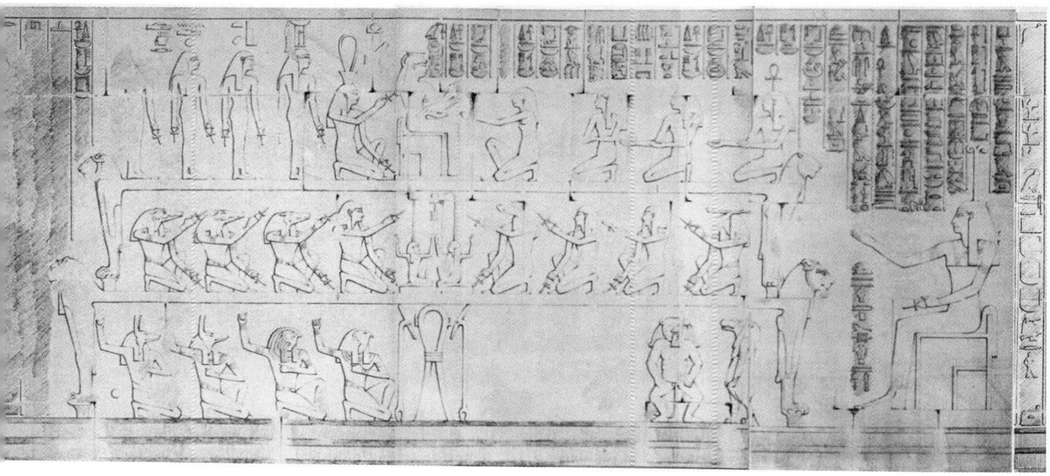

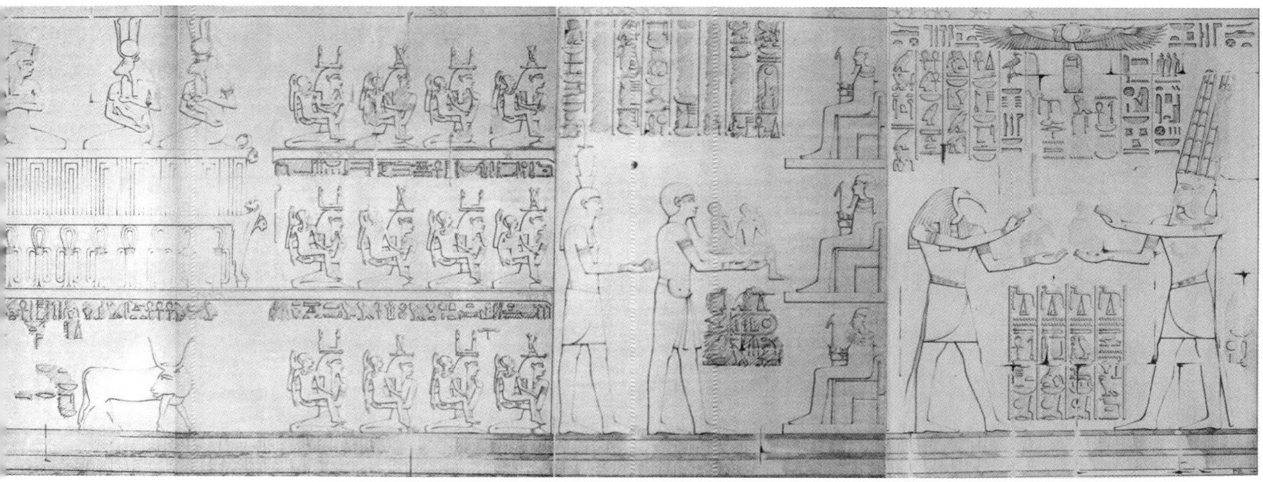

Of course, this fiction ignores the reigns of Thutmose II and III, and is clearly pure propaganda. Yet it was plainly intended to place the advent of Hatshepsut wholly within conventional modes of king-making, beginning with a composite divine–pharaonic parentage, and followed by presentation to the court.[10] Indeed, it is possible that a desire to fulfill the third criterion for kingship—burying one's predecessor—lay behind Hatshepsut's later reburial of Thutmose I. We will return to this in chapter five.

FIGURE 24 Detail of the south wall of the outer hall of Main Sanctuary of Amun at Deir el-Bahari, showing Hatshepsut and Neferure, with the latter restored from Dundee 67.244 and a copy made by Champollion in 1829.

Princess Neferure

Prior to her assumption of kingship, one of the key titles of Hatshepsut had been that of God's Wife. This seems to have been transferred to her daughter Neferure shortly before the beginning of the coregency.[11] The princess appears with this title in the Amun sanctuary at Deir el-Bahari (fig. 24), on a stela from Serabit el-Khadim (fig. 25), and on at least one statue of Senenmut, her long-time tutor.[12] The Serabit stela is interesting in that Neferure is shown as the sole officiant, over whom Senenmut waves a fan, with no sign of her mother or Thutmose III. This would seem to imply that she is here acting for the king(s). Indeed, the Year 11 at the top of the stela is followed by the phrase "under the Person of," implying that the regnal year is that of Neferure herself. This seems unlikely, and is more probably a case of carelessness on the part of the scribe, in either omitting the cartouche of Hatshepsut or Thutmose III, or mechanically adding the *ḫr ḥm n* that so often follows a year date.

Nevertheless, Neferure's solo action indicates the exalted status held by the princess. Yet the idea put forward by some,[13] that she might have been being groomed as a future female pharaoh, goes beyond the extant evidence. She is generally viewed as having died before the end of the coregency, but she seems to have been depicted with Thutmose III on a stela that can be dated on the basis of its contents to Year 23 or slightly later (fig. 26).[14] The cartouche of the figure in question now gives the name of Queen Sitiah, a wife of Thutmose, but it has been altered; the traces of the original name are consistent with having been that of Neferure. This has been used to suggest that Thutmose III married Neferure,[15] but it is interesting to note that the sole title given to the woman on the stela is God's Wife, without the King's (Great) Wife that one would have expected if she had been married to the king. Thus, all that can be stated is that, if the palimpsest name has been correctly read, Neferure will have survived into Thutmose III's sole reign.[16] How long she lived remains wholly obscure.

FIGURE 25 Stela of Neferure, from Serabit el-Khadim (Cairo JE38546).

FIGURE 26 Stela of Thutmose III, shown accompanied by a woman who seems originally to have been named as Neferure, but whose cartouche was later recut to name Sitiah (Cairo CG34013).

There is also another usurped stela on which some have seen the name of Neferure as having been surcharged, in this case by Thutmose III's mother, Iset, but this has been questioned (page 154, fig. 111). At the Deir el-Bahari temple of Hatshepsut, two of Neferure's figures, on the exterior façade of the Amun chapel (visible directly adjacent to the granite doorjambs in fig. 99 top left), have had their headdresses, titles, and cartouches amended to change them into representations of her grandmother, Ahmes.[17]

How to Be a Female Pharaoh

The precedents available to Hatshepsut for a woman being a king were extremely limited, with only one certain example during the previous millennium-and-a-half of Egyptian history.[18] This was Sobekneferu, apparently a daughter of Amenemhat III of the Twelfth Dynasty.[19] There are indications that another of his daughters, Neferuptah, might have been previously groomed for kingship (in particular her unprecedented use of a cartouche), in the absence of a male heir, but predeceased her father.[20] It certainly seems likely that Amenemhat III's immediate successor, Amenemhat IV, was not a direct heir.[21] The exact relationship (personal and chronological) between Amenemhat IV and Sobekneferu is not altogether clear, but Sobekneferu seems to have had a reign of some four years. The remains of a statue show her wearing a conventional woman's dress, but with a royal kilt over it, together with the *nemes* headdress (fig. 27 top).

FIGURE 27 Top: Torso of statue of the female pharaoh Sobekneferu, showing the *nemes* headdress and the kilt worn over her sheath dress (Louvre E27135). Bottom: Nile-level text from Semna, dated to the reign of Sobekneferu (Khartoum).

Much further back in history, Merneith, mother of Den of the First Dynasty, had been buried in the manner of a king, probably on account of her having ruled the country during her son's minority.[22] However, she did not possess any kingly title, and thus probably fell into the category of regent, rather than female king. On the other hand, at this point the royal titulary had not yet assumed the standard forms that would emerge during the Old Kingdom, leaving the matter open to some degree.

When she first became king, Hatshepsut followed Sobekneferu in continuing to be shown in a woman's attire.

FIGURE 28 Two depictions of Hatshepsut as king, but wearing female attire. Left: fragment of cornice from Serabit el-Khadim (location unknown), probably originally carved during the regency, with the nomen added subsequently; right: block from Karnak (Luxor Museum J771).

FIGURE 29 Statues of Hatshepsut from Deir el-Bahari: a. as a woman, wearing *ḫ3t*-headdress (MMA 30.3.3); b. as a woman, wearing *nms*-headdress (MMA 29.3.3 + RMO F1928/9.2); c. as androgynous (MMA 29.3.2); d. as a man (MMA 27.3.163).

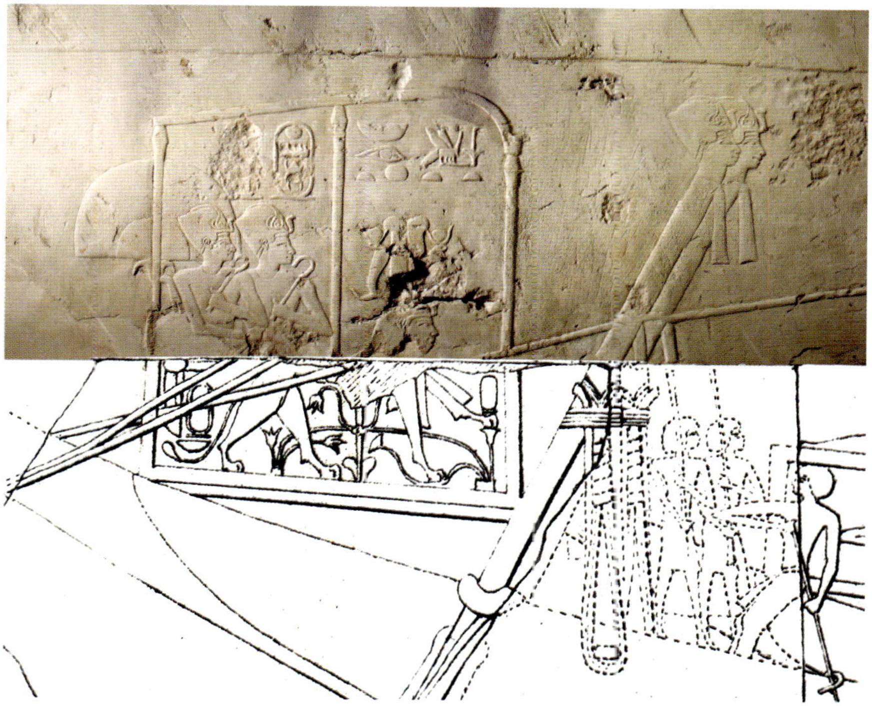

FIGURE 30 Thutmose III and Hatshepsut in their cabin at the stern of the royal bark, from the scene of the transportation of obelisks (fig. 103) in Hatshepsut's temple at Deir el-Bahari (Bournemouth 1922-03-004).

Indeed, her earliest depictions lack any obvious kingly aspects, other than the presence of a kingly cartouche, and the use of a double-plumed headdress (fig. 28).[23] However, as her reign continued, there was a progressive masculinization of her depictions, in both two and three dimensions (fig. 29).[24] Thus, by the end of her period of rule, her iconography was wholly masculine, and were it not for the presence of feminine endings in the accompanying texts, one would have little idea that a woman was being represented (cf. fig. 43). Indeed, by no means all of Hatshepsut's texts use feminine endings, pronouns, and verb forms for her (cf. page 44), making some of her monuments wholly indistinguishable from those of a male pharaoh—except, of course, that no attempt was made to de-gender her name, "Foremost of Noble Women."[25]

The coregency of Hatshepsut with Thutmose III provides us with our first surviving example of how the dynamic of two kings ruling in parallel was dealt with in art.[26] That Hatshepsut was the senior is implied by the number of occasions on which she appears alone, and by the two kings' relative placement when shown together: in two-thirds of the cases she is depicted in the foremost position (e.g., figs. 36, 44, 99), whereas most of the others show the two kings "neutrally" back to back or facing each other (e.g., fig. 123). However, the two are always shown on the same scale, albeit often (but by no means always) with each wearing a different crown, and Thutmose interacts with the gods in just the same way as Hatshepsut. There is no indication that Thutmose III was in any way "set aside." Rather, he was seemingly now "second among pharaonic equals."

One interesting feature found in the titulary of Thutmose III during the coregency is that, on occasion, his prenomen is expanded to read Menkheper*ka*re (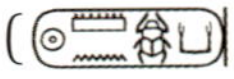, ). This may have been intended to link the king's titulary with those of Thutmose I (Aakheper*ka*re) and Hatshepsut (Maat*ka*re) herself, but examples are quite rare, and the basic form, Menkheperre, continued to be used in parallel, with the *ka*-form never used after the end of the coregency, and was always the version used in private names honoring Thutmose III.

Being a Pharaoh

Administration

The Thutmosid period saw a crystallization of the administration of Egypt, with a basic structure put in place that would survive, with a few adjustments, down to the end of the New Kingdom.[27] It embraced four basic domains: the state itself; Nubia, now a formal viceroyalty; the temples; and the army. These nodes did not exist in isolation from one another. Many individuals held office, or exercised roles, across some or all of them, either simultaneously or in succession. The concept of a standing army was fairly new for Egypt, being an outgrowth of the wars of liberation from the Hyksos, and the imperial expansion into Syria-Palestine and Upper Nubia that followed it.

The state

Since Old Kingdom times, the state administration had been headed by the vizier, who was also head of the justice system. At the time of Thutmose II's death, the office was in the hands of Ahmose-Ametju (TT83), who had been in the position since the time of Thutmose I, when he had succeeded Imhotep (QV46) in this role. Ametju would, however, be joined in office before Year 5 by his son Useramun (TT61+TT131, fig. 31), who seems to have acted alongside him for a brief period. Useramun would continue as vizier until some point between Years 28 and 33 of Thutmose III. His funerary monument contains (in TT131) the earliest version of the text known as the Duties of the Vizier. This sets out the breadth and depth of the responsibilities of the holder of the office, underlining his position as mediator between the king and the broader administration.

Useramun would, like almost all viziers, later also become Mayor of Thebes. However, at the beginning of Thutmose III's reign, and Hatshepsut's regency, this post was held by Amentju's brother-in-law, Ineni, whose career went back to the time of Amenhotep

FIGURE 31 Top: the tomb complex of Useramun (TT61+TT131) on the Sheikh Abd el-Qurna hill, with his false-door inset; bottom: burial chamber of TT61, showing decoration with the Book of *Amduat*.

I. His autobiographical account of the post–Thutmose II transition of power has been quoted above (page 19). Ineni held a wide portfolio of other posts, especially regarding the temple of Amun at Karnak, but probably died before Hatshepsut transitioned to king, as there is no reference to her as pharaoh in his tomb-chapel (TT81).

The post of Chancellor (and also that of First Royal Herald) was held initially by the veteran Ahmose-Pennekhbet, a native of El-Kab. He had fought during the Hyksos campaigns of Ahmose I, and was also a tutor to Princess Neferure. He seems to have died soon after the beginning of the coregency as, while calling Hatshepsut by her queenly titles, he nevertheless calls her by her kingly prenomen, Maatkare. His successor, Nehesy, was certainly in post by Year 9, when he led the Punt expedition (page 42, fig. 33). A second chancellor is known during the coregency, Tiy, and it is possible that the two men were respectively responsible for activities in the north and south, should the identification of Nehesy's tomb as Saqqara Bubasteion I.6 (358/Bub) be correct.[28] Tiy was still in office in Year 25, when he led a mining expedition to the Sinai (page 84). He was buried in Wadi 300, at the southeastern extremity of the Theban necropolis, where all the known burials seem to be datable to the time of Thutmose III and Hatshepsut.[29]

The management and redistribution of the agricultural products of Egypt was a key enabler of the state, with the underpinning crop of grain under the control of the Overseer of the Granary of Upper and Lower Egypt, with separate secretariats for the north and for the south. Minnakht (TT87) was appointed Overseer by Hatshepsut, and had a long career that stretched into the sole reign of Thutmose III (see page 73). An Overseer of the Granary and Scribe of Accounts Nebamun (TT65) may also have served during the reign of Hatshepsut. Another Overseer of the Double Granaries was Minmose, who also continued in office after the end of Hatshepsut's reign, when he served alongside Tjenuna, who had been an official in the household of the God's Wife under Hatshepsut, and may have been appointed to his granary post before the end of the coregency.

Two Overseers of the Houses of Gold and Silver are known from the time of Hatshepsut: Djehuty (TT11) and Senemiah (TT127). The former is known between Years 9 and 16, and was involved in the assessment of myrrh brought back from Punt, and in various building activities at Karnak and at Deir el-Bahari. These included the erection of the western pair of Hatshepsut's Karnak obelisks (page 57). It is not known when his career ended, but his monuments were subsequently mutilated. Senemiah's tenure in the post may have been relatively short-lived, beginning after Year 9, and ending before Thutmose III began his sole rule during Year 21/22.

The Great Royal Herald Inyotef (TT155) appears to have been appointed around the beginning of the regency, serving until the earlier part of Thutmose III's sole reign. A

First Royal Herald, Duawyneheh (TT125), who was also an Overseer of the Granaries of Amun, is also known from the coregency, a man who seems to have been promoted to Chief Steward of the King soon after the end of the coregency.

The Viceroyalty of Nubia had been held until at least Year 2 by Seni, who had been originally appointed by Thutmose I.[30] He may also be the "Senires" who had been Mayor of Thebes prior to Ineni, especially as, prior to gaining the Nubian post, Seni had been in charge of works at Karnak during the reign of Amenhotep I. He seems to have been succeeded (directly or otherwise) by Penre until Year 10, with Inebny-Amenemnekhu (fig. 122) in office by at the latest Year 18, who then served until replaced by Nehi in Year 22/23 (pages 75–77). Inebny-Amenemnekhu's name was later erased on a number of monuments. He was buried in Wadi 300.

Probably operating in parallel with the main administration were the officials of the royal household, led by the Stewards of the King. Senenmut was one holder of the title, but there were at least two others during Hatshepsut's period as king, Amenhotep (TT73) and Wadjetrenput—and possibly Djehutyhotep and Meryre as well. Amenhotep was Overseer of Works on the Two Great Obelisks, indicating overall oversight of the production and erection of Hatshepsut's western obelisks at Karnak. He was also involved in the Nubian campaign(s) of the reign. Wadjetrenput was involved in the building work at Deir el-Bahari, and also in quarrying activities at Gebel Hammam, just north of Aswan.

A Royal Butler named Djehuty (TT110), also holder of various other offices, served Hatshepsut and continued in service under Thutmose III. Royal Butlers seem often to have undertaken various ad hoc tasks for the king, and Djehuty was certainly involved in military matters with Thutmose III, under whom he was also a Royal Herald.

Karnak

As noted below (pages 53–60, 91–99), Hatshepsut and Thutmose III made large-scale investments in the rebuilding and expansion of the temple of Amun at Karnak. The High Priest from the earliest part of Hatshepsut's rule was Hapuseneb (TT67; fig. 32), who had a substantial string of subsidiary titles, as well as an apparently honorary one of vizier (found only once). He also had general oversight of the temples of Egypt, and of many building activities. He was the owner of a shrine (15) at the Gebel Silsila sandstone quarries, probably in connection with his constructional activities (fig. 20). His precise date of appointment is not known, however, although he seems to have served as a senior temple official under Thutmose II, and may have died before Year 17, when a major new phase of Hatshepsut's work at Karnak began (page 57). It is possible that someone else held the high priesthood between Hapuseneb and the next attested incumbent, Menkheperreseneb the Elder, known to have served during Thutmose III's sole reign (see

FIGURE 32 Statues of Hapuseneb (Louvre A134; Bologna KS1822).

page 77). Hapuseneb's name was erased once on one of his statues (fig. 32 right), but was otherwise left untouched, including in his tomb-chapel.[31]

Hapuseneb's senior deputy, the Second Priest of Amun, Puyemre (TT39), was the son of Neferiah, possibly a nurse of Thutmose II, and was also the high priest's son-in-law. As well as his sacerdotal role, Puyemre had, like Hapuseneb, a range of other responsibilities, including concerning work at Deir el-Bahari. It appears that Puyemre had a long career, extending into at least the late 30s of Thutmose III's reign (page 77).

Trade and resources

The role of the Egyptian king embraced, nominally, every aspect of the state and its activities. The latter stretched from the most mundane aspects of administration through great enterprises of both peace and war. All of these aspects are to be seen in records surviving from the period of Hatshepsut's kingship.

The world of the Late Bronze Age was one of extensive trade and exchange connections by land and sea. In the north, Egypt was linked with the civilizations of the Aegean. This is seen especially in the case of the island of Crete, with scenes of Cretans bringing produce found in a number of contemporary tomb-chapels (e.g., fig. 39 bottom),[32] while actual Cretan art adorned at least one Egyptian royal palace (page 90, fig. 68). To the south, there were riverine/cross-desert routes into Africa, and also access via the Red Sea to the Horn of Africa and other coastal destinations. Expeditions are known to have been made from Egypt to the part of this region known as Punt since at least the Fifth Dynasty, when an expedition under Sahure is attested by both reliefs from his pyramid complex[33] and records in the Palermo Stone. Other brief references to expeditions to the place exist from the Sixth, Eleventh, and Twelfth Dynasties, and also from the later Eighteenth and the Twentieth Dynasties. Mentions of the products of Punt range down to Greco-Roman times.

The precise location of Punt has been the subject of debate since the earliest days of Egyptology.[34] However, it is clear that it lay at the southern end of the Red Sea, the general view being that the flora and fauna of Punt are consistent with the Sudanese, Eritrean, and Tigrayan coasts, although there have been some arguments in favor of southern Arabia.

The best-documented trading expedition to Punt comes from the reign of Hatshepsut. It was nominally a response to an oracular command of Amun, "that the ways to Punt should be sought out and the highways to the myrrh-terraces should be penetrated."[35] The date the expedition departed from Egypt is a matter for some debate, as what is ostensibly the announcement of its success (fig. 34) is dated to Year 9, implying that the actual voyage had taken place earlier that year, or perhaps in Year 8. However, it has also been argued that the scene in question is an evocation of the original decision to send the expedition, which would then have taken place during Year 9/10.[36]

The sequence of reliefs commemorating the expedition (fig. 33) begins with the arrival of the fleet at Punt, although the accompanying text describes the journey from an Egyptian Red Sea port, "sailing in the sea, taking the head of the good way toward Gods-Land, journeying in peace to the land of Punt by the army of the Lord of the Two Lands, according to the command of the Lord of the Gods, Amun-nebnesuttawy . . . to bring for him the marvels of every country, because he so loves the Dual King, Lord of the Two Lands, [Maatkare]."

The Egyptian expedition was greeted by the Chief of Punt, Parahu, his wife and family. The wife's unusual physique has been closely observed by the Egyptian artist in the Deir el-Bahari reliefs,[37] who was also keen to render the exotic aspects of the landscape, fauna, and flora of Punt. Then, presumably after negotiations of terms, myrrh trees, sacks of myrrh, ivory, wood, and monkeys (baboons and grivets) were loaded onto the Egyptian ships to return north. After transshipment across to the Eastern Desert (not shown), the fruits of the expedition were carried up the Nile to Thebes. There they were weighed and formally presented to Amun by Hatshepsut and Thutmose III, along

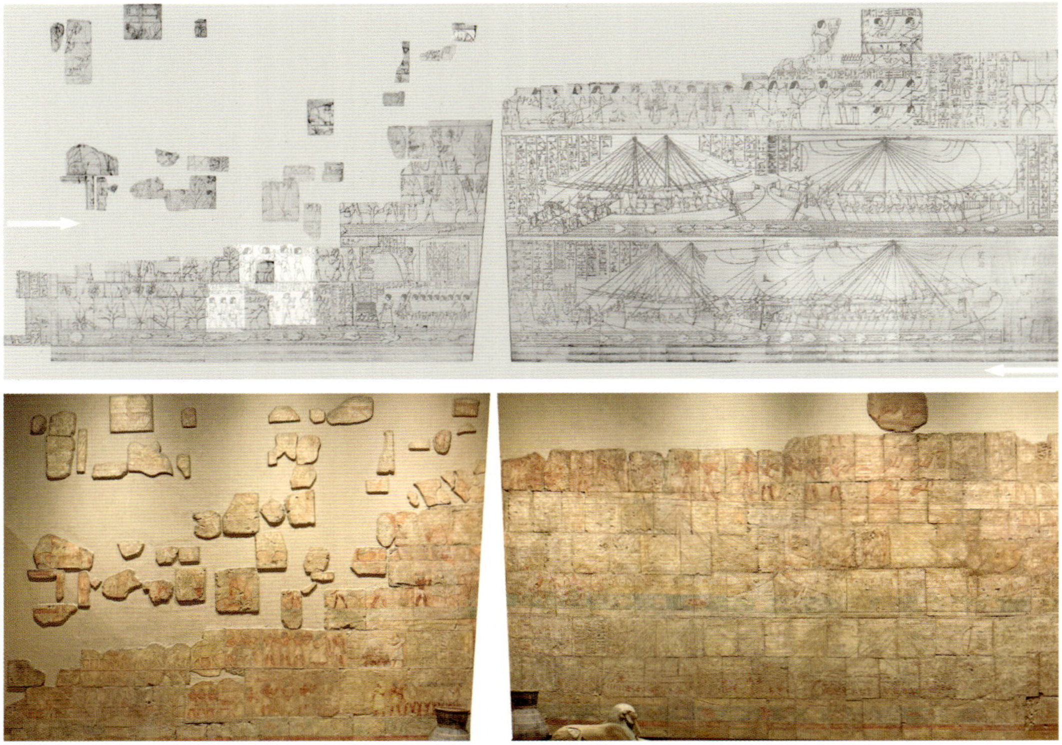

FIGURE 33 Drawing and cast (ROM) of the Punt expedition reliefs at Deir el-Bahari. The elements in white were stolen during the 1870s, although one was later recovered.

with material apparently just arrived from Irem and Nemayu in Nubia. The outcome of the expedition was also presented to the court (fig. 34; but cf. above on an alternate "reading" of the scene). Three of its noblemen were actually represented in the tableau recording the event: Nehesy, the leader of the Punt expedition; an unnamed individual—and Senenmut. The latter's presence in this context further underlines his importance to Hatshepsut.

Closer to home, a stela from Wadi Maghara indicates the opening of a turquoise mine there in Year 16 (fig. 123). The exploitation of the resources of Sinai went back to at least the Old Kingdom, and the temple at Serabit el-Khadim provides evidence of activity at least as early as the late Twelfth Dynasty.[38] The latter saw considerable attention under Thutmose III and Hatshepsut, its pylon and the so-called "Hathor Hanafiya" bearing images of the former, with stelae of Years 11, 13, and 20 certainly belonging to the coregency. Many stelae found there are dated to the sole reign of Thutmose III, but others are without surviving dates, or any indication whether they date to the coregency or the sole reign of Thutmose III.[39]

FIGURE 34 Hatshepsut's speech announcing the decis on to launch the Punt expedition; the first two figures in front of the throne are Nehesy and Senenmut; the th rd, unnamed, figure may represent the broader nobility.

War

The peaceful Punt expedition of Hatshepsut has frequently been contrasted with the extensive military activities of the sole reign of Thutmose III, and the idea that there was a "peace" party that gathered around Hatshepsut, and a "war" party gathered around Thutmose III, has become a staple in the literature.[40] However, one rather suspects that this is simply a projection of the persistent sexual stereotype that women are in some way naturally "peaceful and nurturing," in contrast with the bellicosity attributed to men. While this dichotomy perhaps has some basis in reality, the assumption that a female ruler is more likely to prefer "peace" to "war" is not borne out by history—witness Elizabeth I of England and Catherine II of Russia. The difference is more that male rulers have tended to lead their forces in person, rather than the more remote control sometimes exerted by their female counterparts.

In any case, there certainly was "war" during the period when Hatshepsut was in ultimate control in Egypt, with her leading the army in person in Nubia.[41] A graffito from Sehel, left by the senior official Tiy (for whom see page 38, above),[42] states that he "followed the vital god, the Dual King [Maatkare], may she live! I saw when he [*sic*] overthrew the Nubian bowmen, and when their chiefs were brought to him [*sic*] as living captives. I saw when he razed Nubia, I being in His [*sic*] Person's following" (fig. 35 top).[43] Another official, Djehuty (see page 38), reports seeing the monarch herself collecting booty on the battlefield. A damaged text in Hatshepsut's Deir el-Bahari temple may refer to this action, likening it to Thutmose I's great Nubian campaign, stating that it was in response to Nubian plotting. It includes a statement that Hatshepsut had "destroyed the southern lands" and placed "all lands beneath her feet."

This fighting in Nubia may be that mentioned in the fragmentary autobiographical text in the tomb-chapel of Senenmut (TT71).[44] A more stereotyped reference to military activity in Nubia comes in the form of a scene in the Southern Lower Colonnade in Deir el-Bahari temple that showed Hatshepsut smiting enemies before the god Dedwen, who is leading Nubian captives (for location see fig. 97). A parallel scene, involving Asiatic captives, is to be found in the Northern Lower Colonnade, while both colonnades have depictions of Hatshepsut as an enemy-trampling sphinx (fig. 35 bottom).

Aspirations to parallel operations in the south by a consolidation of her father's gains in Syria-Palestine are contained in a prophecy included in the text describing Hatshepsut's alleged elevation to kingship by her father (page 27, above), that she would "seize the chiefs of Retjenu by violence, those remaining from [her] father's time," and that her "catch should be men by the millions" and "men by the thousands for the temples." It is possible that a campaign led by Hatshepsut into Syria may be indicated by a text at Deir el-Bahari mentioning a royal elephant hunt,[45] as the classic elephant hunting locale was Niy in Syria, where Thutmose III certainly indulged in the activity (page 87).

Toward the end of Hatshepsut's reign, Thutmose III began to be involved in military activity, heralding his extensive warfighting once he became sole king. A Year 20 graffito at Tombos speaks of the king as "one who overthrows him who has attacked him," and of Amun as "one who gave victory," implying some kind of action in Nubia led by Thutmose. A reference in the records of his first Palestinian campaign as sole ruler (Year 22–23) implies that he had captured Gaza on a previous occasion, which could only have been while he was still sharing the throne with Hatshepsut. There is therefore evidence for at least four military campaigns while Hatshepsut was directing the state, at least one of them led by her in person.

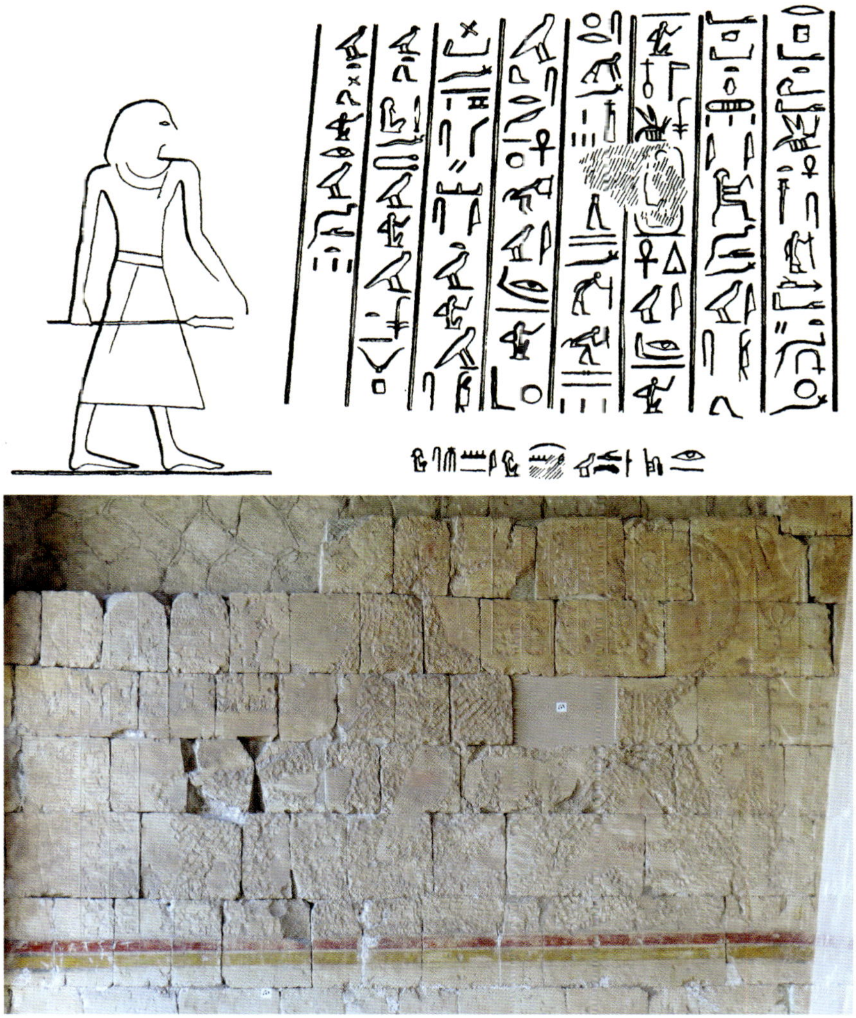

FIGURE 35 Top: graffito of Tiy describing Hatshepsut's Nubian war; bottom: relief on the south wall of the Northern Lower Terrace of the Deir el-Bahari temple, showing Hatshepsut as a sphinx trampling enemies.

Jubilee?

Egyptian kings aspired to celebrate at least one *ḥb-sd*, a festival of rejuvenation, often dubbed a "jubilee." These generally seem to have been first celebrated after a king had been on the throne for thirty years, and then repeated every three/four years thereafter. This was the pattern that would be followed by Thutmose III, other New Kingdom examples including the jubilees of Amenhotep III and Rameses II. However, there are also examples that do not conform to this model, and it has been proposed that Hatshepsut may have held one in Year 16.[46] This idea is based on a number of depictions of her involved in rituals that can be associated with the *ḥb-sd* (e.g., fig. 36), and

FIGURE 36 Scenes on the Chapelle Rouge at Karnak.

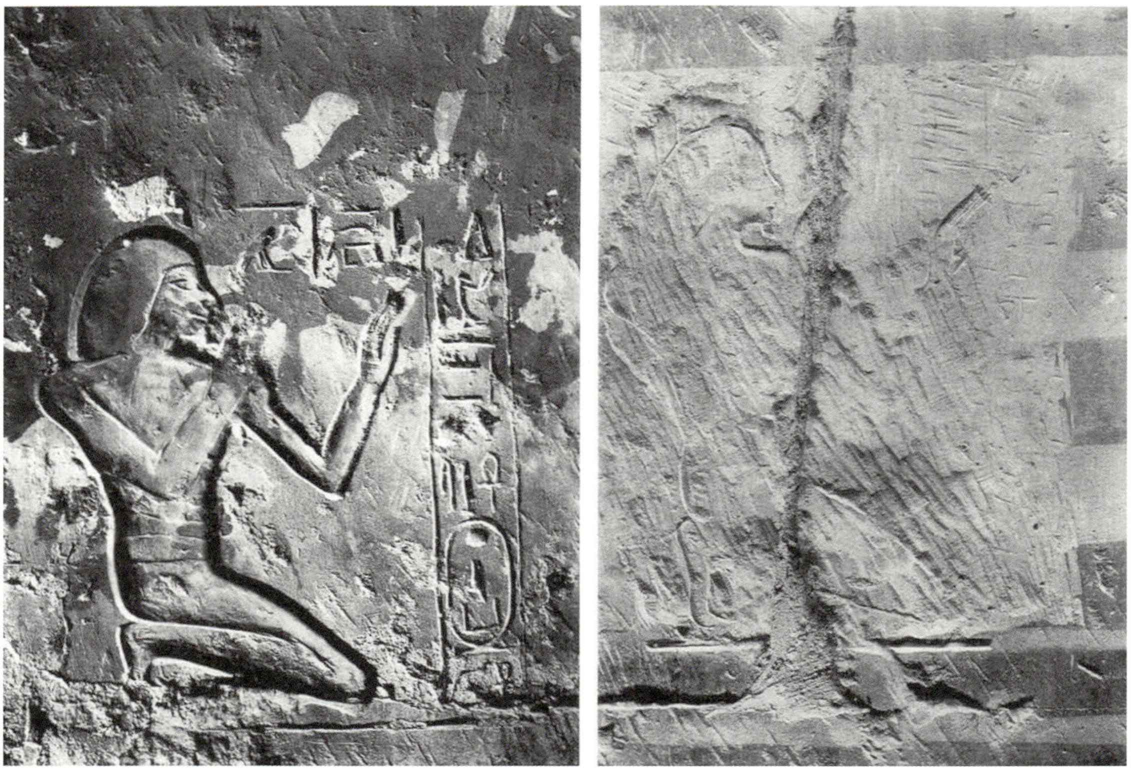

FIGURE 37 Two of the "secret" images of Senenmut. The example on the left is in one of the inner niches of Hatshepsut's Hathor chapel, and the other is in niche D on the Upper Terrace (see fig. 97).

also a mention of a "first occasion of the *ḥb-sd*" on the northern of the pair of obelisks erected by Hatshepsut between Pylons IV and V at Karnak in Year 16 (page 57, fig. 46). However, the context of the text is of a kind that has been demonstrated to be a prospective wish for a jubilee, in this case among the desired results of dedicating the monument to Amun.[47] The depictions of Hatshepsut carrying out activities that also formed elements of the *ḥb-sd* should thus be seen as simply wishes for the future.[48]

Senenmut

A major topic of debate concerning Hatshepsut has been the nature of her relationship with Senenmut. Having lost her husband at a fairly young age, it is unlikely that Hatshepsut would have forgone a desire for a romantic life, especially in a society that seems to have been far less puritanical about sex than those influenced by Judeo-Christian traditions.[49] But the identification of such partner(s) is hampered by the lack of any vocabulary to describe a partner of a female pharaoh. Indeed, it is important to note the difficulties faced by female rulers through history as to the status of any romantic partner other than a crowned king (cf. the case of Catherine II of Russia and her "favorites").

In Hatshepsut's case, she was pushing Egyptian practice to its extreme by claiming pharaonic kingship for herself. It would surely have been a step too far to invent an unprecedented new title of "*hỉ-nsw" ("King's Husband") as a male equivalent of the female royal spouse title of *ḥmt-nsw*. In such a situation, any partner for the female pharaoh would simply hold regular titles of nobility and administration. They would be distinguished purely by the quantity of those titles, and implicit marks of close association with the female pharaoh.

A person who fulfilled all these criteria during Hatshepsut's regency and reign was Senenmut. His prominence during this time is abundantly clear, as evidenced by the existence of no fewer than twenty-seven known statues of him.[50] Wholly unique are the over seventy (mainly kneeling) representations of him in relief within Hatshepsut's memorial temple.[51] Senenmut is depicted in each case "giving praise" to a deity, for the benefit of Hatshepsut and, just once, Thutmose I (fig. 37). They were carved within various doorways of many of the niches and chapels on the Upper and Middle Terraces. Most were located so that when the inward-opening wooden doors of the niches were open, the figures were concealed behind their leaves, but at least one set was visible when the doors were closed. Similar representations of Senenmut have also been noted in the Mut precinct at Karnak,[52] and in the temple of Satet on Elephantine.[53]

Some have alleged that this concealment was because the images were unauthorized, and that their "discovery" contributed to Senenmut's "fall," when most of his representations were destroyed or mutilated (see further below). However, this idea is explicitly contradicted by a text, found twice in the same room (the Northern Room of Amun on the Upper Terrace), which states that Senenmut was acting "in accordance with a favor of the king's bounty, which was extended to this servant in letting his name be established on every wall, in the following of the king, in Djeser-djeseru (Deir el-Bahari) and likewise in the temples of the gods of Upper and Lower Egypt."

A further testament to Senenmut's ability to occupy space within the sacred realm of the Deir el-Bahari temple is the placement of the burial apartments of his tomb complex within its boundaries. While his funerary chapel (TT71) lay high on the Sheikh Abd el-Qurna hill (fig. 39 top), the actual tomb (TT353) lay five hundred meters to the north (fig. 38). Approached from a corridor that opened some sixty meters to the east of the wall of the Deir el-Bahari precinct, the inner chambers of tomb lay within the temple's enclosure (figs. 40 top, 87, 97).[54] Like Senenmut's images in the temple, this has also been called a "secret" and/or "presumptuous" piece of work, but the interment of non-royal individuals in "royal" locales has many parallels. A good analog is the vizier

FIGURE 38 View of Sheikh Abd el-Qurna and Deir el-Bahari, showing the location of the two elements of Senenmut's tomb (TT71 and TT353), and the tomb-chapels of Rekhmire (TT100—fig. 60) and Ametju (TT83). The latter would be the home of Gardner Wilkinson (see pages 170–75) during the early nineteenth century AD.

FIGURE 39 Top: the summit of the Sheikh Abd el-Qurna hill, showing the chapel of Senenmut (TT7—with its stela [Berlin ÄM2066], and rock-cut image of Senenmut and Neferure above the chapel, inset). Three tomb-chapels of the same period are also marked, of Useramun (TT61—see also fig. 31), Re (TT72), and Amenhotep and Amenemhat (TT122); bottom: scene of Cretan gift-bringers in TT71.

FIGURE 40 Top: quarry to the northeast of the temple of Hatshepsut at Deir el-Bahari, which both housed the tomb of Senenmut (TT353), and was later used for dumping broken statues of Hatshepsut. Bottom: first (decorated) chamber of TT353, with its astronomical ceiling bottom. Interestingly, while all names (of Senenmut, his parents, and Hatshepsut) are intact, some of the faces of Senenmut have been attacked, as has that of his father.

Amenemopet (of the time of Amenhotep II), who had his chapel (TT29) on Sheikh Abd el-Qurna, but his burial chamber (KV48) in the Valley of the Kings itself.

These particular honors bestowed upon Senenmut (together with his impressive roster of titles (page 22), and his being singled out for depiction and naming in the Punt announcement tableau) are clearly indications of his exceptional status, and the closeness of his relationship with Hatshepsut. However, there is another piece of evidence that makes it difficult to sustain a view that he was "just" a close associate of the pharaoh. This is his sarcophagus (fig. 41). Curiously, its fragments were found in Senenmut's chapel (TT71), which has no burial chamber, rather than in or near his intended burial place, TT353, for which it had presumably been intended.[55] As reconstructed it is of a singular form, rounded at each end, but is otherwise essentially identical with the final sarcophagus manufactured for Hatshepsut (page 129, figs. 95, 133). Senenmut's sarcophagus has a flat-topped lid, is twelve centimeters shorter, and has some textual variations, but it is quite clear that it was made in the same workshop at Hatshepsut's, probably at the same time.[56]

That a private individual should have such a sarcophagus is particularly remarkable during the Eighteenth Dynasty, when there was a very clear separation between coffins (mummiform containers) and sarcophagi (rectangular outer containers) of kings, and those of others. During the Old and Middle Kingdoms, there was no obvious variation between a kingly sarcophagus and one intended for the burial of another person of high status. During the New Kingdom, things were very different,[57] with stone rectangular

FIGURE 41 The sarcophagus of Senenmut, reconstructed from fragments found in TT71 (MMA 31.3.95+65.274+1971.206).

sarcophagi almost unheard of in private burials, the vast majority being of wood. This includes even such people as Yuya and Tjuiu, the parents-in-law of Amenhotep III. Apart from that of Senenmut, the only known non-kingly Eighteenth Dynasty stone sarcophagi are those of Amenhotep-son-of-Hapu (the extremely prominent official of Amenhotep III, who also had a unique mortuary temple)[58] and Senenmut's near-contemporary, the Viceroy of Nubia, Nehi (fig. 61 bottom). But in neither case was the sarcophagus of royal pattern, that of Amenhotep being of a unique trapezoid form, and that of Nehi a fairly crude piece of simple rectangular form.

This underlines the unique status of Senenmut. The fact that he possessed one of what appears to have been a "his and hers" pair of sarcophagi, with the other owned by Hatshepsut, is highly suggestive, and seems not to have been addressed by the numerous scholars who have denied an intimate relationship between Hatshepsut and Senenmut. Indeed, it seems difficult to explain the situation as other than an ultimate manifestation of an intimate relationship between the owners of these sarcophagi. If this is admitted, the representations of Senenmut at Deir el-Bahari cease to be potential "impertinences," but a means of sharing the eternity of his royal partner, within the bounds of whose mortuary precinct he also placed his burial chamber. While it must be acknowledged that no absolute proof exists as to the nature of Hatshepsut and Senenmut's relationship, the balance of probabilities would seem to support the idea that they were life partners. Thus, Senenmut's exceptional monuments should be seen not as an irregular self-aggrandizement, but a reflection of an intimate relationship with Hatshepsut that was not susceptible to expression in a conventional way.

The "fall" of Senenmut

As already intimated, most of these memorials of Senenmut were subsequently mutilated to a greater or lesser extent.[59] TT353 certainly never received a burial, and as there was nowhere in TT71 for a burial to be made, it would seem that Senenmut fell from grace before, or directly after, his death. However, dating this "fall" is distinctly problematic. There is a lack of consistency between the individual occurrences of mutilation and erasure, a key factor being the fact that while some pieces have the names of both Senenmut and Hatshepsut erased, others have her names left intact and only those of Senenmut taken out—and some have no deletions at all.

The existence of items with the names of both Hatshepsut and Senenmut intact would suggest that the attack on Senenmut's memory was not primarily part of the campaign that was carried out against the female pharaoh two decades after the end of her reign (pages 108–11). But resolving whether Senenmut's "fall" occurred before or after the beginning of the sole reign of Thutmose III is hampered by the equivocal nature of evidence.

If it occurred while Hatshepsut was still pharaoh, one might see it as a result of the collapse of the putative personal relationship between her and Senenmut. If, on the other hand, it took place after the end of her reign, a falling-out with Thutmose III could be posited, and/or a feud between Senenmut and other officials, particularly in the absence of Hatshepsut from the equation. However, as already noted, the evidence for the episode is wholly equivocal and, for the time being at least, no coherent working hypothesis can be proposed.[60]

Builder-king

Karnak and Luxor

Hatshepsut had already commissioned significant works at Karnak while still regent (pages 21–22). Of these projects, the two obelisks were not finished until after she had become king. They may be the pair whose transport from the quarries in Aswan was depicted in Hatshepsut's memorial temple at Deir el-Bahari (fig. 103).[61] They were erected not, as might have been expected, athwart the principal approach to the complex from the west, but at its eastern extremity. They stood outside the Upper Gateway of the eastern enclosure wall that at that time stood some twenty meters east of the main body of the temple. The Upper Gateway was demolished when Thutmose III built his Festival Hall complex and the location of the obelisks swallowed up by a chapel constructed to mark Thutmose's first jubilee (in Year 30). Only fragments of the obelisks, from which Hatshepsut's images were later removed, now survive.

As king, apparently beginning in Year 11,[62] she embarked on an extensive program of construction that would transform the Karnak temple, and would continue into the sole reign of Thutmose III. This program seems to have involved extensive demolitions of earlier structures, and the replacement of limestone with sandstone as the principal building material of the Karnak complex. This change may have been a reaction to the vulnerability of limestone to the flooding that might accompany a particularly high Nile inundation.[63]

At the core of the project was a new shrine to house the bark (ceremonial boat) of Amun, composed of quartzite on a black granite foundation and which, from the color of the former stone, is generally known today as the "Chapelle Rouge" (figs. 36, 43, 69, 85).[64] This replaced a calcite example erected by Amenhotep I, which appears to have been moved west to a new location between Pylon IV and the Dismantled Pylon. The Chapelle was decorated with a wide range of ritual scenes, some of them showing Hatshepsut and Thutmose III acting together (e.g., fig. 44), but Hatshepsut is most frequently depicted on her own, and exclusively so on the interior of the chapel.

There is ongoing discussion as to the exact original location of the Chapelle Rouge, which was subsequently dismantled and its blocks ultimately used as filling for Pylon III

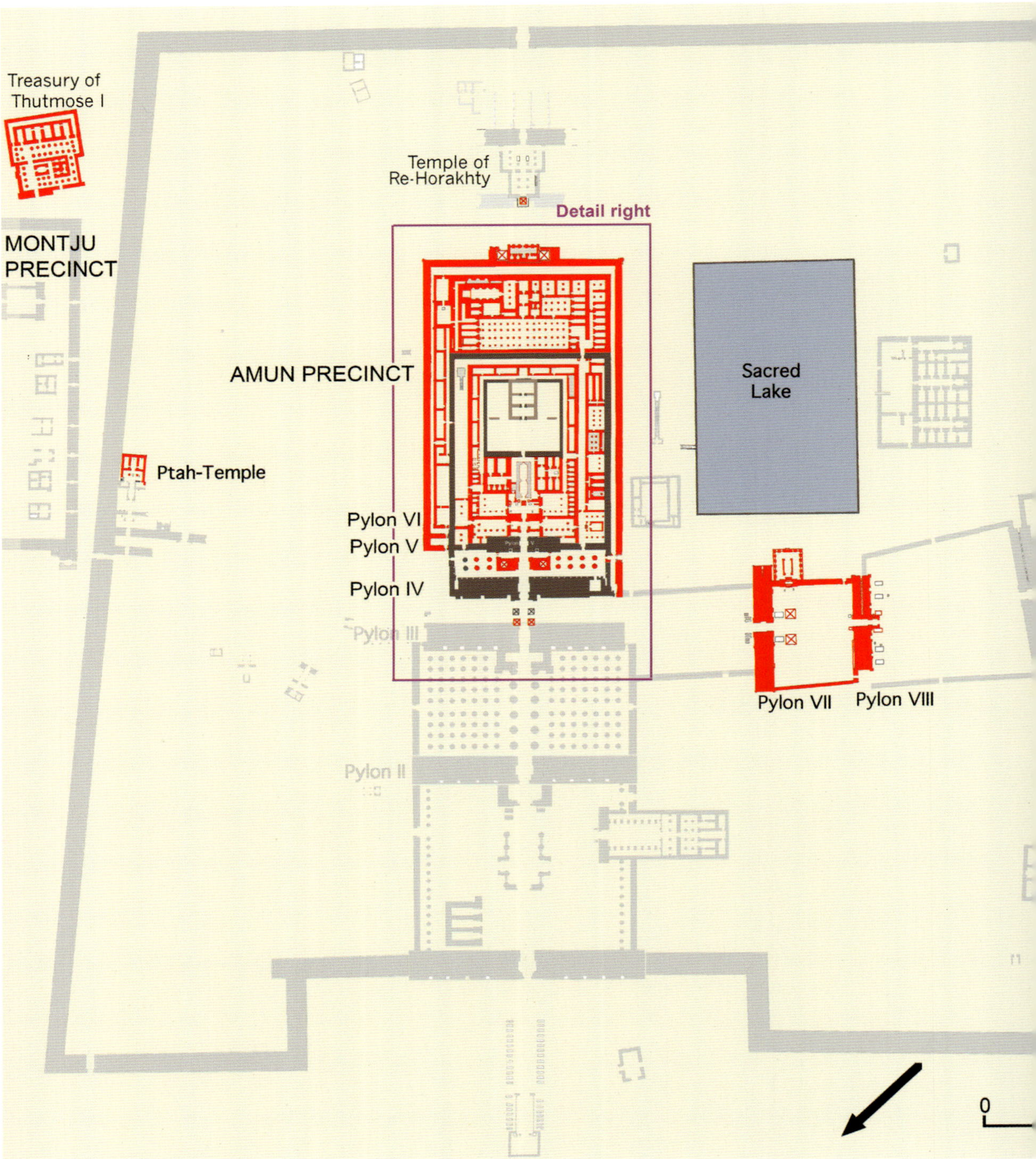

FIGURE 42 Plan of Karnak as it was at the end of the reign of Thutmose III.

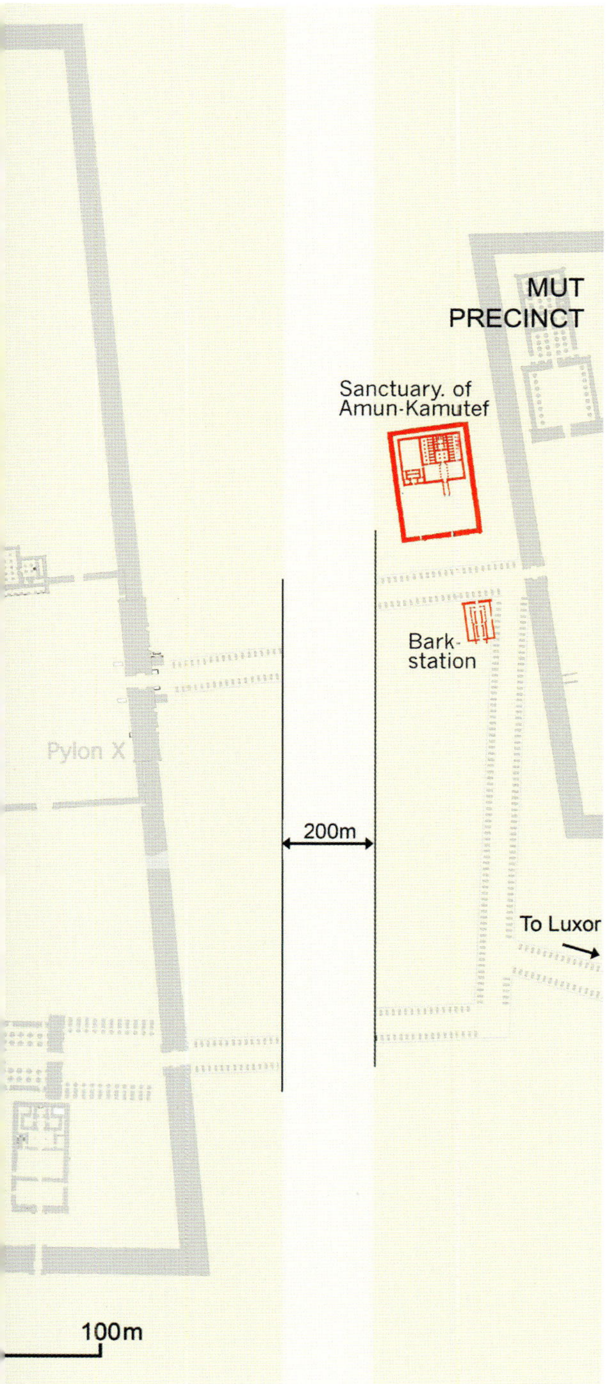
MUT
PRECINCT
Sanctuary. of
Amun-Kamutef
Bark-
station
Pylon X
200m
To Luxor
100m

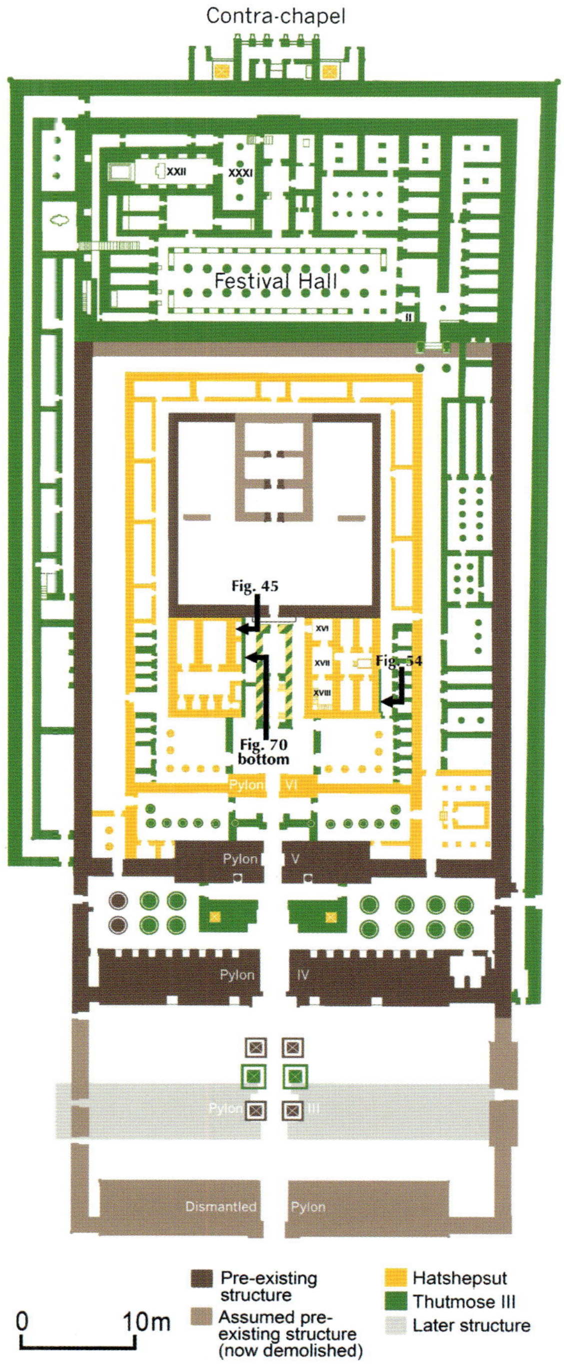
Contra-chapel
XXII
XXXI
Festival Hall
Fig. 45
XVI
XVII
XVIII
Fig. 54
Fig. 70
bottom
Pylon VI
Pylon V
Pylon IV
Pylon III
Dismantled Pylon
0
10m
Pre-existing
structure
Assumed pre-
existing structure
(now demolished)
Hatshepsut
Thutmose III
Later structure

FIGURE 43 The Chapelle Rouge at Karnak, reconstructed from blocks reused in the core of Pylon III.

FIGURE 44 Hatshepsut and Thutmose III shown together on the Chapelle Rouge, with the female pharaoh in the senior position.

FIGURE 45 Scenes of Hatshepsut, formerly in the location marked on fig. 42, from which her images and names were later removed.

by Amenhotep III.[65] However, it certainly formed part of a complex of chapels, replacing earlier structures, known as the Mansion of Maat (*ḥwt m3ʿt*), and was begun on I *3ḫt* 30 of Year 17 (fig. 45). A month earlier, Hatshepsut had erected a pair of obelisks (her second) in the midst of her father's Iunyt Hall, pillars and the roof of which had to be removed to facilitate their introduction (fig. 46); it was now renamed the Wadjyt Hall. Hatshepsut was also responsible for constructing the new Pylon VI,[66] which bisected the courtyard between Pylon V and the façade of the Mansion of Maat, which became two separate colonnaded courts under Thutmose III.

As well as these structures in the main west–east axis of the temple, a new pylon (VIII—fig. 47 top) was erected by Hatshepsut on its north–south axis. This axis, which was already marked by a mud-brick pylon, probably erected by Amenhotep I, and later replaced by Thutmose III's Pylon VII, linked the Amun complex with that of his consort Mut, and with other points further south.

FIGURE 46 The western obelisks of Hatshepsut at Karnak. While the northern example is still standing, the southern one later fell, although the upper portion was little damaged (cf. fig. 124), and has now been placed upright. The top halves had scenes of Thutmose III added flanking the original texts of Hatshepsut, after their lower parts had been sheathed with masonry during the roofing-over of the court in which they had first been erected.

FIGURE 47 Top: Panorama of Thutmosid Karnak. Bottom left: the Mut temple and the junction of the sphinx avenues between the Amun and Mut precincts at Karnak. Bottom right: the Triple Shrine at Luxor temple, constructed by Rameses II incorporating material of Hatshepsut.

Festival Hall
Temple of Re-Horakhty

The temple of Mut (fig. 47 bottom left) certainly went back to the Middle Kingdom, but the earliest standing remains date to the time of Hatshepsut.[67] This included a "Porch of Drunkenness," for a festival at which the excessive imbibing of beer propitiated the leonine deity Sekhmet, and created an epiphanic state that also included sexual activity.[68] Directly in front of the Mut precinct were constructed a sanctuary of Amun-Kamutef (east)[69] and a bark station (west—to temporarily accommodate the bark of Amun when en route to or from its sanctuary).[70]

The latter marked the point where the processional way was diverted around the western side of the Mut precinct toward the site later occupied by Amenhotep III's great Luxor temple;[71] textual references exist to five further bark stations erected by Hatshepsut along the route south. It appears that some kind of sanctuary had existed at Luxor from at least the reign of Ahmose I, if not since the Middle Kingdom.[72] Four granite columns that had originally borne the names of Hatshepsut were incorporated into a triple shrine erected by Rameses II in the forecourt that he added to the temple of Amenhotep III (fig. 47 bottom right). These have been attributed to the sixth bark station of the female king (perhaps on the same site). However, it is also possible that the columns belonged to a more substantial building erected by Hatshepsut, perhaps on the site of the later sanctuary of the Amenhotep III temple.

To the north of the Amun temple at Karnak, Hatshepsut began the reconstruction of the temple of Ptah, a project completed by Thutmose III (page 95),[73] while fragments of hers, including blocks from a chapel of Amun, have been found in the enclosure of Montju.[74] Nearby, the so-called "Gateway of Thutmose I" was erected in the joint names of Hatshepsut and Thutmose III[75] and, 150 meters further east, Hatshepsut contributed to the construction of the building dubbed the "Treasury of Thutmose I."[76]

Western Thebes

As well as her funerary monuments (pages 117–41), Hatshepsut was responsible for a number of structures on the west bank at Thebes, and also the completion of the temple of Thutmose II.[77] The memorial temple of Thutmose III (page 143) was also certainly under construction during the coregency.

At Medinet Habu, work was begun on what would prove to be a most enduring sanctuary, still in use, and still being extended, in Roman times (fig. 48).[78] The temple (the "Small Temple," dedicated to Amun-Re) replaced a Middle Kingdom foundation, which may have been renovated under Thutmose I. Work under Hatshepsut was carried out in two phases, creating a set of inner rooms built over earlier foundations, together with a new colonnaded outer element containing a bark shrine. The temple was still

FIGURE 48 The Small Temple at Medinet Habu.

incomplete and not yet in use when Thutmose III took sole rulership, and the outer elements were subsequently completed to a modified design.

From Western Thebes come blocks from a secondary context that once formed parts of a building of Hatshepsut's known as *ḫ'-3ḫt*.[79] However, there is no scholarly agreement as to whether it was a stand-alone monument, or part of a larger complex. In any case, it was completely demolished by the time of Rameses II.

From north to south

While the major known building works of Hatshepsut are at Thebes, traces are to be found throughout the country, and it is likely that some structures now preserving only the names of Thutmose III were actually begun during the coregency. Nothing of hers seems to be known from the north, but just south of the Middle Kingdom cemetery at Beni Hasan, a rock-cut temple was cut, dedicated to the goddess Pakhat (fig. 49).[80] Now known as the Speos Artemidos or Istabl Antar, a long dedication inscription was inscribed on its façade, boasting of Hatshepsut's achievements. Listed alongside the Punt expedition are a number of temple restorations, including at Ashmunein, twenty kilometers to the west, and at Quseir, sixty kilometers to the southwest. The need for some of these restorations is stated to be a hang-over from the depredations of the Hyksos, "who ruled without Re"—a century earlier. A deep niche was cut further up the same valley, also dedicated to Pakhat, in the names of Thutmose III and Hatshepsut (who is accompanied by Neferure in the principal offering scene).[81]

Blocks at Medamud[82] suggest that work was carried out there by Hatshepsut. South of Thebes, Hatshepsut was responsible for beginning the pylon of the temple at Armant,[83] and was also active at El-Kab, adding a large peristyle court to a structure built by Amenhotep I to replace one of Montjuhotep II of the Middle Kingdom (fig. 50).[84] A statue of Hatshepsut has been found at Edfu,[85] and a gate bearing her names and those of Thutmose III formerly existed at Kom Ombo (fig. 51).[86] At Elephantine, Hatshepsut undertook the construction of the core buildings of the temples of Satet (fig. 52)[87] and Khnum.[88]

In Nubia, a block originally from the temple at Quban attests to Hatshepsut's building work there,[89] at the Second Cataract border between Lower and Upper Nubia. Here, the early Eighteenth Dynasty saw the rebuilding of a number of the Middle Kingdom forts, including the addition of new temples.[90] Hatshepsut's presence as regent in the decoration of that erected at Semna has been noted above (pages 20–21), while she appears as king (as does Thutmose III) in that at Kumma.[91] The main temple in the fortress of Buhen (fig. 53) was built by Hatshepsut, which included depictions of Thutmose II.[92] At Faras, Hatshepsut was responsible for the rock chapel of Hathor-of-Abeshek,[93]

FIGURE 49 View toward the valley of the Istabl Antar, and of the temple and its interior.

FIGURE 50 The temple area at El-Kab in 2003; inset: naos of Thutmose III from the site (Fitzwilliam E.40.1902).

FIGURE 51 Doorway of Thutmose III and Hatshepsut from Kom Ombo (current location unknown).

FIGURE 52 The island of Elephantine and the temple of Satet.

and on Sai Island[94] have been found a number of sealings naming Hatshepsut as king.[95] The lower part of a statue of her as queen was also found at the site,[96] which would suggest work on the temple here during the regency. Further south, at Kerma-Dukki Gel, major work was carried out in the names of Hatshepsut and Thutmose II.[97]

FIGURE 53 The temple from the fortress of Buhen, as reconstructed in the Sudan National Museum, Khartoum.

4 Thutmose Alone

Just as Hatshepsut attributed her kingship to the cumulative gift of her heavenly father, Amun, and her earthly father, Thutmose I, the third Thutmose also set forth an account that placed his right to the throne in the context of the birth-nomination sequence, albeit only employing the second of these elements. It seems clear that the formulation of this text dates from after Thutmose III's assumption of sole rule.

The inscription at Karnak recounting Thutmose III's advent as king (fig. 54)[1] begins by recounting that Amun had destined him for kingship "while in the nest." The text depicts Thutmose, a young prince, as a novice priest in the temple of Karnak, who is sought out

FIGURE 54 Thutmose III's account of his elevation to kingship; for its location, see fig. 42.

by Amun's image while in procession around the Wadjyt Hall (pages 57, 92). Amun then sets Thutmose before "His Person" (either Amun himself or Thutmose II—but perhaps both, in a case of "constructive ambiguity," not uncommon in Egyptian texts), and it is after this that the prince is presented to those assembled in the hall. In the same way that Hatshepsut depicts herself as being made king at the time of her presentation by Thutmose I, the text of Thutmose III has his coronation following directly after his presentation to the court. That this telescoping of events should be seen as standard in this kind of text is demonstrated by the equivalent inscription of Rameses II at the temple of Sethy I at Abydos,[2] which also places that king's coronation directly after his proclamation as heir.[3]

Titles

Following the end of the coregency, the "ka" form of Thutmose's prenomen was never used again—nor was the complementary *n* ever used with the *mn*-sign. Although the rest of his titulary remained extant, alternate Horus, Nebti, and Golden Falcon names were introduced, while epithets were on occasion added to the nomen and/or prenomen (see the appendix to this chapter, pages 115–16). Some of these were location-specific (e.g., *ḥq3-ỉwnw*, "Ruler of Heliopolis"), while others were relevant to the king's jubilees.

The Royal Family

Although it has been suggested that Thutmose III might have married Neferure, the evidence is weak (page 31), and the earliest known wife of the king is Sitiah, referred to in texts as both King's Wife and King's Great Wife (fig. 55 left). Unless there was indeed an earlier spouse, she is likely to have been the mother of Thutmose III's eldest son (*s3-nsw smsw*), Amenemhat, who is known from a text of the end of Year 23, and may be mentioned at Kurgus (fig. 11). Sitiah was the daughter of a royal nurse named Ipu,[4] and is shown as deceased in the king's tomb (fig. 108e). Also noted in the tomb as dead (*m3'-ḫrw*) is another King's Wife, Nebtu; nothing is known about her except that she had an estate whose steward, Nebamun, was buried in TT24.

A third spouse, Meryetre, is also shown in the tomb, but denoted as "alive" (*'nḫ-tỉ*). This woman (more fully Meryetre-Hatshepsut, fig. 56) was Great Wife during the latter part of the reign of Thutmose III, and the mother of the eventual heir, Amenhotep, under whom she became God's Wife.[5] Like Sitiah, Meryetre seems to have been a commoner by birth, probably the offspring of an Adoratrix of the God named Huy (fig. 55 right).[6] She appears on a number of monuments, both of the reign of her husband and that of her son, and it was certainly intended that she should be buried in the Valley of the Kings (page 150). In addition to Sitiah, Nebet, and Meryetre, three other King's Wives, named Menwi, Merti, and Menhet (apparently of Syrian extraction),[7] are known

FIGURE 55 Left: statue of Queen Sitiah; from Tod (Cairo JE37638). Right: statue of Huy, probably the mother of Meryetre, who is depicted with her grandchildren, Prince Menkheperre and Princesses Nebetiunet (on her lap), Iset, Meryetamun C, and Meryetamun D (BM EA1280).

from their joint tomb (page 150); this seems to date around the end of the coregency. It is likely that other junior wives also existed.

Apart from Princes Amenemhet and Amenhotep, other known children of Thutmose III include Prince Menkheperre, Princesses Nebetiunet and Iset, and two more daughters, both named Meryetamun (one presumably born after the other's death). As they all appear on the statue of Huy, probably the mother of Meryetre, it would seem that they were all offspring of the latter. A Princess Baketamun is named on a fragment of a faience votive object from Deir el-Bahari, which also bears the cartouche of Thutmose III,[8] and a deceased Princess Nefertiry is shown alongside the aforementioned queens in the king's tomb. A further possible son of Thutmose III, Siamun, is depicted on the statue of an official which may date to the reign of Thutmose III.[9] Interestingly, Siamun's

FIGURE 56 Top: Queen Meryetre, shown with Thutmose III in his Deir el-Bahari Hathor chapel (see fig. 129). Bottom: as depicted with her husband in the Small Temple at Medinet Habu.

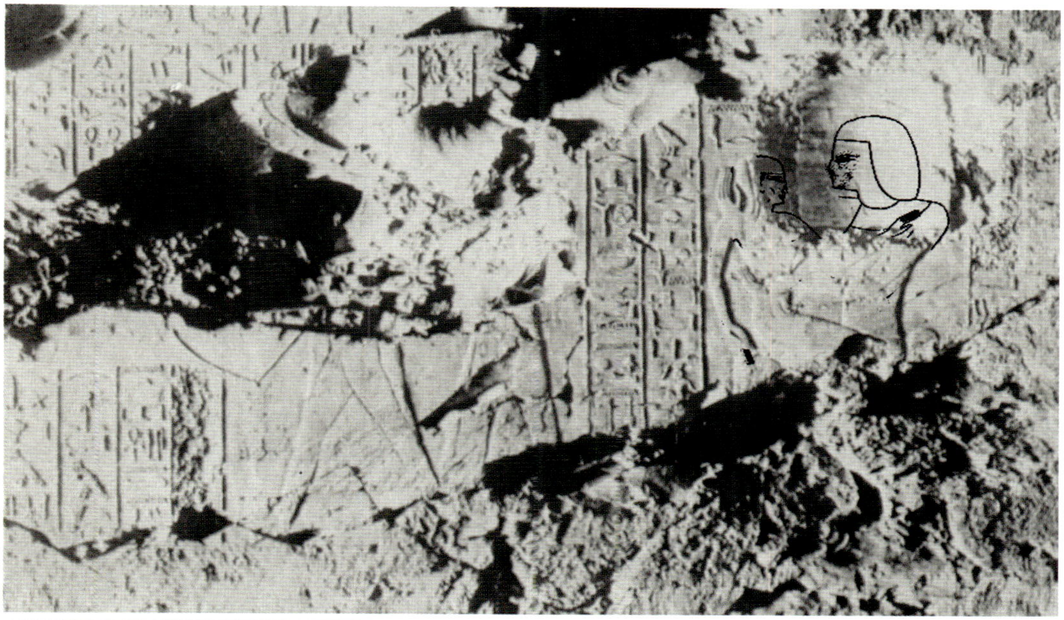

FIGURE 57 Top: photograph and sketch of scene of Prince Amenhotep being taught to shoot by Min in TT109. Bottom: as king, the prince shooting arrows through a thick copper target; from Karnak (Luxor Museum J129).

FIGURE 58 Benermerut with a Princess Meryetamun; from Karnak (Cairo CG42171).

name has here been partly erased, which may be linked with a conflict that wracked the royal family at the end of the reign of Amenhotep II (see pages 154–55).

Prince Amenhotep states (as King Amenhotep II) that he came to the throne at the age of eighteen,[10] which would place his birth around Thutmose III's Year 36. As usual with royal children, his education was entrusted to senior officials, and he is shown being taught archery by Min, Mayor of Thinis, in the latter's tomb-chapel (TT109—fig. 57), and may also appear in the anonymous TT143.[11]

Of the Princesses Meryetamun, one of them is depicted on the lap of her tutor, Benermerut (fig. 58), while the younger Meryetamun is shown with her father in his Hathor shrine at Deir el-Bahari (for which see page 101). This latter depiction seems to have been carved (or at least finished) under Amenhotep II, since Meryetamun is given the title of King's Sister—and also God's Wife, presumably passed to her by her mother, Meryetre, after the death of Thutmose III.

The Administration of the State

There is no evidence for any extensive change in the officials of the realm when Thutmose III became sole ruler.[12] There seems to have been some rebalancing of authority, the vizierate becoming more powerful, certainly in the south, at first in the person of the incumbent Useramun, and then in that of his nephew and successor, Rekhmire, who was in post by Year 33. The latter had extensive responsibilities regarding the Karnak precinct and its furnishings, also holding the post of Steward of Amun. This had long been a key office held by Senenmut. The breadth of his activities led to Rekhmire's tomb-chapel (TT100) being an important source of illustrations of workshop activity of the period (fig. 60). Since Rekhmire's tomb-chapel has no burial complex, he may have been granted burial in the Valley of the Kings. This would certainly be the case with the later vizier Amenemopet, who combined his chapel on Sheikh Abd el-Qurna (TT29) with a shaft tomb (KV48) in the Valley.

FIGURE 59 Tombs on the Sheikh Abd el-Qurna hill datable to the time of Thutmose III and Hatshepsut.

The reign of Thutmose III seems to have marked the division of the vizierate between northern and southern incumbents, presumably reflecting the sheer volume of activities that now fell within the purview of the office. Thus, in addition to the southern Rekhmire, we know of two northern viziers under Thutmose III, Ptahmose (who also held the Memphite high priesthood)[13] and his probable successor, Neferweben.[14]

As noted above (page 38), the Chancellor Tiy was still in office in Year 25, but by Year 28 he had been succeeded by Sennefri (TT99), who had been appointed Northern Chief Spokesman late in the coregency; he was still in office in Year 35. Sennefri's activities included a voyage to Byblos to procure cedar for use at Karnak, and involvement in the turquoise mines of Sinai. He was also the mayor of a number of towns, and the tutor of one of the king's sons; one of Sennefri's daughters became a royal nurse. A final Chancellor known from the reign is Min, who was also Great Chief of Upper Egypt and Judge in Lower Egypt. His son Sobekhotep would later hold the post of Chancellor during the reign of Thutmose IV.

The control of the granaries remained under the incumbents of Hatshepsut's reign, Minnakht being an Overseer of the Granary of Upper and Lower Egypt until at least Year 36. Tjenuna was succeeded by Iamnedjeh (TT84), although the latter accompanied Thutmose III to Syria as a First Royal Herald in Year 33. At the end of the reign, the title of Overseer of the Granary of Upper and Lower Egypt was borne by Minnakht's son Menkheper(reseneb) (TT79), who served into the reign of Amenhotep II.

FIGURE 60 The tomb-chapel of Rekhmire (TT100), including scenes of brick-making, statue manufacture, and the bringing of foreign tribute. At the top left, the upper false door (now Louvre C74) is shown restored to its former location.

Djehuty had been Overseer of the Houses of Silver and Gold under Hatshepsut, but it is unknown whether he continued in office after the end of her reign. All we know is that Benermerut (fig. 58) and Ptahhotep were in the role by Year 45, with another Djehuty (TT80+TT104) holding the title at the end of the reign of Thutmose III, and serving into that of Amenhotep II. A number of Royal Butlers served Thutmose III, following on from Djehuty, known in that role during the time of Hatshepsut (page 39). One, Qenamun, was also Mayor of Memphis, while others included Neferperet and Montjuiwy (TT172).

Another Mayor of Memphis was Hemy, while various other towns' chief officials are known from the reign. A number had wider responsibilities as well, Paheri of El-Kab having been a royal tutor as far back as the time of Thutmose I (page 11). The Mayor of Thinis, Satepihu, was involved in the extraction of Hatshepsut's second pair of obelisks, while the Herald Inyotef also fulfilled that mayoral role, combining it with that of the Chief of All Oases. Another Thinite mayor was Min (TT109), who was additionally tutor to the future Amenhotep II (fig. 57).

Nubia had been conquered as far as the Abu Hamed Reach under Thutmose I (page 12), with military activity taking place there during the coregency (page 44). Now, a text apparently dating to Year 22[15] mentions rhinoceros hunting in a remote land named Miu, probably to be placed between Abu Hamed and the Sixth Cataract. However, that Abu Hamed was still regarded as a permanent frontier is suggested by the addition of a near-duplicate of Thutmose I's tableau on the same rock at Kurgus (fig. 11), presumably as a restatement of this locale being the southern limit of Egyptian permanent dominion. Indeed, in contrast to the extensive military expeditions into Syria-Palestine, there is very little indication of such activity in Nubia during Thutmose III's sole rule.[16]

The most substantive piece of evidence on this matter is a Year 50 rock inscription at Sehel.[17] This speaks of the king traversing a canal through the First Cataract, having defeated his enemies. However, it is unclear whether this was a true military operation or simply an armed royal progress. Indeed, a pacified status for the region is suggested by the fact that it was under Thutmose III that the first major building works seem to have been undertaken in Upper Nubia (pages 102–106, below). From at least Year 31 the Nubian dominions provided a steady stream of resources to Egypt, and in Year 47 a stela was erected in the area of Gebel Barkal (fig. 82 left), whose locale was now becoming the imperial center in Upper Nubia. The text of the stela rehearsed the king's career to date, and recorded a speech delivered at Barkal by the king, in which he set out aspects of the way in which Egyptian rule over the region would function.

The key office of viceroy was held by Nehi through much of Thutmose III's sole rule,[18] and who left memorials and inscriptions at Buhen, Semna, Sai Island, Kumma,

FIGURE 61 Monuments of the Viceroy of Nubia, Nehi. Top left: statue from Deir el-Bahari (Nubian Museum). Top right: pyramidion from his tomb (Florence 2608). Bottom: sarcophagus (Berlin ÄM17895).

Sehel, Qasr Ibrim, and Aniba. It is unknown when Nehi left office, as no other viceroy is known until Usersatet, attested under Amenhotep II. Nehi was buried at Thebes, in the hitherto little-used Qurnet Murai necropolis, in the now-lost tomb TTD1 [perhaps TTK-274-] (fig. 61).

Operating the Temples

Thebes

Although for some time a matter for debate, it now seems that there were two High Priests of Amun named Menkheperreseneb during the reign of Thutmose III.[19] Of them, Menkheperreseneb the Elder was the owner of TT86, and was in office after Year 33, and was also involved in the building of Thutmose III's Deir el-Bahari temple (page 101). Menkheperreseneb the Younger, his nephew, was the owner of TT112, and had none of the additional responsibilities held by the earlier pontiff Hapuseneb, many of which now fell under the remit of the vizier.

Puyemre initially maintained his position as Second Priest of Amun, at least into the 30s of Thutmose III's reign, to which time the decoration of his tomb can be dated.[20] However, a number of later holders of the title are known (although it has been suggested that some actually served the cult of Amun of Deir el-Bahari, rather than of Karnak). These are a further Menkheperreseneb, Amen(?)hotep (a son of the Vizier Rekhmire), Merymaat (a son of the Vizier Useramun), a Pehueker, an Ahmose, and Amenhotep-Sise (TT75), who lived into the reign of Thutmose IV. A Third Priest of Amun at Karnak was Khaemheryibsen (TT98), but it is not certain whether a Fourth Priest Kaemamun functioned there, rather than at a temple at Thebes-West. In Karnak's Precinct of Mut, Qen (TT59), was High Priest of Mut.

The priesthood was supplemented by administrative personnel, headed by the Steward of Amun. The first post-Senenmut incumbent seems to have been Roau, who was probably succeeded by Sendjehuty. Amenhotep (TT97), who was a High Priest of Amun under Amenhotep II, also listed the steward's office among his titles, which role he may previously have exercised under Thutmose III.

Elsewhere in Egypt

Only a few temple officeholders are known from elsewhere in Egypt. A man named Sennefer, apparently a native of Sedment, held both the titles High Priest of Re at Heliopolis and High Priest of Ptah at Memphis. However, it is unclear whether he held them consecutively, or, quite exceptionally, simultaneously. Another Memphite pontiff was Ptahmose, who also served as northern Vizier (page 73). At Abydos, Nebwawy was both High Priest and Steward of Osiris into the reign of Amenhotep II; a number of other staff of Osiris's temple are also known. The regular combination of sacerdotal and civil posts in provincial centers is demonstrated by the dual roles held by Iamnefer, who was at the same time Mayor of Neferusy, and High Priest of Thoth.

The Warrior Pharaoh

As already noted (page 44), it is likely that Thutmose III had been involved in military activity during the coregency. However, once he was sole pharaoh, campaigning became a major feature of the remainder of his life.[21] Our knowledge of these comes from the set of Annals that Thutmose III caused to be inscribed on the walls of the complex of rooms and structures whose construction had been begun by Hatshepsut, and continued after the end of the coregency (figs. 62, 70).

As is stated in the Annals themselves, they were based on a war diary maintained on campaign, later transcribed onto a leather roll, and kept in the archives of the Karnak temple. The General and Royal Scribe Tjanuny states, in his tomb-chapel (TT74),[22] that

FIGURE 62 The southern face of the west tower of Pylon VII at Karnak, showing Thutmose III smiting enemies, with a list of conquered towns below. For the whole pylon, see fig. 73.

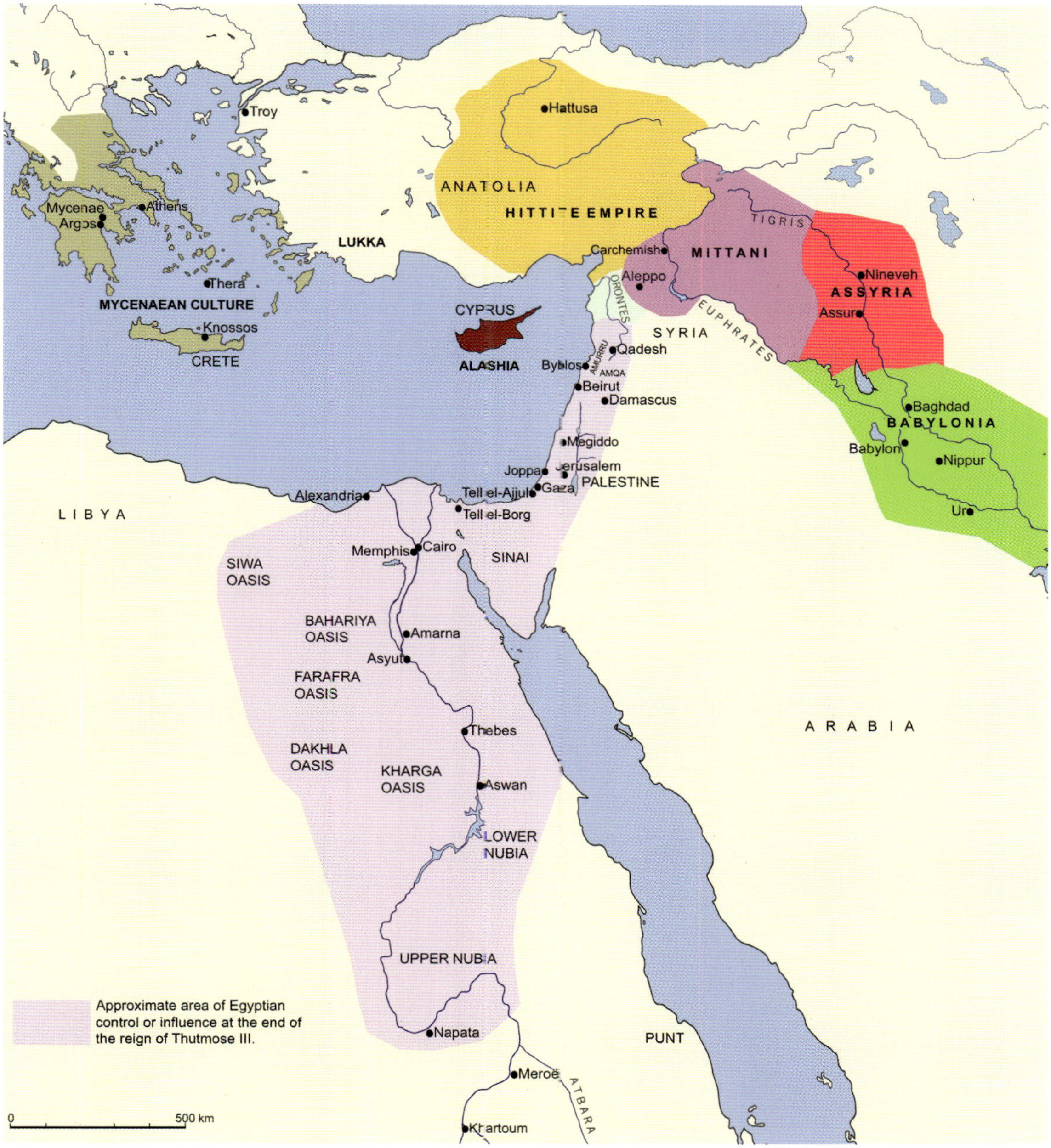

FIGURE 63 Map of the Near East, with the approximate extent of the major powers and their spheres of influence during the second half of the Eighteenth Dynasty.

he "followed [Thutmose III] and saw the victories of the king in every country . . . and recorded the victories which he won in every land, putting (them) in writing according to the facts." It is accordingly clear that he was responsible for maintaining the war diary for at least some of the campaigns, although, given his long service after Thutmose III's death, into at least the reign of Thutmose IV, he may not necessarily have undertaken the task during Thutmose III's very earliest campaigns.

Megiddo

Thutmose I had brought most of Syria-Palestine under Egyptian influence, but it is unclear how solid the Egyptian position remained during the following years. It seems that by the time that Thutmose III attained sole rule, Egyptian interests were threatened by the rulers of the cities of Tunip and Qadesh, in northern Syria. They were vassals of the state of Mitanni (also known as Naharin), the eastern part of which straddled the upper waters of the Euphrates, which had marked the limit of advance of Thutmose I. Heading a coalition of local potentates, the ruler of Qadesh and his allies now occupied the city of Megiddo (Tell el-Mutesellim) in northern Palestine (known as Retjenu to the Egyptians). The city occupied an important strategic location, where a number of trade routes coincided. The official account of the opening of Thutmose III's long-term campaigning in the region begins on IV *prt* 25 of Year 22.[23]

> [His Person passed the fortress of] Tjaru[[24]] on the first campaign of victory [to smite those who attacked] the borders of Egypt . . . . Year 23, I *šmw* 4 . . . (arriving) at . . . Gaza. [Year 23], I *šmw* 5, departure from this place . . . to overthrow that wretched enemy, to extend the borders of Egypt. Year 23, I *šmw* 16, (arrival) at the town of Yehem. [His Person] ordered a consultation with his valiant army, saying: "That wretched foe of Qadesh has come and entered into Megiddo and is [there] at this moment. He has gathered to him the princes of [all] the foreign lands [that had been loyal] to Egypt, as well as those from as far as Naharin."

The debate in the Egyptian camp concerned the best means of approaching Megiddo from Yehem. The latter lay some thirty kilometers southwest of Megiddo, separated from it by the mountainous Carmel Ridge (fig. 64). There were three possible routes between the two points: one to the north of the mountains, one to the south of the mountains, and one through the mountains. The first two were easy to traverse, but were long, would certainly be watched by the forces based at Megiddo, and the use of either would result in any battle taking place some distance from the city, which was the Egyptians' target.

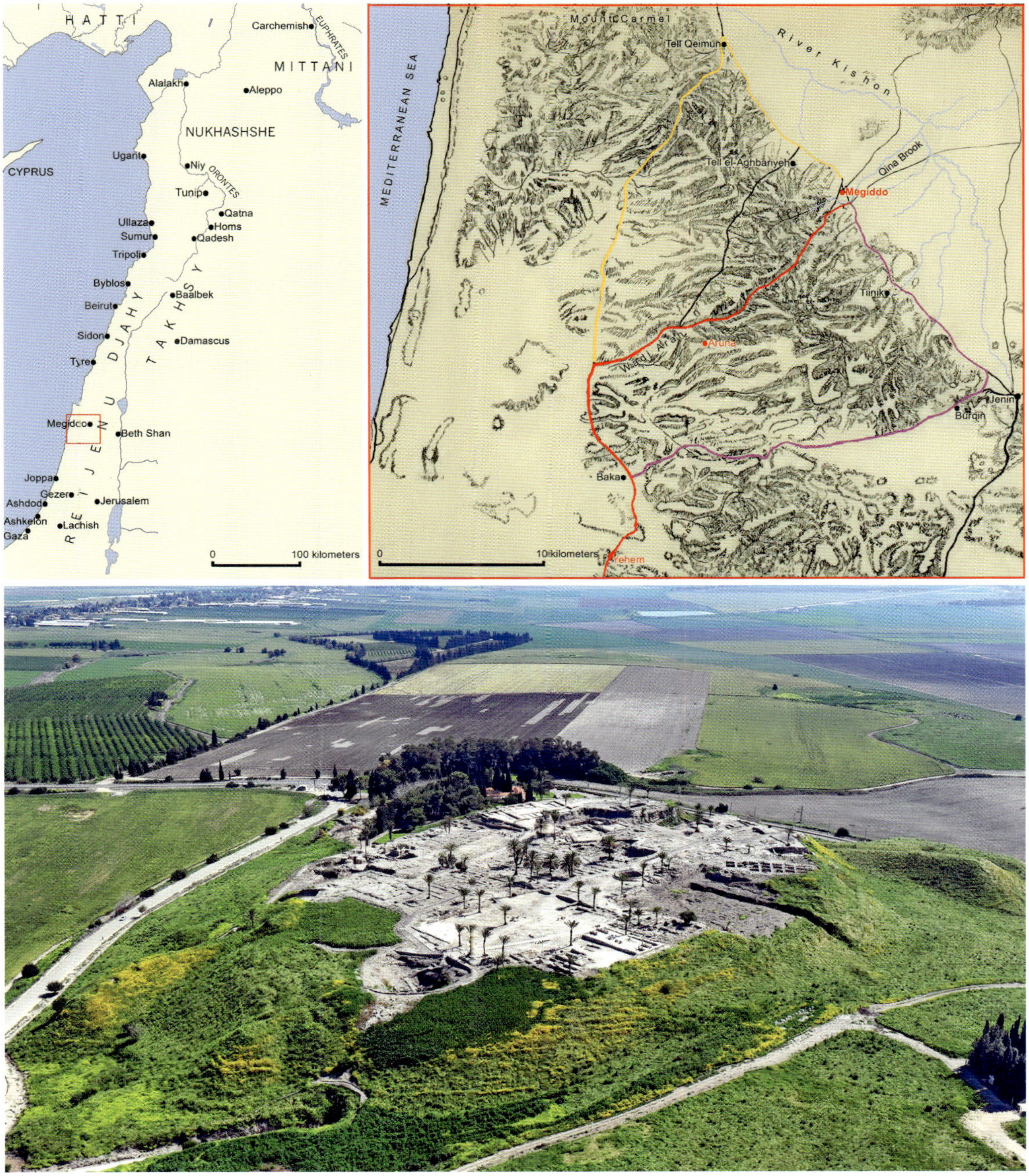

FIGURE 64 Top left: the coastal region of Syria-Palestine. Top right: the region of Megiddo, showing the three principal routes to approach the city from the southwest. Bottom: the site of Megiddo, from the southwest.

The third route followed the Wadi Arah, a narrow pass through the center of the mountains, via a place known as Aruna, and led directly to Megiddo.[25] The king's view was that the difficulty of the route, requiring the army to advance in single file, would make it unlikely that Megiddo would expect attack from that direction. The Egyptian senior officers are depicted in the Annals as being doubtful.

> "How will it be to go [on] this road which becomes narrow, when it is [reported] that the enemies are waiting there [beyond and they] are numerous? Will not horse go behind [horse] and [soldiers] and people too? Shall our vanguard be fighting while the [rearguard] waits here in Aruna, unable to fight? . . . . May our valiant lord proceed on whichever of [these] seems best to him, (but) do not make us go on that difficult road!"

This kind of depiction of the king in debate with his advisors is a common trope in Egyptian texts, with the king invariably opting for the daring course of action, in contrast to the views of his more timorous officials.[26] Accordingly, Thutmose's response was to exclaim:

> "I swear, as Re loves me, as my father Amun favors me, as my nostrils are refreshed with life and dominion my majesty shall proceed on this Aruna road! Let him of you who wishes go on [the other roads]. Let him of you who wishes come in My Person's following. Or they will say, those foes whom Re abhors: 'Has His Person gone on another road because he is afraid of us?' So they will say." They said to His Person: ". . . Do [as you wish]! We are followers of [Your Person] wherever Your Person goes! A servant follows his lord." [His Person ordered that] the whole army be told: "[Your valiant lord will guide your steps on] this road which becomes narrow." [For His Person had taken] an oath, saying: "I shall not let [my valiant army] go before me from [this place!]"

Accordingly, the Egyptian army pressed on to Aruna, where the march through the last section of the mountains began. The van of the army emerged from the pass while the rear was still at Aruna, and found that the enemy army had been divided to watch the two "expected" routes around the mountains. Concerned that the king might strike without his whole force being with him, the generals urged that he await the passage and arrival of the rearguard before attacking:

> "May our valiant lord listen to us this time. May our lord watch for us the rearguard of his army with its people. When the rearguard has come out to us in the

> open, then we shall fight against those foreigners; then we shall not be concerned about the rearguard of our army!" His Person halted in the open, and he waited there to watch the rearguard of his valiant army. Now, when the last of the lead troops had come out from this road, midday passed. His Person arrived to the south of Megiddo, on the shore of the Qina Brook, when the seventh hour was in (its) course of day. A camp was laid out for his majesty, and the whole army was told: "Prepare yourselves! Make your weapons ready! For I will engage in combat with that wretched foe in the morning." . . .

At dawn on I *šmw* 19,[27] the Egyptian army deployed for the attack on Megiddo. One division took up station on a rise to the northwest of the city, one on a hill south of the Qina Brook, and a third in the center, under the personal command of the king. On the Egyptian attack, the enemy forces fell back on Megiddo, abandoning their equipment to find shelter within the city walls, being "hoisted up into the town by pulling at their garments. For the people had shut the town behind them, and they now [lowered] garments to hoist them up into the town."

Unfortunately, the enemy horses and "chariots of gold and silver" that now lay between the Egyptian armies and the city's walls proved too much of a distraction, and rather than storming the city before the enemy could enter and its gates be secured,

> His Person's troops . . . set their hearts to plundering the possessions of the enemies . . . at this moment, when the wretched foe of Qadesh and the wretched foe of this town were being pulled up hurriedly so as to admit them into their town.

Accordingly, while in possession of a vast store of booty and prisoners, there was now the need to lay siege to Megiddo, within which was shut up "every prince of every [northern] land." A ditch was dug around it, reinforced by a wall, and, at length,

> the rulers of this foreign land came on their bellies to kiss the ground to the might of His Person, and to beg breath for their nostrils, because of the greatness of his strength and the extent of the power of [Amun over all foreign lands].

With them came tribute, including slaves, precious metals, semiprecious stones, food and drink, cattle, sheep and goats, luxury and household goods, weapons, chariots, and horses. In addition, the fields of wheat around Megiddo were requisitioned by the Egyptians, the harvest carried out under their direction yielding 207,300 sacks of wheat. The surrendering local rulers were allowed to keep their cities, but were now firmly marked out as vassals of the Egyptian king. This was to be the basis of Egyptian control in Syria-Palestine: to do so via native rulers, who were to be kept under close scrutiny, and with their children to be sent to Egypt for education, and simultaneously to be hostages against their fathers' good behavior (see pages 86–87, below).[28]

Having secured Megiddo, the army moved northwest, where the cities of Yenoam, Nuges, and Herenkeru (exact locations unclear)[29] were subdued and gave tribute, and a fortress was constructed. The king then gathered his booty and returned toward Egypt, reaching Thebes around five months after his army had first left Tjaru. There, a series of celebrations took place, culminating in a ceremonial presentation of offerings to Amun.

Beyond Megiddo

Thutmose III clearly felt that the Megiddo campaign was emblematic of his military endeavors in Syria-Palestine, and no later operation was recounted in anything approaching the same detail. Rather, the focus of later parts of the Annals is generally on booty taken and gifts received. Thus, having secured much of Palestine for Egyptian authority by his Year 22/23 campaign, the king spent most of the summers of the next two decades in the field. These expeditions were a mixture of armed tours and more proactive military ventures. That of Year 24 involved the receipt of tribute from the chiefs of Palestine, together with two sets of gifts sent from Assyria, far to the east, reflecting the development of what was becoming an intricate system of gift exchange between the major independent powers of the eastern Mediterranean region.[30]

Year 25's expedition is interesting. In addition to the "subjugation" of an area of the region, it involved the collection of fauna and flora, images of which (fig. 65) were included in one of the rooms that he was incorporating into his Festival Hall complex at Karnak (pages 92–95). The same year saw a mining expedition to the Sinai, led by the Chancellor Tiy (fig. 66 left).

The next known campaign into Syria-Palestine was in Year 29. This was counted as the "Fifth" campaign, suggesting that some operation, the record of which is now lost, had occurred in Year 26, 27, or 28 (a mining expedition went to Sinai in Year 27—fig. 66 right). The Year 29 campaign extended into the coastal region of what is now Lebanon (known as Djahy to the Egyptians), against forces loyal to the ruler of Tunip, northwest of Qadesh. During this operation, the city of Waret (probably near Tripoli) was taken, and then a fleet of cargo ships. Next, the city of Ardata, just southeast of Tripoli, was seized, along with its grain and fruit harvest (followed by the felling of the trees), suggesting that Egyptians were there in late summer.

Year 30 saw Thutmose III finally dealing with the home city of his old enemy the ruler of Qadesh. Rather than marching through Palestine, the army took ship along the

FIGURE 65 Parts of the "Botanic Garden" reliefs in Room XIII of the Festival Hall complex at Karnak.

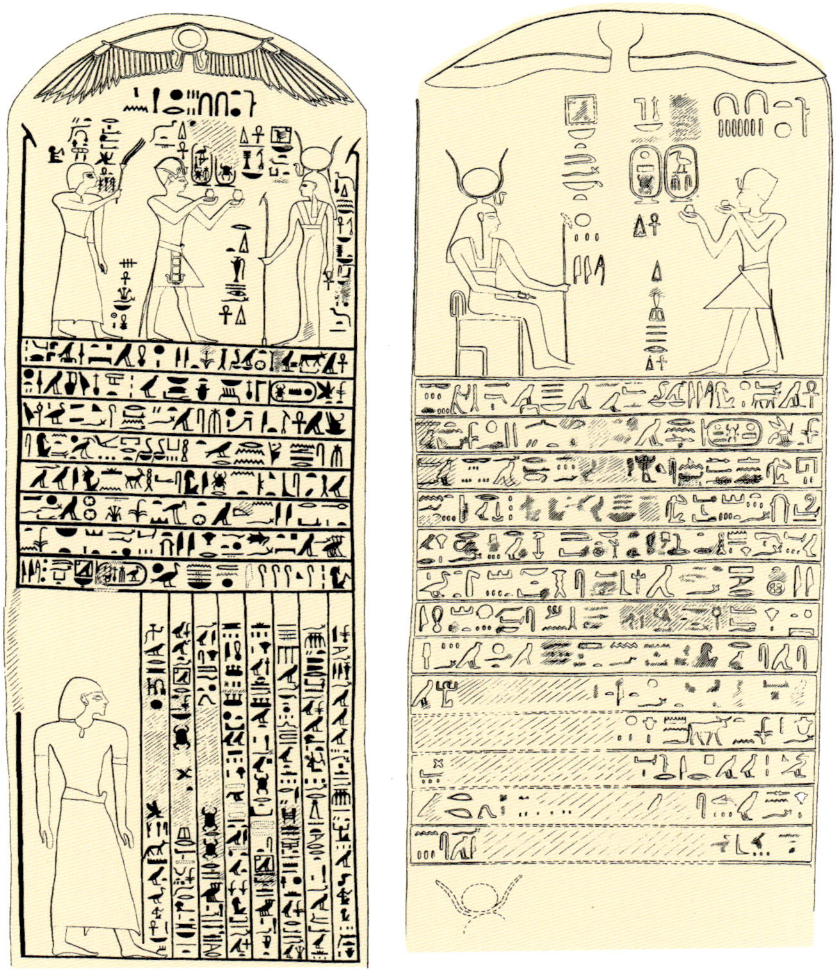

FIGURE 66 Stelae at Serabit el-Khadim, commemorating mining activities in Years 25 and 27 of Thutmose III, the former under the direction of the Royal Acquaintance Simontju.

coast and were landed on the Levantine shore, perhaps at the port of Byblos, before proceeding northeast overland to Qadesh. Unfortunately—unlike the later battle of Qadesh under Rameses II, two centuries later—the surviving official account of the attack on the city is laconic at best: "Arrival at town of Qadesh; sacking it, cutting down its fruit trees and harvesting its grain."

The army then moved on to the towns of Sumur, apparently on the coast to the northwest of Qadesh (at Tell Kazel?), and Ardata (again), both of which were dealt with in the same way as Qadesh. The capture of these towns was accompanied by a rounding up of the sons and brothers of the local rulers, who were then to be transported to Egypt. There they would remain until one was needed to succeed his father or sibling in the rule of a Syro-Palestinian polity. By that time it was hoped that such individuals would be Egyptianized and willing to follow Egyptian "advice" in their conduct of matters of state. Thirty-six such persons were taken away on this occasion, accompanied by 181 servants, 188 horses, and forty ornately decorated chariots.

Thutmose was back in the region in Year 31, seizing the town of Ullaza, a little further up the coast from Sumur, the prisoners including the commander of the army of a son of the ruler of Tunip. Year 32 was seemingly taken up with preparations in Egypt for the great campaign of Year 33. Thutmose having consolidated his hold over Palestine and southern Syria by the defeat of Qadesh, the king's road was open to Mitannian territory further north. Thutmose I had reached the Euphrates; now, Thutmose III crossed it and defeated the king of Mitanni in battle, before returning south, to the town of Niy, north of Tunip. At the point where he had crossed the Euphrates, the king erected a stela on the east bank, opposite that of his grandfather on the west side of the river. Interestingly, among those from whom the king received gifts this year were the Hittites, just beginning to emerge onto the Late Bronze Age world stage.

It was probably at this point that the king undertook an elephant hunt that is recorded in the Year 47 stela of Thutmose III from Gebel Barkal (fig. 82 left), as well as in the autobiographical text of one his army officers, Amenemheb-Mahu (TT85).[31] According to the latter, the king confronted 120 elephants, and Amenemheb states that he came to the king's aid, cutting off the trunk of an animal that Thutmose was fighting. Amenemheb, who would continue in royal service into the reign of Amenhotep II, includes a number of anecdotes concerning his service in the wars of Thutmose III, including the capture of Qadesh in Year 30.

Among the king's senior army commanders[32] was General Djehuty. He became the hero of a folk tale,[33] set during the campaigns of Thutmose III (or possibly Amenhotep II), in which he infiltrates Egyptian soldiers into the town of Joppa in sacks carried by pack animals. As with many officials, Djehuty had a range of non-military responsibilities as well, and his now-lost tomb at Saqqara yielded a range of rich items.[34] Other generals in the service of Thutmose III included Tjanuny (TT74), whom we have noted above (pages 78, 80) as being responsible for keeping at least some of the campaign war diaries, and who would serve into the time of the king's grandson, Thutmose IV.

In the wake of his achievement of crossing the Euphrates—the furthest that ancient Egyptian armies are known to have penetrated in this direction—Thutmose received presents from Babylon and the Hittites. The next year's expedition seems to have comprised little more than accepting the surrender of various towns on the Lebanese coast and the region of Nukhashshe, which lay to the south of Aleppo. Gifts were also received from, apparently, the king of Cyprus,[35] which lay only a short distance from what was now an Egyptian-dominated Levantine shore.

Year 35 saw resistance to Egyptian hegemony in Syria from the king of Mitanni, resulting in a battle at Aranu, probably somewhere in Nukhashshe. This was an Egyptian victory, spoils including 180 horses and sixty chariots. Although we know that the next two years also saw campaigns, the Annals are missing for this period, but resume for Year 38, when the king was back in Nukhashshe. In Year 39, Thutmose III was further south, in Palestine, on a punitive expedition against *š3sw*-nomads, as well as undertaking the now-usual collection of tribute.

In Year 40, gifts were received from Assyria, as well as tribute from the chieftains of Palestine. The latter was repeated the following year, when gifts were again forthcoming from Hatti. These were received during a campaign that seems to have included the sacking of one or more towns in an unknown location. Year 42's operations appear to have been more extensive. They first focused on the lands of the Fenkhu (Phoenicians), starting with the conquest of the town of Irkata (probably Tell Arqa), southeast of Sumur. Thutmose then headed northeast, destroying the town of [...]kana en route to his long-standing antagonist, the city of Tunip. Here, he followed his usual approach of sacking the town, taking its grain and fruits, and chopping down its orchards.

Captives included troops from Mitanni, the campaign being rounded off by the sacking of three towns in the vicinity of Qadesh, and a siege of the city itself. Amenemheb describes this action in the autobiographical text, which includes the anecdote that Amenemheb himself had cut down a mare sent out by the King of Qadesh to distract the stallions of the Egyptian chariot teams. Gifts were again sent by Hatti, and also the otherwise unknown location of Tanaya, which included a jug of "Keftiu (Cretan) workmanship."

The Year 42 expedition seems to have marked the end of the king's active campaigning in Syria-Palestine, rounding off two decades of intensive military activity. That Thutmose III felt that he was drawing a line is indicated by his formal command "to record the victories that he had won from Year 23 to Year 42, when this inscription was recorded on this divine booth, that he might be given life forever." Much of the booty from the campaigns (and gifts received from further afield) was devoted to the enlargement of the Karnak temple complex, where a wall was devoted to its formal presentation (fig. 70 bottom). The king's victories were widely trumpeted on various monuments, one of the most remarkable being a stela in which his successes were celebrated partly in verse (fig. 67).

While Thutmose's successors would also campaign in Syria-Palestine, none would emulate him in crossing the Euphrates, and their activities seem to have been essentially devoted to maintaining the status quo in the region, putting down revolts and suppressing other disorder. As the dynasty progressed, Mitanni went from a foe to a valued ally of

FIGURE 67 The "Poetical" stela of Thutmose III, with its last section in verse; from Karnak (Cairo CG34010).

Egypt. As such, it was part of a "concert of nations" that endured until Mitanni fell victim to Hittite and Assyrian expansion in the latter part of the fourteenth century.

Nevertheless, northern Syria would remain an area of shifting allegiances—with Qadesh switching its fealty on more than one occasion. The region would be the theater of conflict between Egypt and Hatti during the latter years of the Eighteenth Dynasty and the first decades of the Nineteenth. This would culminate in a peace treaty between Rameses II and the Hittite Hattushilish III in the former's Year 21.[36]

Trade and Diplomacy

We have already noted that gifts were delivered to the Egyptian king by various powers beyond the areas of his conquests. The exchange of gifts was an important part of international relations, although often conflated with tribute from defeated or dependent polities in public presentations. The management of such material from abroad involved many officials in Egypt, and as a result depictions of presentations are to be found in a number of tomb-chapels of the Eighteenth Dynasty (e.g., fig. 60 bottom).

Among the places from which goods came was Crete (fig. 39 bottom). A connection between the island's Minoan culture and Egypt is to be seen in a remarkable set of Cretan-style frescoes that were painted on the walls of a palace at Avaris that seems to date to around the time of Thutmose III (fig. 68).[37] Their significance remains unclear, but the presence of such works on Egyptian soil, apparently executed by Cretan artists, clearly attests to some quite intimate link.

FIGURE 68 Part of the area occupied by the city of Avaris (Tell el-Daba), and reconstruction of a Minoan-style fresco in the Thutmosid palace there (Allard Pierson Museum, Amsterdam); inset: fragment F12.

The Monumental Pharaoh

Karnak

Hatshepsut had initiated a comprehensive rebuilding of many parts of the temple complex at Karnak, and this work was continued and expanded by Thutmose III after he became sole pharaoh (fig. 42).[38] Of elements still in progress at the end of the coregency, the Chapelle Rouge was completed by Thutmose, with the dedication text at its upper level in the king's sole name (fig. 69). Its doorways were inscribed in his name as well.

FIGURE 69 Façade of the Chapelle Rouge, with detail of part of the uppermost course of blocks, decorated entirely by Thutmose III. The gray granite gate was also wholly in the name of this king.

Nevertheless, the chapel was later dismantled and replaced by a new bark shrine at some time prior to Year 42. This replacement shrine of Thutmose III was itself dismantled in the fourth century BC, and replaced by one in the name of Philip Arrhidaeos, half-brother and successor of Alexander the Great.[39]

West of the area of the bark shrine, columns were added to the courtyard between the Mansion of Maat and Pylon VI, the area between the latter and the bark shrine becoming a covered vestibule. In constructing the vestibule, Thutmose reused the granite doorways that had been manufactured in his name as part of the completion of the Chapelle Rouge complex, which was now being taken down. The vestibule continued between Pylons VI and V, and then beyond the latter into the Wadjyt Hall.

This hall was returned to its pre-Hatshepsut status as a covered space. A dozen new columns were added to match the surviving original pair of Thutmose I, and the lower parts of the obelisks of Hatshepsut were sheathed in masonry to produce massive piers, which served together with the pillars to support the new roof of the hall.[40] A pair of obelisks were erected between Pylon IV and the Dismantled Pylon (fig. 70 top left), between the obelisks of Thutmose I and Thutmose II. Like the obelisks of his father, Thutmose III's obelisks here were probably taken down when their site was overbuilt by Amenhotep III's Pylon III, less than a century later.

Many of the wall surfaces of Hatshepsut's Mansion of Maat and Thutmose III's architectural additions were covered with his military Annals, and with texts relating to his donations to, and works at, Karnak (fig. 70 top right, bottom). The south wall of the Mansion of Maat complex received Thutmose's retrospective account of his elevation to the throne (pages 67–68, fig. 54). Some walls built under Hatshepsut (e.g., those of Rooms XVI–XVIII) had been left blank, and so could be decorated from scratch, but others had their existing adornments erased or/and covered with new layers of masonry to receive new decoration by Thutmose III (e.g., figs. 45, 70 bottom).

The "core" temple was enclosed on three sides by a new girdle wall, with a number of rooms placed between it and the earlier original girdle wall on the north, and also to the inner wall of the latter on the south. Among structures erected on the north were chapels replacing earlier ones of Amenhotep I, which had been demolished during building works by Hatshepsut and Thutmose III in the area.

As well as these additions and amendments to the scheme of core buildings initiated by Hatshepsut, a wholly new complex was erected between the rear of the original Middle Kingdom sanctuary and Hatshepsut's first pair of obelisks to the east. Any structure that may have been placed here by Hatshepsut will have been demolished. Named the *3ḫ-mnw* and generally referred to today as the Festival Hall, Thutmose's project, initiated on I *šmw* 2 of Year 23, comprised a main hall and a subsidiary set of chapels

FIGURE 70 Top left: upper part of one of the obelisks of Thutmose III. Top right: part of the annals of Thutmose III, on Pylon VI. Bottom: Thutmose III's gifts to Amun, including two obelisks, as depicted on the north wall adjacent to the bark shrine (see fig. 42).

FIGURE 71 Thutmose III's Festival Hall at Karnak. Bottom left: main hall, with "tent pole" columns; bottom right: Room XXXII, from the north, showing its large altar.

(including ones dedicated to Sokar, Horus, Amun-Kamutef, the sun, and the deified king), halls, and related spaces (fig. 71).

The main hall is unusual in that its columns are of a unique "tent pole" shape, while a number of the rooms to which it gives access are without parallel in their decoration. We have already noted the depictions of plants and animals encountered during the king's military campaigns, which adorn Room XXXI (fig. 65) and some of the surrounding spaces.[41] Room XXXI gives access to an inner sanctuary (figs. 42, 71 bottom right). Room II was decorated with images of the king making offerings to the seated figures of a large number of earlier kings, and has been dubbed the Chamber of Ancestors (fig. 72). This has often been dubbed a "king list," but unlike such documents known from the early Nineteenth Dynasty (cf. page 172), the kings are not consistently in chronological order, and it may be that the seated figures actually represent statues of ancient pharaohs that existed in the Karnak temples during Thutmose III's reign.

Moving to the north–south axis at Karnak, Thutmose commissioned a sandstone pylon (VII) to replace an old brick example that had hitherto marked the beginning of the processional way toward the Mut and Luxor complexes. The pylon was fronted by a pair of obelisks (one now in Istanbul) and a pair of colossi (fig. 73), with its east tower connected to that of Pylon VIII by a wall. A door in this wall led to a calcite bark shrine, the core of which was built for the king's first jubilee in Year 30, with an ambulatory added for the subsequent jubilee of Year 33. It is likely that this shrine was associated with rituals on the adjacent Sacred Lake, which seems to have been dug during the time of Thutmose III.

One obelisk commissioned by Thutmose III (fig. 74 left) was not erected until the reign of his grandson, Thutmose IV (see page 155). It has been suggested that its solitary nature, and long-delayed erection, may have been owing to an accident befalling its intended mate, quite possibly to be identified with an obelisk of appropriate size that remains in a quarry at Aswan (fig. 74 right).[42]

Behind the Festival Hall complex, a contra-chapel, facing east, was built to mark the king's first jubilee, incorporating a statue of Thutmose and Amun, carved from a single block of calcite (fig. 75). The structure, fronted by a series of sheathed ("Osirid") figures of the king, incorporated the bases of the eastern obelisks of Hatshepsut. On the northern edge of the Amun precinct, Thutmose completed the Ptah temple reconstruction begun by Hatshepsut (figs. 76, 118 left). Fragments of structures of Thutmose III have been found in various other locations around Karnak but, given the way in which blocks of dismantled buildings were moved around for reuse over time, these cannot necessarily indicate building work by the king in the areas where they were found. There are also a number of structures mentioned in texts of the reign that cannot necessarily be identified with known remains at Karnak.

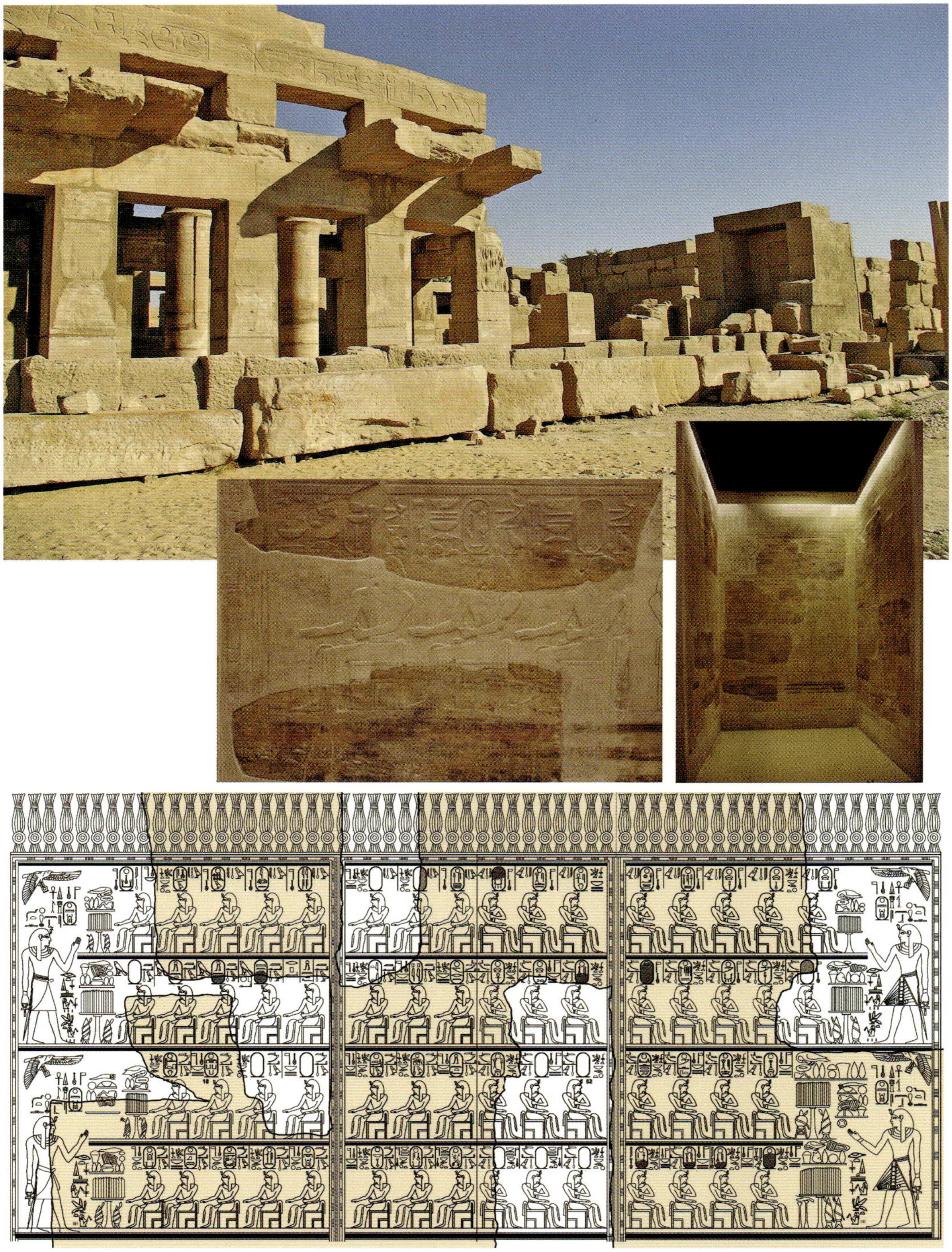

FIGURE 72 The Chamber of Ancestors (Room II) in the Festival Hall complex (now Louvre E13481*bis*).

FIGURE 73 Top: south face of Karnak Pylon VII, showing the obelisk bases in front of it, and the stump of the eastern obelisk. Bottom left: the upper part of the obelisk from here, now in Istanbul. Bottom right: detail of the obelisks as shown in the relief illustrated in fig. 70 bottom.

FIGURE 74 Left: the obelisk quarried and partly inscribed by Thutmose III, erected by Thutmose IV as a single obelisk in what would become the temple of Re-Horakhty, removed to Rome in AD 357, and now outside the Lateran Palace. Right: the unfinished obelisk in the North Quarries at Aswan, perhaps intended to be its mate, but abandoned owing to a flaw in the rock.

FIGURE 75 The contra-chapel behind the Festival Hall, seen from the east.

FIGURE 76 The original part of the temple of Ptah at Karnak, as built by Thutmose III, with the added portico of Ptolemy III.

FIGURE 77 Top: part of the remains of the temple of Thutmose III at Deir el-Bahari, directly south of, and above, that of Hatshepsut, whose Hathor chapel is visible at the top right. Bottom left: rear wall of Thutmose III's chapel of Hathor (see also fig. 129). Bottom right: statue of Thutmose III from his temple (MMA 07.230.3+Cairo JE90237).

Western Thebes

In addition to his memorial temple (pages 142–43), Thutmose III was active in a number of places on the Theban west bank, in some cases as a continuation of work begun during the coregency (in particular at Medinet Habu, pages 60–62), in others with new foundations. A chapel of Wadjmose, the son of Thutmose I (page 11), may have been founded earlier, but work was certainly carried out on it under Thutmose III.[43]

Thutmose III's major non-funerary monument in the area was at Deir el-Bahari. Known as *ḏsr-3ḫt* ("Sacred of Horizon"), it was built between Years 43 and 49, between, and above, the temples of Montjuhotep II and Hatshepsut (figs. 77 top, 96, 97).[44] As with the earlier temples at the site, the topography of the area chosen for *ḏsr-3ḫt* required that the structure be arranged in terraces, joined by ramps, and approached by a causeway from the edge of the desert. The roughly square upper terrace, the largest, was partly rock-cut and partly built from rubble, supported by a retaining wall, and lay above the level of Hatshepsut's Upper Terrace. Construction, utilizing both sandstone and limestone, was begun in Year 43, under the supervision of the Vizier Rekhmire, and was probably completed early in the reign of Amenhotep II.

Like the other two temples, Thutmose III's structure was a reception point for the Beautiful Festival of the Valley, during which the barks of the triad of Amun would visit the west bank from Karnak—which lay directly opposite Deir el-Bahari. The temple's formal dedication remains unclear;[45] the complex also incorporated a sanctuary to Hathor (fig. 77 bottom left),[46] whose cult was an important aspect of the site, Hatshepsut's temple having previously incorporated a large shrine to her. Votive offerings to Hathor continued through the New Kingdom.

Given the date of its construction, paralleling the likely start of the proscription of Hatshepsut, it is likely that the temple was explicitly intended to overmatch its neighbor, which may now have been in the process of mutilation. Although ultimately destroyed by rock falls, probably around the end of the New Kingdom, Thutmose III's temple has preserved vast numbers of fragments of very high-quality relief and statuary (fig. 77 bottom right).

North to south

A stela from Buto[47] attests to building activity by Thutmose III there, and it is likely that other Delta sites received attention during the reign. At Heliopolis, stelae recording the king's works in Year 47 are known,[48] while blocks, doorjambs, and fragments of one or two granite obelisks were found in the temple area.[49] Two more obelisks of the king erected at the site were moved to Alexandria under Emperor Augustus to form part of the Caesarium (pages 165, 205–207; fig. 135). In the Memphite region, only a few

FIGURE 78 Thutmose III's pylon of the temple of Montju at Armant, as depicted in scenes of the Festival of Montju in the tomb-chapel of the First Prophet of Menkheperre, Khonsu-Ta (TT31), dating to the reign of Rameses II.

small items bear the name of Thutmose III, but a memorial temple of the king (cf. page 143, below) seems to have existed there, to judge from the fact that a steward of such a temple was buried at Saqqara during the late Eighteenth Dynasty.[50]

Little can be attributed to the king in Middle Egypt, although work was certainly carried out at Abydos.[51] South of Thebes, the temple at Armant was greatly enlarged, including the addition of a pylon (fig. 78).[52] At Tod (fig. 79), Thutmose III was responsible for adding a bark sanctuary to the north of the main axis,[53] as well as a pronaos to the main temple, which was replaced in Ptolemaic times.[54] A little further south, Thutmose III continued Hatshepsut's building work at El-Kab, with possibly a further phase of activity during the late 40s of his reign.[55]

Nubia

On the border of Nubia, Thutmose III continued work on Hatshepsut's projects at Elephantine, undertaking much of the decoration of the temple of Khnum. In Lower

FIGURE 79 The bark shrine of Thutmose III at the temple of Montju at Tod.

FIGURE 80 Nubian temples of Thutmose III. From the top: Amada; Ellesiya in its original location; and as Turin S.18016.

FIGURE 81 Gebel Dosha, containing a chapel of Thutmose III, including a scene of the king offering to the deified Senwosret III.

Nubia, the temple at Amada (fig. 80 top)[56] was probably founded late in Thutmose III's reign, as most of the building was decorated by Amenhotep II, with its reliefs divided between him and his father (fig. 86; cf. pages 112–14). Further south, rock chapels were cut by Thutmose III at Ellesiya (fig. 80 bottom) and at Gebel Dosha (fig. 81). At Kerma-Dukki Gel, a further phase of work was undertaken during Thutmose III's sole reign, including the erection of two new temples.[57]

FIGURE 82 Left: the Gebel Barkal stela of Thutmose III (MFA 23.733), found in Court 501 of the temple of Amun at Gebel Barkal (right). Since this court was constructed seven centuries after the days of Thutmose III, the stela had clearly been originally erected elsewhere.

A number of mentions have been made of the stela of Year 47 of Thutmose III that was found at Gebel Barkal, the holy mountain of the Nubian variant of the god Amun (fig. 82). However, it is unclear where it was originally erected, as it was found in court B501 within the Great Temple of Amun. This element was not built until seven centuries after the death of Thutmose III (cf. page 161) and, indeed, the earliest surviving part of the whole temple is to be dated a century after Thutmose III, under Akhenaten. The earliest datable sanctuary anywhere at Barkal comes from the reign of Thutmose IV, so it is unknown where Thutmose III's stela was originally placed. It is possible that it may have been first erected in the city of Napata (probably modern Sanam, on the opposite side of the river), which seems to have been established by the Thutmosids as the capital of the southern portion of their Nubian province.

Representing the King

Over the five decades of Thutmose III's reign, there was an evolution of the way in which the facial features of the king were rendered.[58] In his very earliest years, during the regency, it would appear that the king's representations closely followed those of Thutmose I and II (e.g., fig. 83a). Under the coregency, there seems to have been a coordination between the representations of Hatshepsut and Thutmose III (e.g., fig. 83b).

Following his transition to sole rule, a rather more "personal" style developed, with a closer resemblance to Thutmose III's actual appearance, as indicated by a comparison between sculptures made for the Festival Hall at Karnak (e.g., fig. 83c, d) and the royal

FIGURE 83 Statues of Thutmose III: a. Cairo TR 14.6.24.11; b. MMA 08.202.6; c. Cairo CG42053; d. Luxor Museum J2 (ex-CG42054); e. Vienna ÄS70; f. NMEC.

mummy (fig. 127d). During the 40s of his reign, the "standard" facial features of the king changed, with the nose becoming straighter and the eyes more horizontal (e.g., fig. 83e, f). It has been suggested that these adjustments were intended to remove the areas of similarity between the official portrait of Thutmose III and that of Hatshepsut, an idea reinforced by the fact that the change takes place at the same time as the attack on the monuments of Hatshepsut (see just below). Indeed, some earlier two-dimensional representations were actually recarved as part of this process.

The Cancellation of Hatshepsut

Nothing is known as to how Hatshepsut was regarded following the end of the coregency. However, twenty years later there began an assault on her monuments that systematically attempted to destroy her images and textual mentions wherever they occurred.[59] For many years, it was assumed that this occurred soon after the end of the coregency. However, since the 1960s it has been clear that it did not begin until after Year 42 (see pages 199–200), and may, indeed, have been concentrated in the very last years of Thutmose III's life.

This process, found throughout Egypt and Nubia, was manifest in a number of ways.[60] In many two-dimensional cases, images and/or names of Hatshepsut—or entire tableaux—were carefully erased and smoothed, with the intention of adding new material in the space so treated. In others, where the wall was to be concealed by another structure (e.g., fig. 45), the images and names of Hatshepsut were simply mutilated and left in that state (e.g., fig. 84). Further examples fell between the two approaches, with just some preliminary shaving that left the original scheme fully comprehensible: only figures and names of Hatshepsut were fully erased. This is seen particularly in the outer porticoes at Hatshepsut's Deir el-Bahari temple, including in their Punt, obelisk-transport, and divine-birth sequences (figs. 22, 33, 34, 103). In the case of the Deir el-Bahari temple, it appears that the ultimate intention was to rededicate it to Thutmose II; some figures of Hatshepsut that had previously been destroyed were then replaced by new ones of the second Thutmose. One assumes that the overall intent was to follow the high-priority deletion of images and names of Hatshepsut with more thorough erasure and dressing for redecoration, but this was never done. This may suggest that the death of Thutmose III occurred while the proscription program still had time to run.

That the process was interrupted can also be seen where new material was added or figures of Hatshepsut were relabeled. For example, in the Hathor chapel in her temple at Deir el-Bahari, nearly all the cartouches of Hatshepsut were erased, but only half were ever reinscribed, while in the Lower Anubis Shrine on the same terrace, none were reinscribed. A similar situation is also to be seen in the Solar Cult Complex. Where substitutions were actually carried out, in almost all cases it was Thutmose II who replaced

FIGURE 84 Erased image and names of Hatshepsut, in the outer hall of the Main Amun Sanctuary (top) and Lower Shrine of Anubis (bottom) in her temple at Deir el-Bahari.

the female pharaoh, with rare instances of Thutmose I, and even fewer of Thutmose III. This would be much to the confusion of modern historians (pages 194–96).

The Chapelle Rouge is an interesting case.[61] Left incomplete at the end of the coregency, it was completed by Thutmose III, whose royal figures are the only ones that appear on its uppermost blocks and on some of its gates (pages 91–92, fig. 69). However, fairly

FIGURE 85 Adjacent blocks on the Chapelle Rouge east, with some displaying erasures of names and figures, and others completely intact. This indicates that the erasures postdated the dismantlement of the chapel, when the blocks were separated from each other.

soon afterward, the decision was taken to replace it by a wholly new bark shrine (page 92), and the Chapelle Rouge was dismantled. It was while the remains lay in a blockyard that the proscription was begun, with the result that figures and names of Hatshepsut were now erased—but only where they were easily accessible. Thus, many which could not be reached by the mutilators remained untouched (e.g., figs. 43, 44). This scenario is demonstrated by the fact that there are cases of adjacent blocks where one has intact images of Hatshepsut, but the other has had her image and name completely erased (e.g., fig. 85). In any case, all blocks from the Chapelle Rouge were eventually used in the foundations of Pylon III by Amenhotep III, some eight decades later.

In contrast to this nuanced treatment of two-dimensional representations of Hatshepsut, her statuary was attacked remorselessly, and generally reduced to fragments. Such treatment is most visible at Deir el-Bahari, where Hatshepsut's statuary was hauled away from her temple, broken up, and dumped in a former quarry on the north side of the temple causeway (fig. 40 top), and in a depression between the causeways of Hatshepsut and Montjuhotep II. Even the engaged statues that formed an integral part of the façade of the uppermost colonnade of the temple (fig. 98) were cut away, to allow them to be taken for destruction. It may be that the amount of effort required to destroy all this statuary was a reason why the erasure of the portico decoration at Deir el-Bahari had only been summarily carried out when a halt was called.

The late date of the onslaught on Hatshepsut makes it difficult to explain, but it is instructive that it was only the images and names of Hatshepsut as *king* that were attacked—not those as queen. This might suggest that it was not Hatshepsut as a person that was viewed as anathema, but the fact that she had acted as a king. There is no evidence that her burial was desecrated (cf. page 160).

In any case, the process seems to have come to a halt on Thutmose III's death, or very soon afterward. Despite many suggestions over the years,[62] including the idea that Amenhotep II might have played an important role in the instigation of the attacks on Hatshepsut,[63] it has to be admitted that, in the present state of knowledge, the reasons for the attack on Hatshepsut's monuments remain ultimately obscure.

The End

As Thutmose III passed his fiftieth regnal year, he was probably in his late fifties,[64] and almost completely bald (fig. 127d). As revealed by CT scans (pages 200–201), he was by then suffering from moderate spinal osteoarthritis and some calcification of the heart. The king's teeth were, however, in good condition.[65]

It has often been proposed that during his very last years he shared the throne with his late-teenaged (see page 72, above) son, Amenhotep II.[66] This scenario is based on two pieces of separate data. First, the autobiographical text of Amenemheb (page 87) states that

> the king completed his lifetime of many years, splendid in valor, might and triumph, from Year 1 to Year 54, III *prt* last day, under the [Person of] the Dual King Menkheperre, true of voice. He ascended to the sky, joining the sun, his divine limbs mingling with him who made him. When the morning brightened, the sun arose and the sky shone, and the Dual King Aakheperure, the Son of Re, Amenhotep-netjerheqaon, given life, was established on the throne of his father, and he assumed the royal titulary.[67]

However, second, a stela of the Viceroy of Nubia, Usersatet, gives the coronation day of Amenhotep II as IV *3ḫt* 1.[68] This has generally been interpreted as indication of a coregency between the two kings of at least four exact months, with most scholars adding one or more years to this period.[69] In corroboration, some anomalies as to the numbering of the campaigns of Amenhotep II have been cited, together with the alleged "joint" decoration of the temple of Amada (fig. 86).

The coincidence of the institution of a coregency an *exact* number of months prior to the elder king's death is slightly worrying, and it has been suggested that *prt* had simply been written in error for *3ḫt* (or *3ḫt* for *prt*) in the two private accounts involved.[70] This would seem to be supported by a statement in Amenemheb's text that Amenhotep II's accession occurred the morning after Thutmose III's death, with no allusion to any previous regality on Amenhotep's part. However, a better solution would seem to be that while Amenemheb is speaking of the *physical transition* between the reigns, Usersatet is referring to the *ceremonial coronation* of Amenhotep II, which for purely practical reasons is likely to have happened some time after the king had become king (as in many modern monarchies).[71]

The allegedly corroborative data is in any case equivocal. In particular, while the decoration at Amada is clearly divided between Thutmose III and Amenhotep II, in no case are the kings shown acting together, in the way that we see on many of the monuments of the coregency of Hatshepsut and Thutmose III (and we see later in the case of Akhenaten and Neferneferuaten).[72] Indeed, the alleged "joint" decoration at Amada is rather similar to later cases where Sethy I mixed representations of his deceased father into his work at Karnak, and as Rameses II did with Sethy I when completing the latter's unfinished work. While these instances were once thought to be indicators of coregency, it now seems clear that this was not so in either of these cases.[73]

It is perfectly possible to argue that Amenhotep II undertook the decoration of the Amada temple soon after his father's death as a memorial to him—just as would be

FIGURE 86 Wall from the inner part of the temple at Amada (fig. 80 top), with parallel scenes of Thutmose III (right) and Amenhotep II (left).

the case at the beginning of the Nineteenth Dynasty. While memorials of this kind are quite rare—contrasting with the usual self-centered approach to monument-building—Amenhotep II's status as an eighteen-year-old following a father who had reigned for over half a century might have led him to recognize the desirability of making such a gesture to link himself firmly with his glorious predecessor.

Having noted above the fact that the iconography of the alleged Thutmose III–Amenhotep II association differs entirely from that of the unequivocal coregency between Hatshepsut and Thutmose III, it is perhaps worth considering the whole institution of coregency in ancient Egypt.[74] From the early days of Egyptology, it has been assumed by most scholars that coregency was a regular feature of the Egyptian monarchy. However, with the exception of the cases of Hatshepsut and Thutmose III, and Akhenaten and Neferneferuaten, where the kings are shown unequivocally acting together, and a handful of examples (all but one in the Twelfth Dynasty), where double dates giving the equivalent years of the reigns of joint rulers are provided,[75] all other proposed cases[76] are based on circumstantial data only. Indeed, many have been conjured up to bolster wider historical or chronological scenario(s), rather than addressing anything directly linked with the reigns upon which a given coregency is being imposed by the modern scholar.

On this basis, it seems wisest to be profoundly skeptical about any potential coregency where no examples of representations of true joint activity or double dates exist. One should be particularly so where contrary statements exist in contemporary documents (as in the case of Amenemheb). On this basis, the most likely reconstruction of the transition between the reigns of Thutmose III and Amenhotep II is the simple one of the old king breathing his last, and his son taking the throne the next morning in accordance with long-time precedent. Following the rituals of embalming, Amenhotep II will have carried out the interment of his father in accordance with time-honored custom, and commenced a reign that would last for three decades.

Appendix to Chapter 4 The names of Thutmose III after Year 22

	Hieroglyphs	Transliteration	Translation
Horus		*kꜣ-nḫt ḫꜥ-m-wꜣst*	Strong bull, appearing in Thebes
	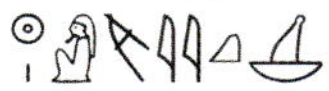	*mry-rꜥ qꜥi-ḥḏt*	Beloved of Re, high of the White Crown
	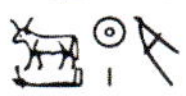	*kꜣ-nḫt mry-rꜥ*	Strong bull, beloved of Re
		*kꜣ-nḫt ḫꜥ-m-mꜣꜥt*	Strong bull, who appears as *maat*
		*kꜣ-nḫt ḥꜥ m mꜣꜥt*	Strong bull, who rejoices in *maat*
Nebti		*wꜣḥ-nsyt mi rꜥ m pt*	Enduring of kingship, like Re in the sky
		*sḫꜥ mꜣꜥt mry-tꜣwy*	Who makes *maat* appear, beloved of the Two Lands
		*ꜥꜣ-šfyt m tꜣw nb*	Great of majesty in all lands
		*šsp-ꜥnḫ n itmw ḫpr m ḫpri ḥtp bꜣw ḥr mꜣꜥt.f*	Living image of Atum, appearing as Khepri, with whose offerings the Souls of Heliopolis are content
Golden Falcon		*ḏsr ḫꜣ(w) sḫm-pḥty*	Holy of appearances, powerful of might
	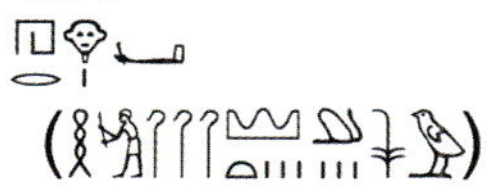	*ḥr ḥir nḫt (ḥwi ḥqꜣw ḫꜣswt pḥw sw)*	Pleased with victories (who smites the rulers of foreign lands who approach him)
		*ꜥꜣ-ḫpš ḥwi pḏwt-9*	Great of strength, who smites the 9 Bows
	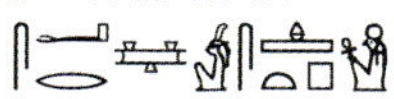	*sꜥr mꜣꜥt sḥtp rꜥ*	Who elevates *maat* & makes Re content

Prenomen		*mn-ẖpr-rꜥ stp-n-rꜥ*	Established manifestation chosen of Re
		*mn-ẖpr-rꜥ sꜥꜣ-n-rꜥ*	*- ditto -* whom Re has made great
		*mn-ẖpr-rꜥ nb-ẖpš*	*- ditto -* the strong-armed
		*mn-ẖpr-rꜥ nẖt-ẖpš*	*- ditto -* the strong-armed
		*mn-ẖpr-rꜥ tit-rꜥ*	*- ditto -* image of Re
Nomen		*ḏḥwty-ms(w)*	Thoth is born
		*ḏḥwty-ms(w) nfr-ẖpr*	Thoth is born, perfect of manifestation
		*ḏḥwty-ms(w) nfr-ẖprw*	Thoth is born, perfect of manifestations
		*ḏḥwty-ms(w) smꜣ-ẖprw*	Thoth is born, united of manifestations
		*ḏḥwty-ms(w) ḥqꜣ-mꜣꜥt*	Thoth is born, ruler of *maat*
		*ḏḥwty-ms(w) ḥqꜣ-iwnw*	Thoth is born, ruler of Heliopolis
		*ḏḥwty-ms(w) ḥqꜣ-nṯr*	Thoth is born, divine ruler
		*ḏḥwty-ms(w) ḥqꜣ-wꜣst*	Thoth is born, ruler of Thebes

5 Houses of Eternity

In contrast to later in the New Kingdom, when kings were buried as a matter of routine in the Valley of the Kings at Thebes, and many members of the royal family were buried in the Valley of the Queens, the locations of the tombs of pharaohs and their families were much less standardized during the first decades of the Eighteenth Dynasty. Although the rulers of the Seventeenth Dynasty had been interred at Dra Abu'l-Naga in Western Thebes,[1] the founder of the Eighteenth Dynasty, Ahmose I, had built a pyramid at Abydos. It is likely that he was buried there, although the king's body was probably translated to Thebes by Amenhotep I, or perhaps Thutmose I.[2]

Amenhotep I certainly constructed his tomb at Thebes, but there has been much debate over its location, with the most likely option being a tomb behind Dra Abu'l-Naga.[3] Likewise problematic is the burial place of Thutmose I,[4] which is tied up with a number of questions concerning the funerary arrangements of Hatshepsut as king. We have already noted the possibility that Thutmose II may originally have been buried in the Wadi Gabbanet el-Qurud.

The Tombs of Hatshepsut

In any case, at some point prior to her coming to the throne in her own right—whether on becoming regent, or on the accession of her husband Thutmose II—Hatshepsut had founded a tomb in the Wadi Sikkat Taqa el-Zeide. The tomb[5] was located, like a number of later royal tombs, at the bottom of a natural chimney in the rock. The intent was that the tomb's location would soon be obliterated by the deposition of debris carried by floodwater running off the high desert and emptying into such water-worn routes (fig. 88). In its plan (fig. 89 top), the tomb follows a pattern established with the sepulchers

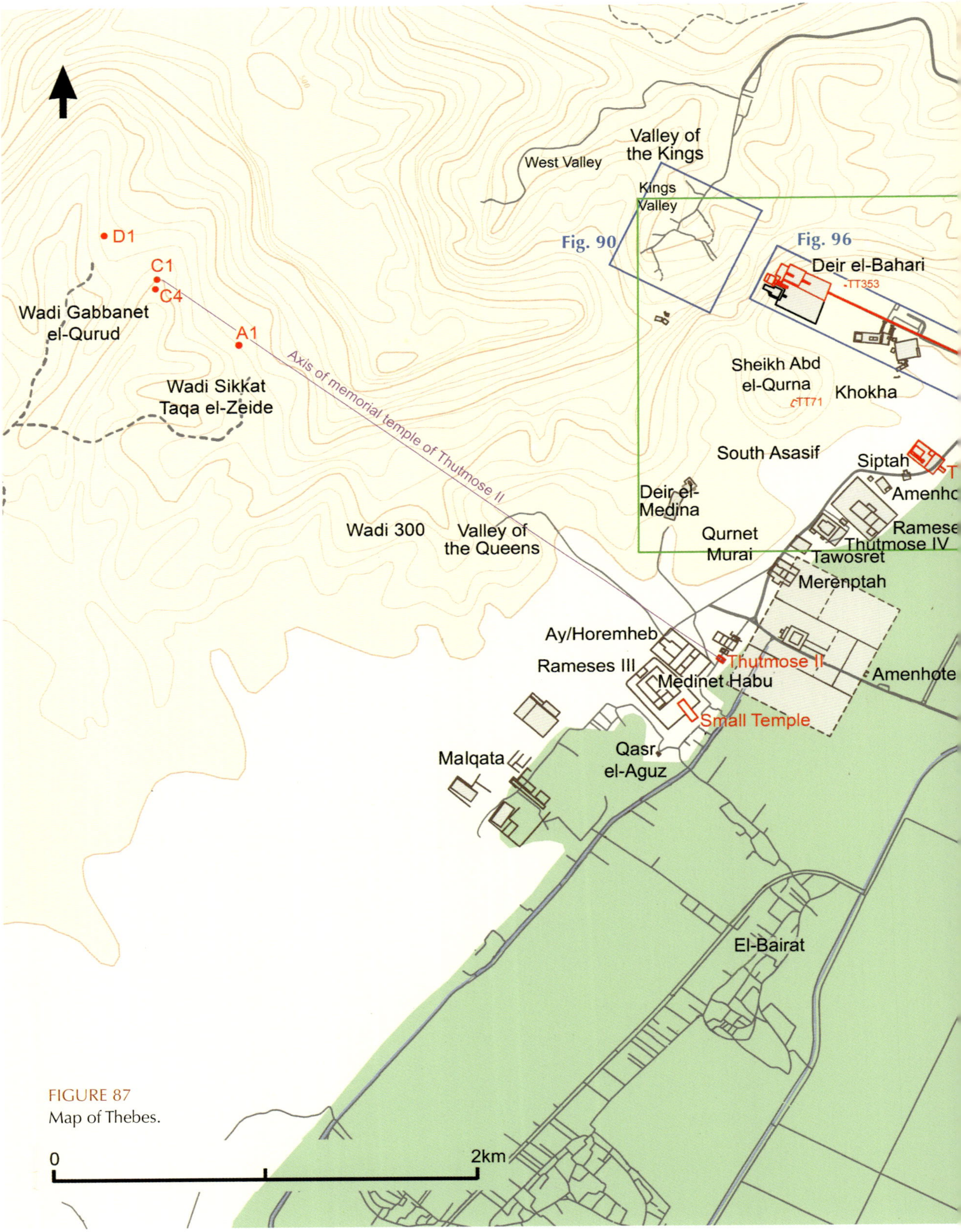

FIGURE 87
Map of Thebes.

Carter House
Abu'l-Naga
El-Tarif
Qurna
Amenhotep I
Sethy I
se I
II
Fig. 42
Karnak
El-Gezira Bairat
Luxor

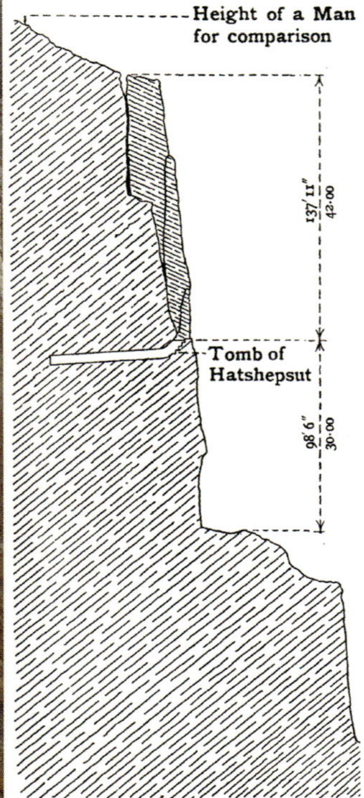

FIGURE 88 Hatshepsut's tomb in the Wadi Sikkat Taqa el-Zeide lies at the bottom of this cleft.

of Amenhotep I and his wife Meryetamun B (and is also seen in the putative tomb of Thutmose II), in that it has a bent axis, which would become standard for pre-Amarna royal tombs. The tomb was never used, but a quartzite sarcophagus (fig. 89 bottom) was found in what would have been the antechamber. This piece is the earliest firmly dated example in an evolutionary sequence of outer containers for the royal mummy that continued until the reign of Amenhotep III.[6]

Subsequently, having become pharaoh, Hatshepsut switched her intended place of burial to the Valley of the Kings (fig. 90). There, her definitive sarcophagus and associated canopic chest were found in the final chamber of tomb KV20. This sepulcher is of

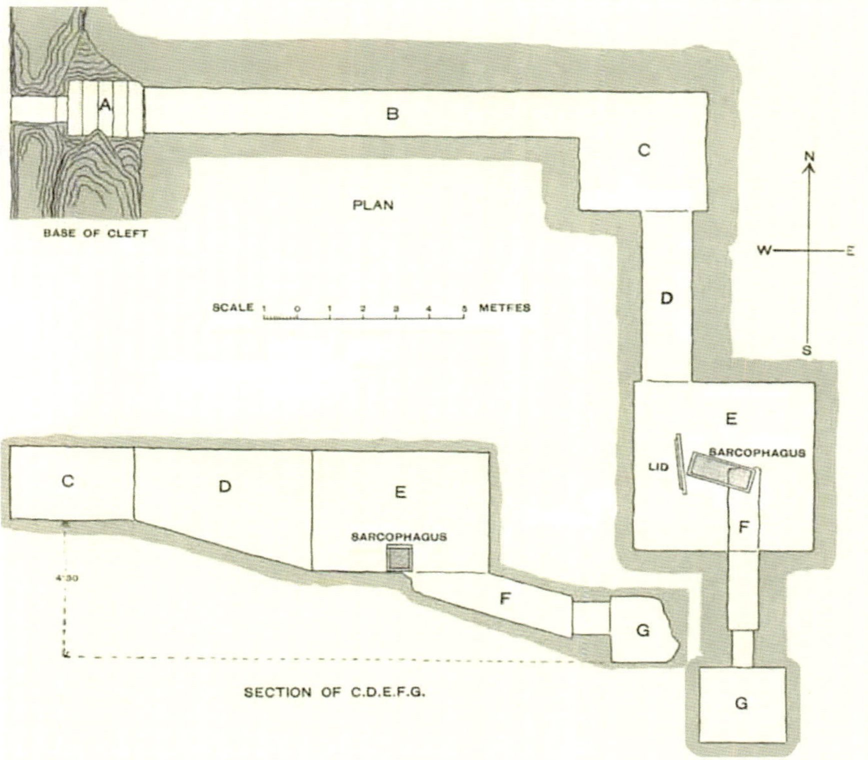

FIGURE 89 Top: plan and section of Hatshepsut's tomb in Wadi Sikkat Taqa el-Zeide. Bottom: the sarcophagus from the tomb (Cairo JE47032). Its decoration was based on that of coffins of the Middle Kingdom, including an eye panel that had become obsolete many decades before, when mummies were no longer placed on their left-hand sides.

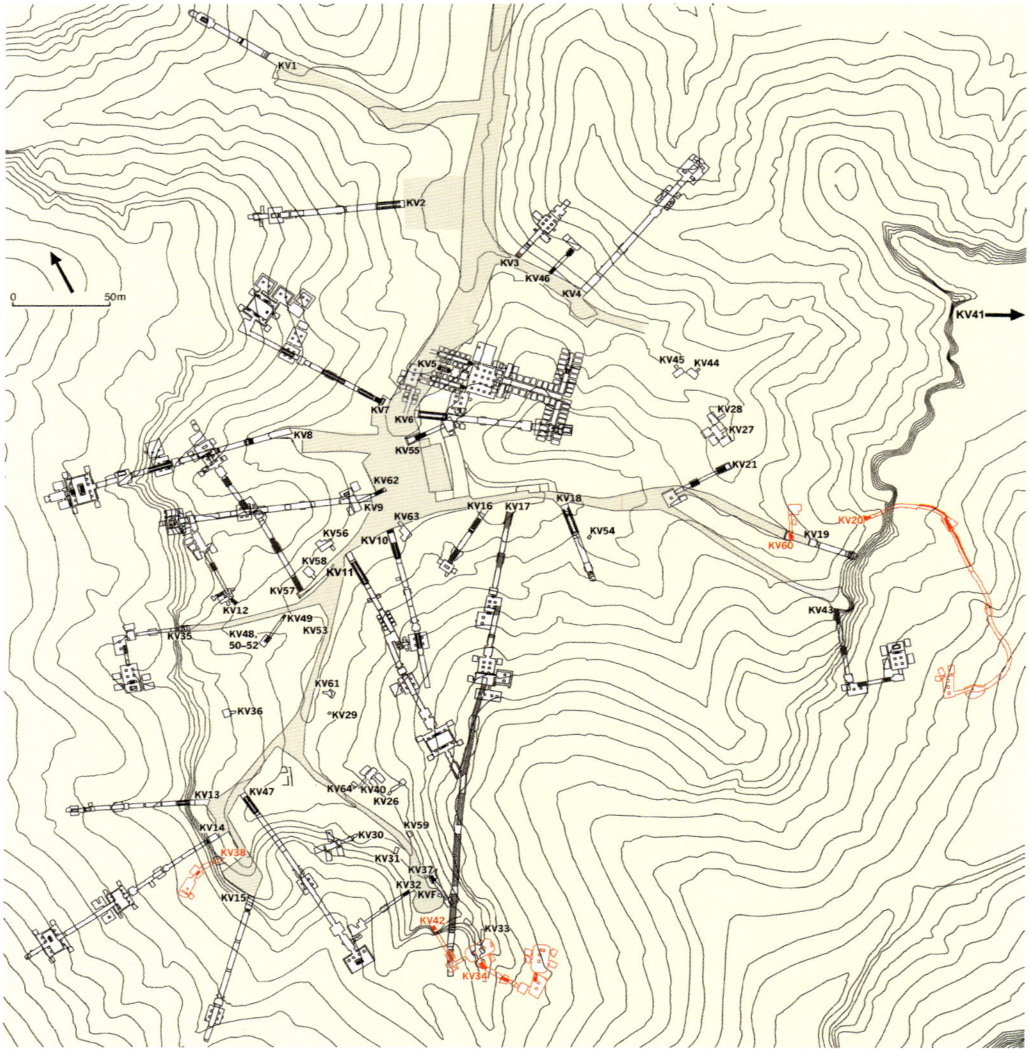

FIGURE 90 The main part of the Valley of the Kings, with tombs of the time of Thutmose III and Hatshepsut shown in red.

a sinuous form, its corridors over two hundred meters in length and descending over ninety meters vertically below its entrance level (fig. 91).[7] It terminates in two large chambers, the innermost equipped with three subsidiary chambers, and with its ceiling supported by three columns. The curved shape of the tomb, gradually deviating to the right from the axis of its entrance, is generally attributed to the poor quality of the rock, although the passages of the tomb that formed part of the pyramid complex of Ahmose I at Abydos were very far from straight.[8]

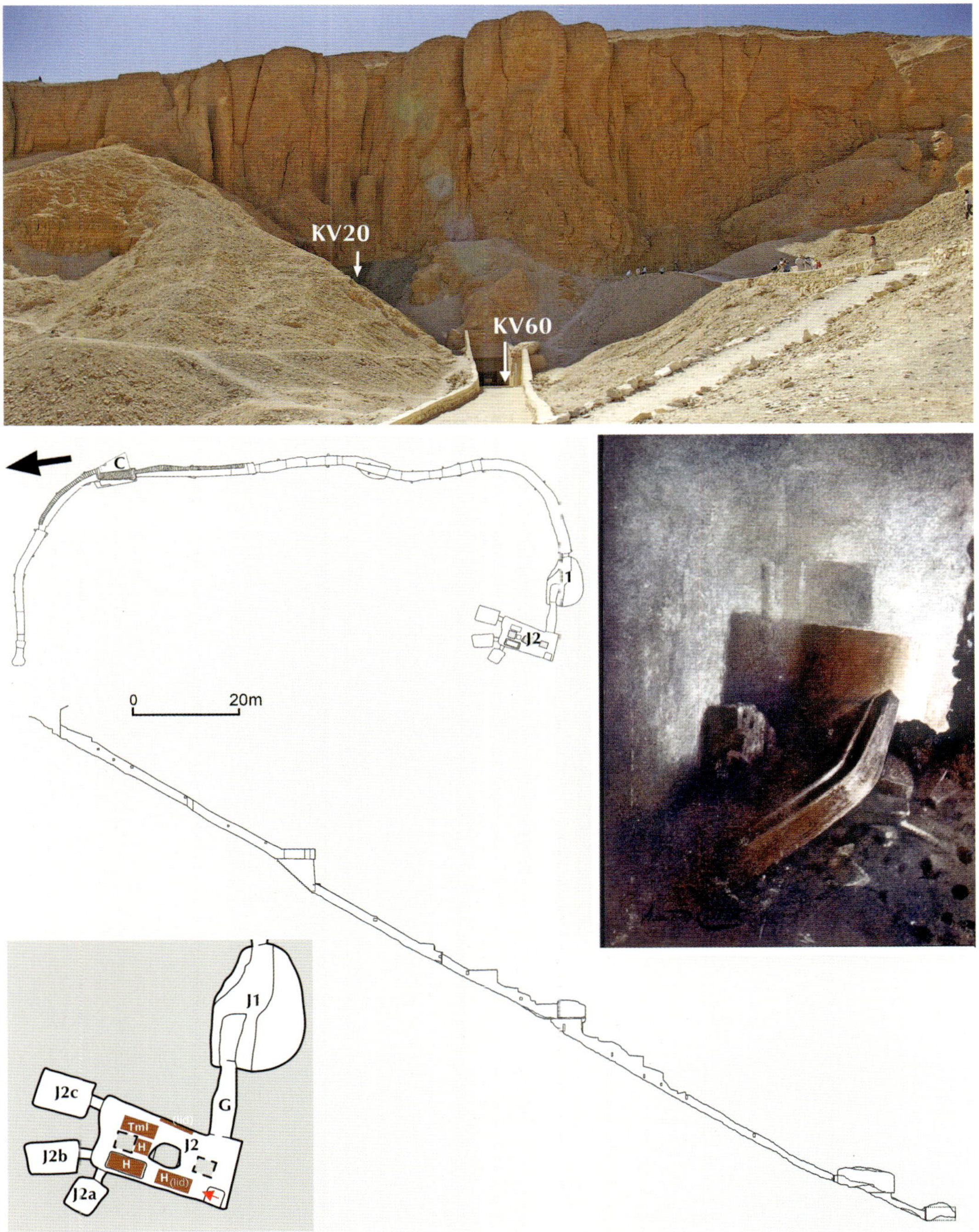

FIGURE 91 Top: view of the area of KV20. Bottom: plan and section of KV20. Inset: painting of the burial chamber as discovered, showing the sarcophagus of Hatshepsut and its lid (figs. 95, 133).

FIGURE 92 Top: block from the lining of the burial chamber of KV20, with part of the Book of *Amduat* (Cairo TR 10.12.14.13). Bottom: part of the wall of the burial chamber of Thutmose III in KV34.

FIGURE 93 The initial sarcophagus of Hatshepsut as king, reworked for Thutmose I; from KV20 (MFA 04.278).

The rock was certainly not of the best, and KV20 has the distinction of being the only tomb in the Valley of the Kings to have its burial chamber (J2) lined with limestone blocks to provide a ground for decoration. On this lining was applied the Book of *Amduat* (fig. 92 top), a composition that seems to have originated at this time, and which would be an important component of the decoration of kings' tombs throughout the rest of the New Kingdom. It is the earliest of a series of texts that describe and illustrate the sun god's passage through the twelve hours of the night, from his "death" at sunset to his rebirth at dawn.[9] It would later be supplemented by a series of further "books" that followed it in dealing with aspects of the sun god's nocturnal journey. Throughout the New Kingdom these books were used only in royal tombs—with the single exception of one of the very early examples, in the burial chamber of the tomb of the vizier Useramun (TT61—fig. 31).[10]

Since foundation deposits outside KV20 named Hatshepsut, it was long assumed that the tomb had been cut for her, as a replacement for the Wadi Sikkat Taqa el-Zeide sepulcher. However, as well as her own equipment (page 129), the burial chamber also contained a sarcophagus for Thutmose I. This had originally been made for Hatshepsut herself, soon after she became pharaoh, but had then been extensively altered (including recarving the whole exterior and crudely lengthening the interior) for her father (fig. 93).[11]

FIGURE 94 View of the burial chamber of KV38, and the sarcophagus and canopic chest (Cairo JE52344, JE36416) found there.

This has often been explained as a reburial from the place where Thutmose had been laid to rest some years earlier, usually identified as tomb KV38,[12] a small sepulcher with an oval burial chamber of a type employed by Thutmose III in his tomb (see page 147). When found, KV38 contained a sarcophagus and canopic chest that had been manufactured from scratch for him by Thutmose III, as is clear from the design of the sarcophagus and a dedication inscription on its side (fig. 94 bottom left).[13] If KV38 were indeed Thutmose I's original tomb, Hatshepsut will have removed her father from his tomb and re-interred him in her own. Then, at some point after the end of Hatshepsut's reign, the mummy of Thutmose I will have been translated back to his original tomb by his grandson, who donated containers for the body and its viscera.

However, it has also been argued that only the innermost chamber of KV20 was the work of Hatshepsut, the remaining parts of the tomb having already been constructed for Thutmose I.[14] In this case, not only the sarcophagus and canopic chest in KV38 would have been the work of Thutmose III, but also the tomb itself. In this scenario, the body of Thutmose I would have been first interred in the chamber J1 of KV20, presumably in a wooden sarcophagus, given the lack of any traces of a stone example. Then, the tomb will have been taken over by Hatshepsut (adding foundation deposits outside) and extended, the new burial chamber housing both monarchs. Subsequently, Thutmose III will have removed Thutmose I to a new tomb (KV38), equipped with a stone sarcophagus and canopic chest.

As mooted above (page 30), it is possible that Hatshepsut's reburial of Thutmose I may have been intended as part of her legitimation as a king, through the concept that an individual's heir was the person who carried out their interment. This certainly seems to be the reason why Ay was depicted on the wall of Tutankhamun's burial chamber carrying out his predecessor's funeral.[15] It is possible that Thutmose III's further reburial of Thutmose I may have been similarly motivated, although it may simply have been a view that the old king deserved a tomb of his own. Whether or not this might have been connected with Hatshepsut's cancellation is unknowable, although on practical grounds the exhumation of Thutmose I might have taken place in parallel with Hatshepsut's funeral.

Returning to the question of the potential appropriation of KV20 for Hatshepsut, the idea that the cutting of the definitive burial chamber (J2) of KV20 should be attributed to her, while superficially attractive, presents some practical issues. If the tomb was indeed already occupied by the burial of Thutmose I when taken over by Hatshepsut, any extension of the tomb would have required the temporary evacuation of the king's mummy, given issues of security and the huge amount of dust that would have been raised by the extension work. In light of this, if KV20 had indeed been cut for Thutmose I, it seems far more likely that the king had built the whole tomb, including

FIGURE 95 The sarcophagus (a) and canopic chest (b) of Hatshepsut from KV20 (Cairo JE37678, JE30872). Presumably originally deriving from the tomb are (c) a fragment of coffin including the titles of a female pharaoh (Luxor Museum), found in the tomb of Rameses XI, and two shabtis (d. Museum Meermanno, The Hague, 79.130; e. Musée d'Aquitaine, Bordeaux, 9087).

J2 and its lining. In this case, just the (re)foundation deposits, and possibly the decoration of the burial chamber, would be attributed to Hatshepsut.[16] A fact offered in support of the burial chamber being the work of Hatshepsut has been its sharing an architectural module with the Deir el-Bahari temples.[17] However, the same proportions are found in the likely burial chamber of Amenhotep I,[18] making the point irrelevant.

While no definitive statement is yet possible, the best working hypothesis would seem to be that on becoming pharaoh, perhaps after contemplating remaining in the Wadi Sikkat Taqa el-Zeide, Hatshepsut decided to appropriate the tomb of Thutmose I. This could be seen as combining the advantage of a ready-made tomb with an ability to present it as an act of legitimation, including the "upgrading" of her father's burial by the donation of a stone sarcophagus of the latest type (albeit second-hand!).

Having abandoned her first sarcophagus in the Wadi Sikkat Taqa el-Zeide, and repurposed her second for her father, Hatshepsut had a third one made (figs. 95a, 133). In contrast to the rectangular forms of her previous two, this one was made in the form of a cartouche, which would be the standard form for a royal sarcophagus until the time of Amenhotep III. As already noted, the new sarcophagus was made as a set with that of Senenmut, and in its decoration it largely followed the redecoration applied to the sarcophagus donated to Thutmose I. The same scheme was also employed on the sarcophagus made for Thutmose III (fig. 114). A further quartzite item made for Hatshepsut was her canopic chest (fig. 95b).[19] This took the form of a typical shrine, with a cavetto cornice and a torus molding, but the lid is lost. Textually, the chest follows canopic equipment dating to the Middle Kingdom, and the Seventeenth Dynasty, from which two royal canopic chests survive.[20]

When excavated in 1903 (pages 190–92), KV20 was found to contain, apart from the chest and the two sarcophagi, only fragmentary stone vessels, belonging to both Thutmose I and Hatshepsut, together with pieces of other vessels of pottery and faience, a fragment of carved wood, and pieces of a faience shabti coffin.[21] While nothing deriving from an actual shabti figure is reported from the tomb, two examples survive in museums (fig. 95d, e). Also clearly originating in the tomb are fragments of a coffin preserving the titles of a female pharaoh who can only be Hatshepsut, found along with other debris from the recycling of royal funerary furniture in the tomb of Rameses XI (fig. 95c).[22]

The Memorial Temple of Hatshepsut

Preliminaries

In every high-status burial, the tomb itself was linked with an offering place. That of Hatshepsut comprised the great temple at Deir el-Bahari, separated from tomb KV20 by the curtain of cliffs that define the eastern side of the Valley of the Kings. KV20 lies directly behind the site of the temple and the axis of its entrance stair descends directly toward the site of the temple, intersecting with the latter in the area occupied by the Solar Cult Complex (fig. 105). However, as discussed above, it actually deviated to the right, leaving the burial chamber far from the temple. The tomb would, however, have had to have been twice its actual length to have reached even the westernmost extremity of the temple.

This fact has been used as an argument for KV20's original construction by Hatshepsut, but the original memorial temple of Thutmose I has never been positively identified (but see pages 138–39 for what seems to have been a substitute, built by Hatshepsut), and it is possible that it might have been placed (or at least planned to be placed) somewhere at Deir el-Bahari. Certainly, a temple of his predecessor, Amenhotep I, had been built there, but was later overbuilt by Hatshepsut's monument.[23] Might this also have been the case with the temple of Thutmose I?

The evolution of the laying-out of Hatshepsut's temple can be traced via a series of her foundation deposits—the only ones hitherto found at the site (marked "FD" on fig. 96).[24] They fall into three groups. The first set (G, H, I, J, and K) simply follow the line of the northern part of the original eastern enclosure wall built by Montjuhotep II, which was then rebuilt by Hatshepsut to accommodate the upper end of her causeway.

The second group of deposits (A, B, L, and M) mark out the eastern half of Hatshepsut's Middle Terrace, part of the temple that could only be constructed after the demolition of the brick temple of Amenhotep I. This suggests that they belong to a final phase of the construction of Hatshepsut's temple.[25] In the directly preceding phase, it may have been intended to comprise just what is now the Upper Terrace and the western half of the Middle Terrace, thus allowing the retention of the Amenhotep I temple. Interestingly, this truncated Middle Terrace would have terminated on a line running directly south from the entrance to the tomb of Meryetamun, the wife of Amenhotep I (TT358).

The third group of deposits (C to F and N) are particularly intriguing, as deposits C to F are aligned, not with any axis of the Hatshepsut temple, but with that of the Amenhotep I structure.[26] Furthermore, deposit N lies slightly north of a western extension of the latter's east–west axis. This would suggest that Hatshepsut's first plans for a temple were constrained by the presence of a structure with the same orientation as that of Amenhotep I. Might this have been a temple of Thutmose I, left unfinished at his death, which Hatshepsut could have planned to appropriate, just like the king's tomb? If deposits D and E flanked the axis of this putative structure, it could have lain between the southwest corner of the Amenhotep I temple and the northern axial wall of the Montjuhotep II complex. Perhaps significantly, an extension of the axis of this potential temple of Thutmose I coincides with KV20 halfway along its length (fig. 105).

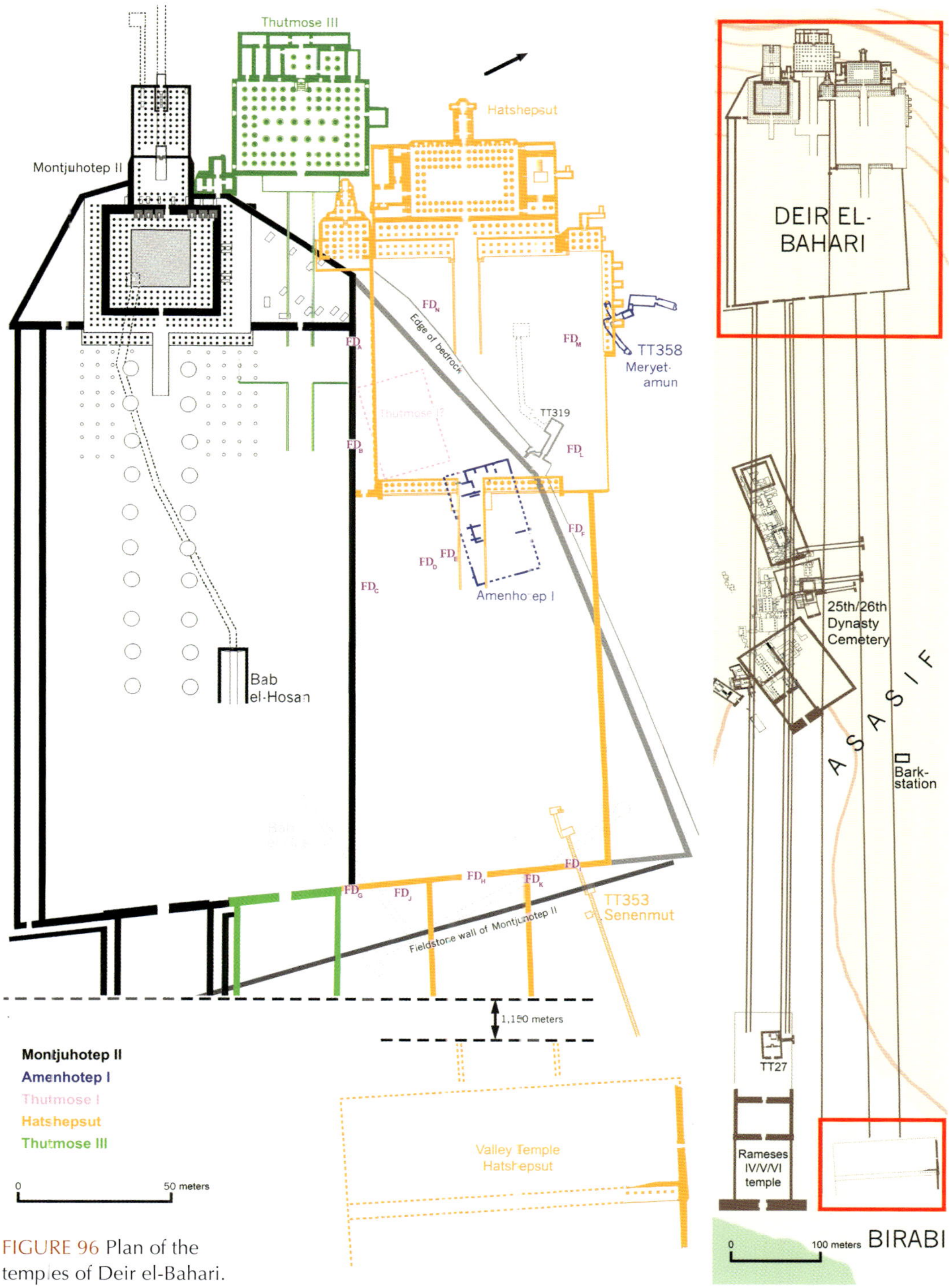

FIGURE 96 Plan of the temples of Deir el-Bahari.

However, a temple defined by deposits C to F and N, whether originally that of Thutmose I or a Hatshepsut original, would be limited in size by the main northern enclosure wall of Montjuhotep II on the south, and the rising ground to the north, with an edge defined by a further wall of Montjuhotep II, and incorporating the tomb of the Eleventh Dynasty Queen Neferu (TT319—see fig. 96).[27] In addition, any processional approach from the desert edge would need to deviate to the south by around 20 degrees to enter the temple, in contrast to the perfect alignment of the Montjuhotep II temple. Accordingly, the original alignment was abandoned, and the major tasks of cutting down and grading of the rising ground to the north (cf. fig. 98 top), and extensive filling to the south, were accepted to create Hatshepsut's actual memorial temple.

As noted above, it is possible that the original design of the structure allowed the preservation of Amenhotep I's temple, but whatever initial qualms might have been present at destroying the Amenhotep I structure (and burying TT319), these were overcome. Any guilt was seemingly assuaged by the provision of a "tourist entrance" to TT319 within the new temple,[28] and moving Osirid statues from the demolished temple of Amenhotep I to the nearby temple of Montjuhotep II.[29] This was probably accompanied by the additions and restoration work undertaken around the time of Hatshepsut at the temple *(mn-ỉst)* that Amenhotep I had built in front of Dra Abu'l-Naga to align with his probable tomb there.[30]

The temple of Djeser-djeseru

The final version of Hatshepsut's temple (figs. 97, 98)[31] represents the earliest preserved example of a New Kingdom "memorial temple" (referred to by the Egyptians as a "mansion of millions of years").[32] This kind of structure differed from the mortuary temples attached to royal tombs of earlier epochs in that, rather than being dedicated exclusively to the cult of the dead king, it also incorporated major sanctuaries of Amun and Re-Horakhty (the Solar Cult Complex), and lesser chapels of other deities. Not only this, but the royal cult arrangements were relegated to the southern part of the temple, with Amun's occupying the main axis (and that of the solar cult the northern).

These major sanctuaries occupied the uppermost terrace of the three that ultimately comprised the temple (fig. 98). The form of the structure was clearly influenced by the adjacent funerary temple of Montjuhotep II (fig. 97 top). However, a more recent parallel may be seen in the western part of the pyramid complex of Ahmose I at Abydos, which culminated in a temple against the western cliff.[33] Colonnades, with sheathed statues of Hatshepsut, flanked the granite gateway that gave access to the peristyle court that dominated the terrace. At the back of the court, on the central axis, was the principal sanctuary, of Amun-of-*ḏsr-ḏsrw* (the ancient name of the

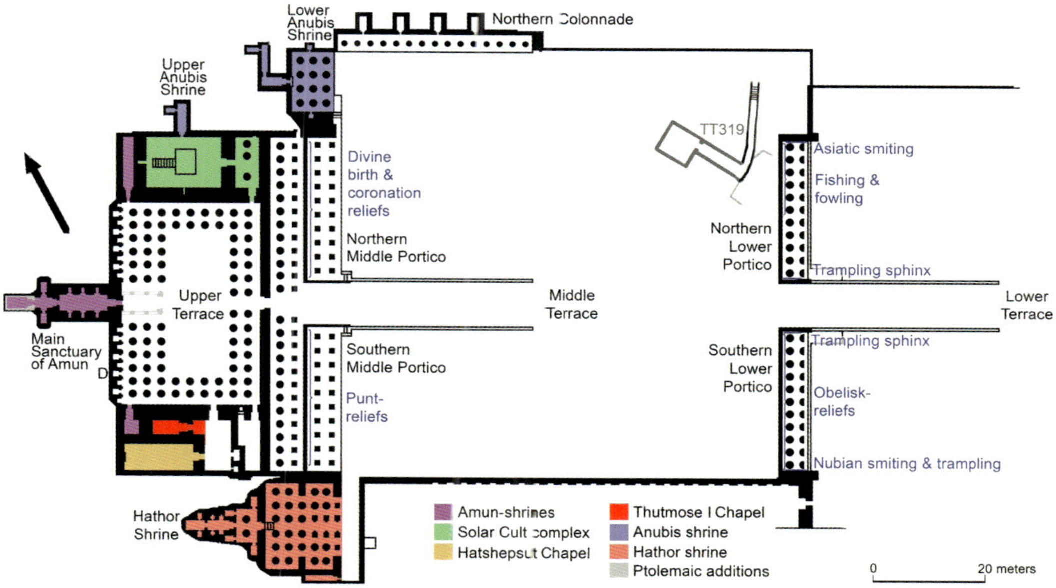

FIGURE 97 Top: aerial view of Deir el-Bahari; note the Eleventh Dynasty tomb-chapels overlooking the causeways of the temples and their approaches. Bottom: plan of the temple of Hatshepsut.

FIGURE 98 Top: the Upper and Middle Terraces of the temple of Hatshepsut; note how only the northern (right-hand) portion of the Middle Terrace is rock-cut. Middle: part of the Northern Upper Portico, with the head of one of its engaged statues (Cairo JE56262). Bottom: the rear of the Upper Terrace, including the Ptolemaic Portico in front of the Main Sanctuary of Amun, added when the latter's inner niche was enlarged into a sanctuary of Imhotep and Amenhotep-son-of-Hapu.

temple: "Holy-of-Holies").[34] This Main Sanctuary of Amun comprised two main rooms, with a niche at the rear.[35] Both Hatshepsut and Thutmose III were shown offering in both spaces, Neferure also being present in the first room only (e.g., fig. 24). Also included in the decoration of the complex were the deceased Thutmose I and II, Queen Ahmes, and Princess Neferubity (figs. 7, 24, 99). The inner niche was enlarged during Ptolemaic times to become a sanctuary for the cult of the deified architects Imhotep and Amenhotep-son-of-Hapu (see page 157).

FIGURE 99 Top left: the gateway of the Main Sanctuary of Amun in the temple of Hatshepsut; the cartouches on the jambs all now belong to Thutmose III, but Hatshepsut's Horus name remains intact, and the feminine t-sign is still present in the royal titles (see also fig. 125). On the lintel, Hatshepsut's cartouches have been altered to those of Thutmose II. Top right: the outer hall of the Main Sanctuary of Amun; for a detail of tympanum, see fig. 84. Bottom: detail of the upper part of the eastern end of the north wall of the sanctuary, showing Hatshepsut, Thutmose III, and Neferure.

At the northern extremity of the Upper Terrace lay the Solar Cult Complex, a court with an open-air altar dedicated to the sun god in his manifestation as Re-Horakhty.[36] This was accessed via a columned vestibule opening into the northeast corner of the peristyle. Leading off this sun court was a small room, dedicated to Anubis, but also including a niche featuring Hatshepsut's parents (fig. 6).

A doorway in the southwestern corner of the peristyle led into a vestibule, which gave access to the chapels of the royal cult. The larger belonged to Hatshepsut herself,

a

b

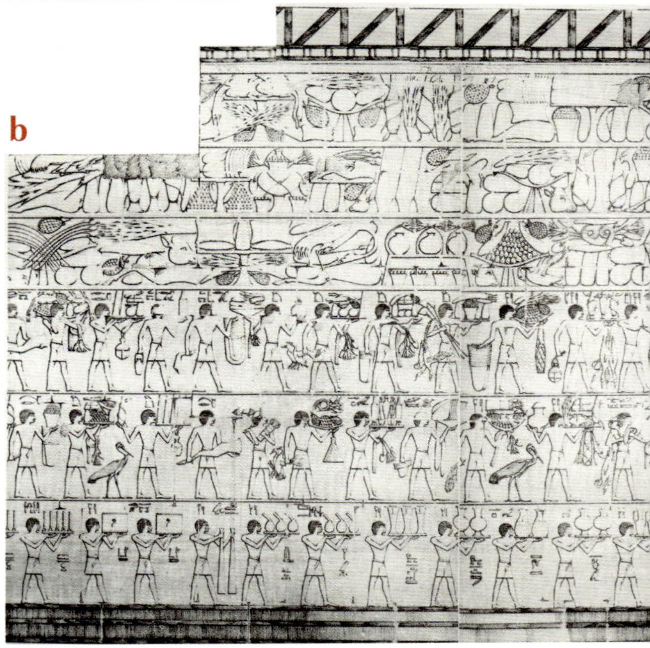

FIGURE 100 The funerary chapel of Hatshepsut, with (b) a drawing of the south wall, a surviving part of the vaulted ceiling, and (c) the tympanum over the false door. The mutilated false door became an altar in Christian times, and an image of Christ Pantokrator was painted on it.

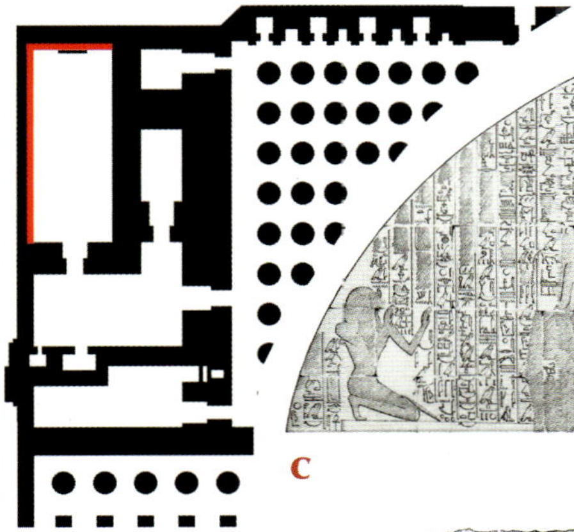

c

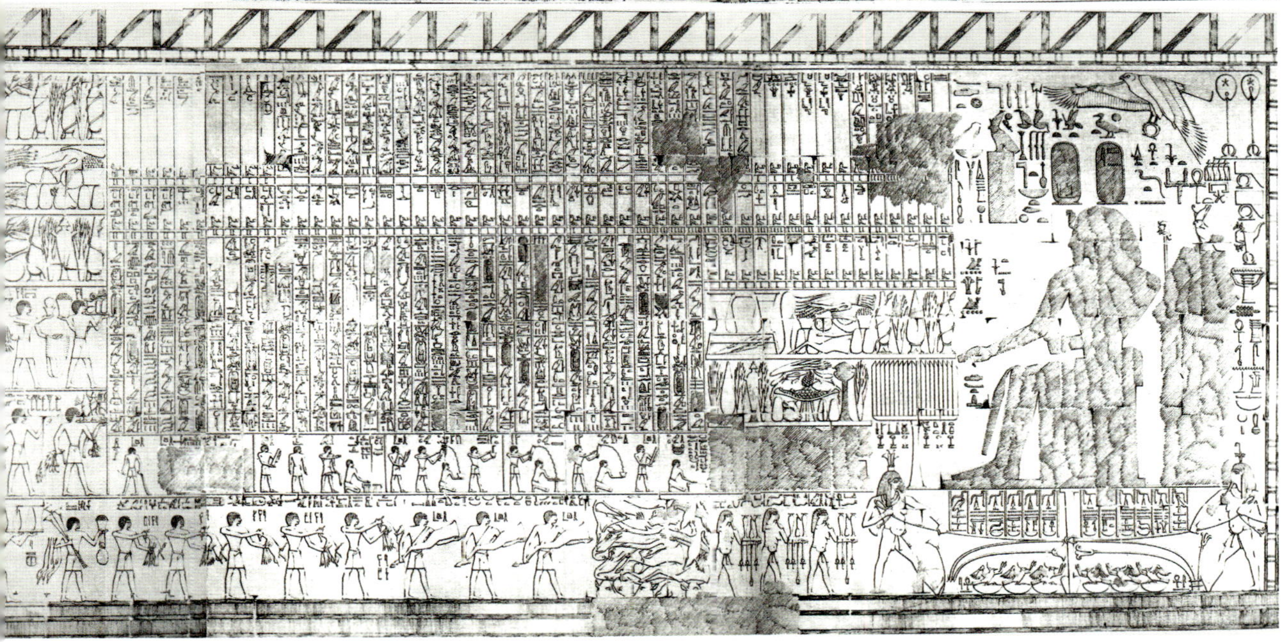

FIGURE 101 Part of Hatshepsut's Divine Birth sequence (see fig. 22 for complete drawing), showing the mutilation of much of the relief, but with the principal figures of Queen Ahmes left intact.

its walls adorned with extensive offering scenes,[37] and the vaulted ceiling showing the pharaoh adoring the hours of the day and night (fig. 100). At the back was placed the false-door stela, the focus for offerings to the dead pharaoh. Adjacent to the room, on the north, was placed the very similar, but much smaller, chapel dedicated to Thutmose I, with his false-door stela at the back.[38]

Since a chapel for Thutmose I was included in Hatshepsut's temple, and one for Rameses I was also included in the memorial temple of his son, Sethy I, it has been assumed that provision for a king's father was a standard part of the New Kingdom memorial temple. However, that of Rameses III, the only other such monument where the relevant part of the building survives, does *not* include such an element, and it is instructive to note that the original arrangements for Thutmose I and Rameses I present problems. As already discussed in the former case (pages 130–32), there is a suspicion that his unfinished temple was appropriated by his successor, and this seems likely to have been the case for Rameses I as well.[39] In these circumstances, the "paternal" sanctuaries provided by Hatshepsut and Sethy I may have been created to be the primary funerary chapels of Thutmose I and Rameses I, rather than a manifestation of some kind of father cult.

In the case of Thutmose I, however, a new separate temple was subsequently erected by Hatshepsut dedicated to him, named *ẖnmt-ʿnḫ*. It lay on the edge of the cultivation, just over halfway between the valley building of Hatshepsut and the memorial temple of Thutmose III (see fig. 87).[40] Fragments of relief indicate that the decoration

of its sanctuary was essentially a duplicate of that of the chapel of Thutmose I at Deir el-Bahari, with its forecourt including battle scenes. Its association with Thutmose I is confirmed by a list of temples in the Chapelle Rouge.[41]

In the Hatshepsut temple, the Upper Terrace was fronted by porticoes adorned with engaged statues of the temple's owner depicted with a sheathed body (fig. 98 middle). From this, a ramp descended to a further terrace. As noted above, this Middle Terrace may have been a later addition, to an original scheme for Hatshepsut's temple that left the temple of Amenhotep I in place, in which case the ramp will have been much longer, extending all the way to ground level. In the event, however, the Amenhotep temple was demolished and the Middle Terrace created by filling the area with chippings, which were supported to the east by retaining walls, which formed the backs of the Lower Terrace colonnades (see below).

The Southern Middle Portico at the rear of the Middle Terrace contained representations of Hatshepsut's expedition to Punt (fig. 33), and the northern example those of her divine birth and coronation sequence (figs. 22, 23, 101). At either extremity of the Middle Terrace was a chapel. The one at the southern end was dedicated to the goddess Hathor (fig. 102); the northern belonged to Anubis. Adjacent to this was the Northern Colonnade, running along the north side of the court, equipped with four niches. This structure was never finished, and was built directly over the old tomb of Queen Meryetamun. Toward the eastern end of the court was a staircase that gave access to the ancient tomb-chapel of Queen Neferu.

FIGURE 102 The Hathor shrine of Hatshepsut.

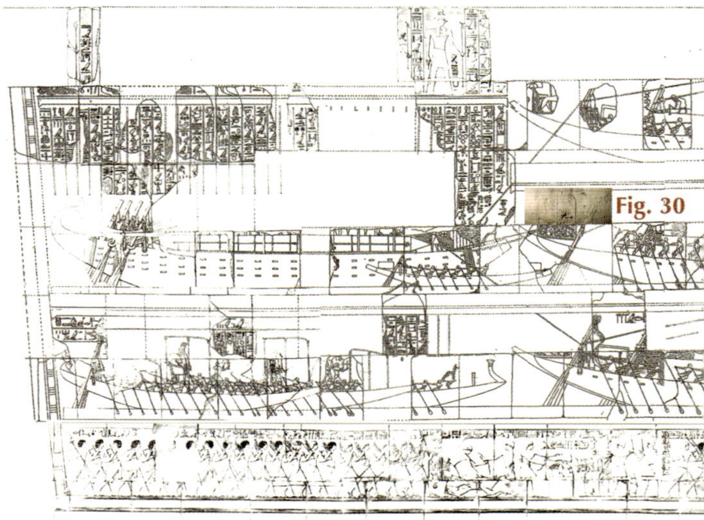

A final ramp led down to the ground-level Lower Terrace, flanked by further colonnaded porticoes. The northern and southern walls of these included images of Hatshepsut smiting and as a sphinx (fig. 35 bottom; cf. page 44), while the decoration of the rear wall of the Northern Lower Portico included images of Hatshepsut fowling, fishing, and offering to the gods, although only fragments of these survive. The Southern Lower Portico was adorned with reliefs depicting the transport of obelisks from Aswan to Karnak (fig. 103; cf. page 53), and various scenes concerning temple construction.[42]

Beyond the final ramp, a path flanked with six or seven pairs of sandstone sphinxes led eastward toward a gate in the temple's enclosure wall, from which a causeway, lined with some thirty further pairs of similar sphinxes,[43] led for half a kilometer toward the edge of the cultivated land. At this point lay a bark station,[44] beyond which the causeway continued onward for a similar distance to Hatshepsut's unfinished valley temple. This acted, like its Old and Middle Kingdom predecessors, as a formal portal to the whole temple complex. Although apparently far from completion, it was robbed for stone in later times, and only ever partially excavated (page 187). The structure was built on two levels, the Upper Terrace being composed of rubble filling, fronted by a retaining wall that was probably to form the back wall of a colonnade. Its form was therefore very much consistent with that of the main memorial temple.[45]

FIGURE 103 The transport of obelisks, as shown in the southern colonnade of the First Court, including the block shown in fig. 30.

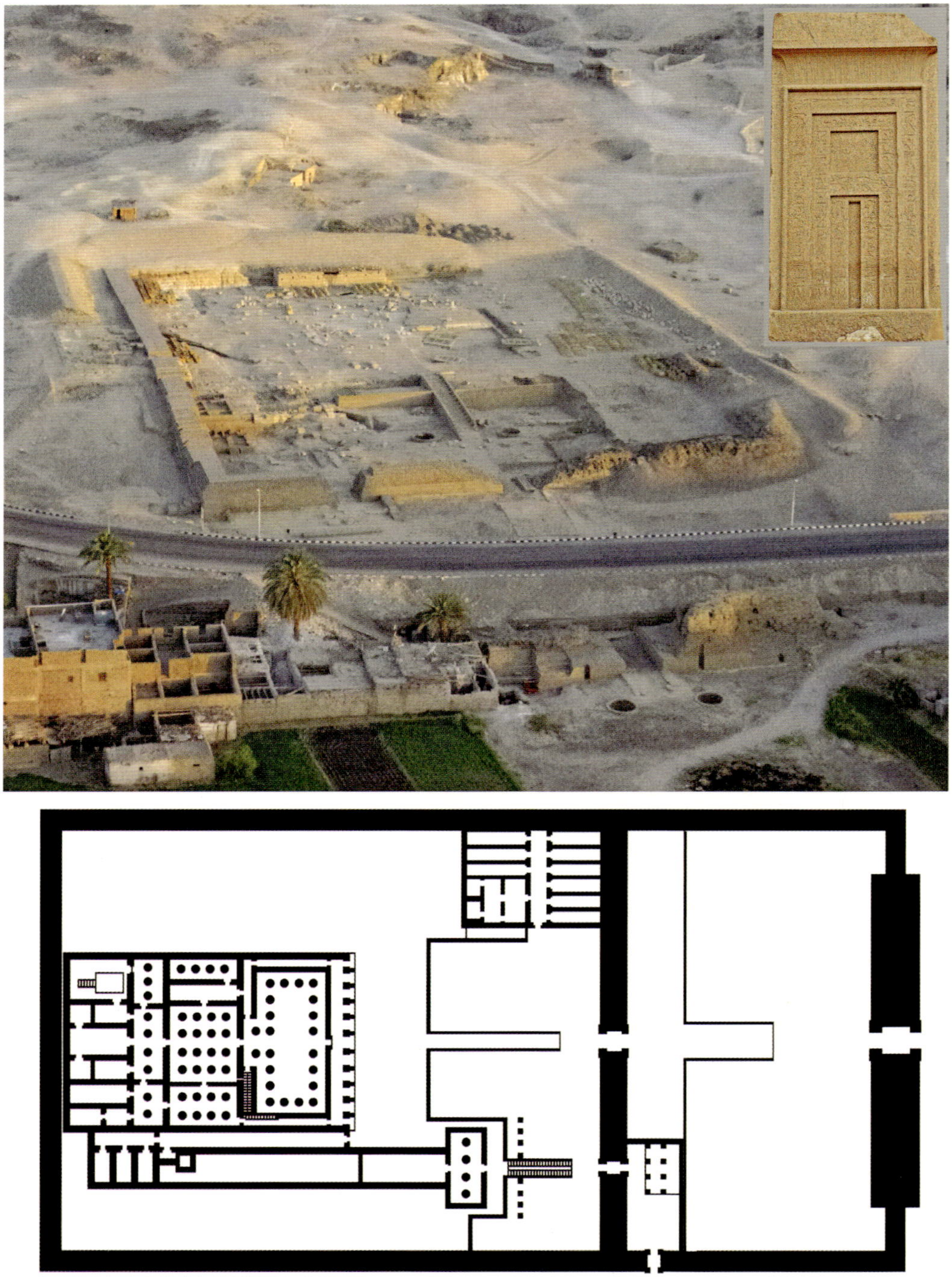

FIGURE 104 Plan and aerial photograph of the memorial temple of Thutmose III, as it was in 2013, with its false-door inset.

The Memorial Temple of Thutmose III

Since Egyptian kings normally began construction of their funerary monuments soon after their accession, work on the Theban memorial temple and tomb of Thutmose III will have begun early in his reign. The temple, named *ḥnkt-ʿnḫ* (fig. 104),[46] is listed as a functioning monument during the coregency with Hatshepsut, and was constructed around five hundred meters southwest of the valley temple of Hatshepsut's Deir el-Bahari complex. It also lay in front of the Sheikh Abd el-Qurna hill, where many of the officials of the time were buried (fig. 59). Its first phase comprised a structure on two levels, the Upper Terrace being partly rock-cut, partly the result of filling and grading, supported by a brick retaining wall. This formed the main body of the temple, fronted by a portico of sheathed figures of the king.

Behind this lay a peristyle court, which in turn gave access to a hypostyle hall, and finally the sanctuaries, arranged as at Deir el-Bahari. A Lower Terrace was later added, fronted by a large brick pylon, while a Hathor sanctuary was subsequently inserted to the south of the main temple axis, equipped with its own ramp and portico leading up from what was now the middle terrace. Only a few fragments of the decoration of the temple survive, the most significant being the false-door stela from the sanctuary of the king himself. As noted above (page 102), the king may have had a second memorial temple in the Memphite area, perhaps close to the edge of the desert below the plateau of the Saqqara necropolis.[47]

The Tomb of Thutmose III

The king's tomb (KV34—fig. 106)[48] lay some distance from KV20, at the opposite end of the Valley, high above the valley floor. As with KV20 and Hatshepsut's tomb as regent, it was cut at the foot of a natural chimney in the rock to aid long-term concealment. A connection with the king's memorial temple may have been intended by the fact that if the latter's axis is extended westward, it intersects the Valley of the Kings only a hundred meters east of the king's tomb. That this was not coincidental is suggested by the fact that a very similar relationship exists between the temple and tomb of Amenhotep II, while the final axis of Hatshepsut's Deir el-Bahari temple runs an even shorter distance to the east of the entrance to KV20 (fig. 105). A relationship also exists between the axis of the temple of Amenhotep I and Ahmes-Nefertiry in front of Dra Abu'l-Naga, and the probable tomb of Amenhotep I.[49] As noted on page 24, Wadi Gabbanet el-Qurud tomb C4, potentially that of Thutmose II, lies close to the extended axis of the temple of that king.

If these temple–tomb spatial relationships were indeed intentional, this would indicate that the architects of the early New Kingdom royal tombs were attempting to perpetuate the intimate link between the temple and burial place that had existed

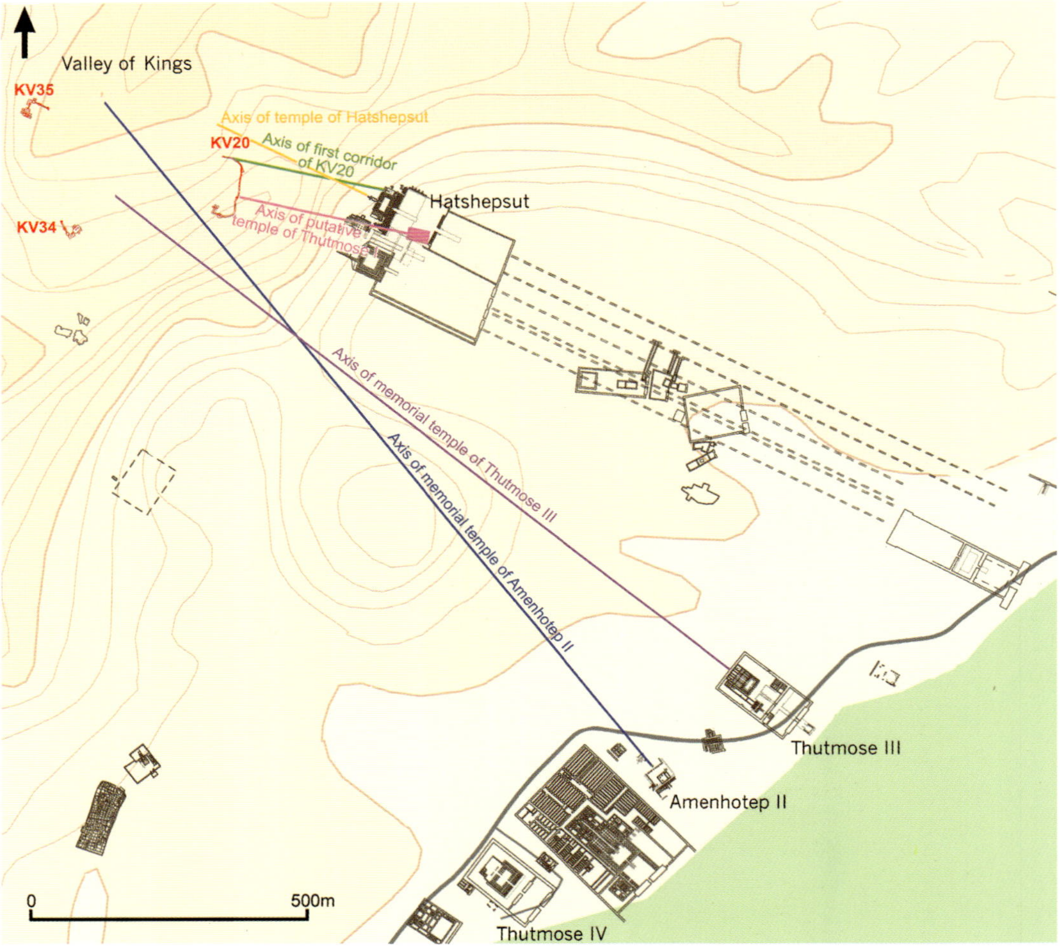

FIGURE 105 The axial alignments of the memorial temples of the middle of the Eighteenth Dynasty.

during the days of the pyramids. A precursor to the new approach should probably be seen in the case of the last Egyptian royal pyramid, that of Ahmose I, the deconstructed elements of whose complex were spread along a single axis, stretching a kilometer across the desert at Abydos.[50] Later monuments, however, from Thutmose IV onward, show no potential correlations with their associated tombs. This may simply be a matter of practicality, since available sites for both tombs and temples after the time of Amenhotep II were such that such correlations were no longer possible.

KV34 had the "bent" plan that is first seen in the tomb of Amenhotep I, and would continue down to that of Amenhotep III (fig. 106). It began with two sets of steps and

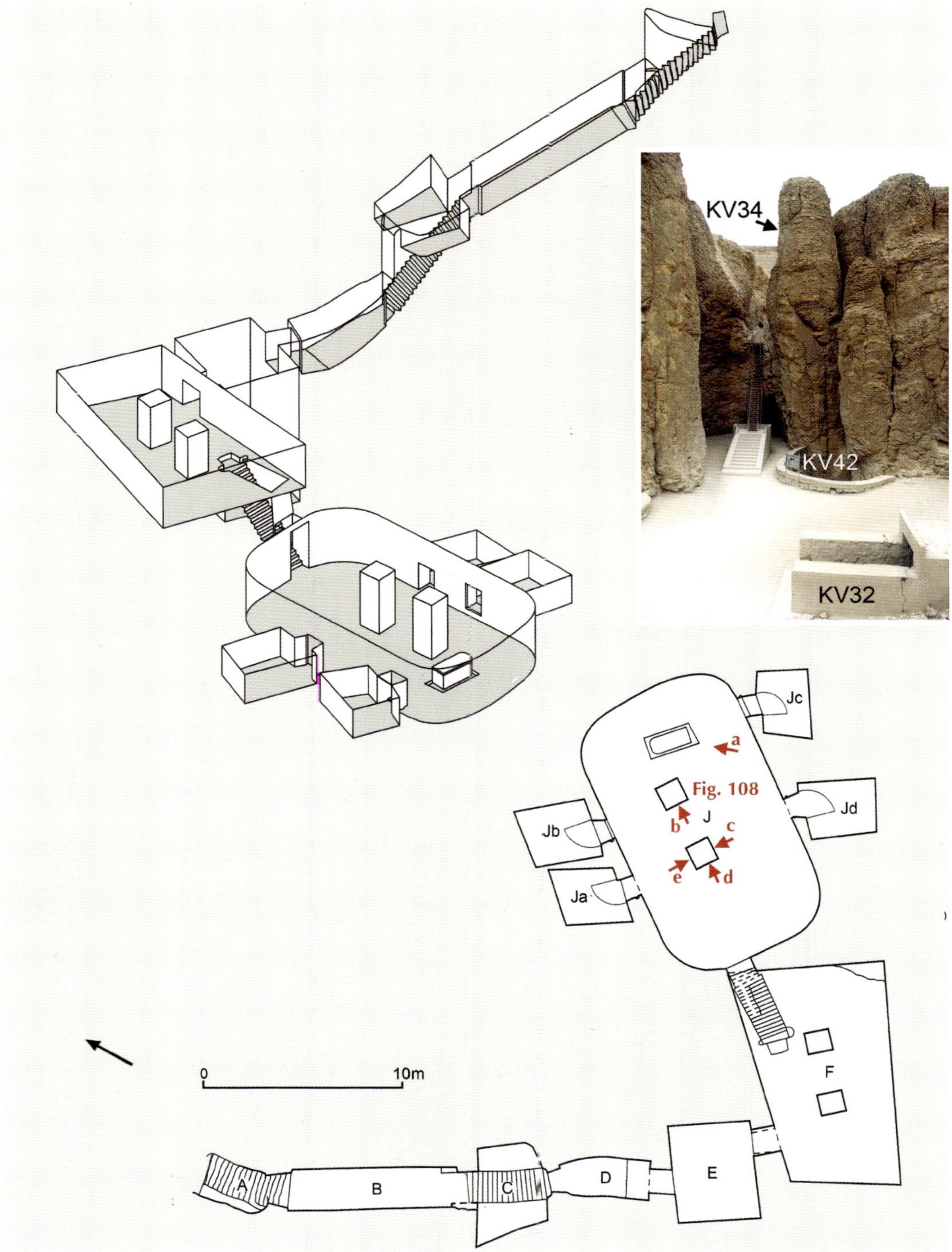

FIGURE 106 Plan, axonometric section, and view of ascent to the entrance of the tomb of Thutmose III (KV34).

FIGURE 107 The outer rooms of the tomb of Thutmose III. Top: shaft room E, with *kheker* frieze surmounting the "sky" sign. Bottom: the antechamber, with detail of the list of underworld deities that adorns the space.

two corridors, all somewhat roughly cut, which led to a square chamber. The walls of the room were whitewashed and topped with a *kheker* frieze (fig. 107 top). The preparation of the wall below the frieze suggests that further decoration was contemplated, but never carried out; the ceiling was adorned with five-pointed yellow stars on a deep blue background. The floor of this room was cut away after the funeral to form a shaft some nineteen meters deep.

A doorway, once sealed and painted over to match the rest of the wall, led into the antechamber, its roof supported by a pair of pillars. The shape of the room is rather odd, each wall being of a different length; it was adorned with long lists of the denizens of the Underworld, many of whom were not found outside the restricted world of the royal tombs. In keeping with the fashion of the period, the texts and figures were drawn in pen on a golden-yellow background, in the imitation of a papyrus roll (fig. 107 bottom).

A sunken stairway in the floor of the chamber led down into the burial chamber. Constructed on an oval plan, this was probably intended to represent a royal cartouche (fig. 108a). The chamber's walls were adorned with the earliest intact version of the "papyrus-written" *Amduat*, seen in fragmentary form in Hatshepsut's sepulchral chamber. Two pillars supported the roof, five faces of which hosted an abbreviated version of another funerary "book," the Litany of Re (fig. 108b–d). The sixth pillar face, however, was given a unique scene. This depicted the king with three wives and a daughter, and then suckled by his mother, "Iset," in the guise of a tree. It is unclear whether this is meant to be his earthly mother or the goddess Isis—or perhaps the two fused together. This would be the first and last time that members of a royal family would be included in the decoration of an orthodox royal tomb (fig. 108e).[51]

Four small annexes, all roughly cut and undecorated, opened out of the burial chamber, and were intended to hold funerary equipment, some fragments of which survived when the tomb was excavated in modern times. These annexes had been closed by wooden doors, but all other openings in the tomb, where closed, had been blocked with masonry.[52] All images and texts in the tomb appear to have been applied during the funerary ceremonies, perhaps as part of the "activation" of the magical mechanism that was the tomb.

Thutmose III's sarcophagus (fig. 114) was very similar to the final example of Hatshepsut, having probably been manufactured in parallel with it and that of Senenmut. No canopic chest is known, but it presumably conformed to the same naos form as that of Hatshepsut and the one later manufactured by Thutmose III for the reburial of Thutmose I (fig. 94). It may have been removed from the tomb in the Late Period, when the sepulcher seems to have been entered to allow the copying of the sarcophagus's decoration for use on that of a contemporary noble (page 162, fig. 117).

a

b c d e

FIGURE 108 The burial chamber of KV34, with decorated column faces (see fig. 106): b. demons and abbreviated Book of *Amduat*, part 1; c. text and demons; d. abbreviated *Amduat*, part 2; e. upper register: the king and his mother Iset in a boat, preceded by two men carrying the standards of Horus and Nefertum. Lower register: king followed by Queens Merytre, Sitiah, and Nebtu, and Princess Nefertiry; and king suckled by a tree. The latter is labeled as "his mother Iset"—probably a double entendre linking his earthly mother with the goddess Isis (Iset).

FIGURE 109 The surviving coffin of Thutmose III, stripped of its gilding; from TT320 (NMEC CG61014).

Of the nest of coffins that the sarcophagus of Thutmose III once held, only one survives, albeit in a poor condition (fig. 109).[53] Made of gilded and inlaid wood, it had been adorned with the *rishi* feathered pattern[54] that appears to have been employed for all royal coffins from the Seventeenth Dynasty down to the Twenty-first. However, almost all of its gilding and underlying gesso and inlay were removed during the late New Kingdom or/and the early Third Intermediate Period (see pages 158–59).[55] The royal mummy was also badly damaged by robbers and later rewrapped, mainly with new linen, but including an original shroud, inscribed with spells from the Book of the Dead and dedicated by Amenhotep II.[56]

Tombs of the Royal Family

The wadis of the southern part of the Theban necropolis, which had hosted the queenly tomb of Hatshepsut, continued to be used for royal family interments through the reign of Amenhotep III.[57] In particular, the next valley beyond the Wadi Sikkat Taqa el-Zeide, the Wadi Gabbanet el-Qurud, already noted as hosting the potential tomb of Thutmose II (pages 23–24), contains a number of tombs datable to the time of Thutmose III, in very similar situations to the Hatshepsut tomb. One (D1), with a single corridor and chamber, contained the burials of three wives of Thutmose III, Menwi, Merti, and Menhet, and remained intact until robbed early in the twentieth century AD (see page 193, below).[58] Another (C1) has been attributed to Neferure, on the basis of her cartouche being found inscribed on a rock nearby.[59] This tomb has a "bent" axis, but yielded no artifacts, although possible blocking stones found nearby suggest that it may have received a burial. This tomb lies directly above C4, which may be the sepulcher of Thutmose II.

The Valley of the Kings was certainly used for royal family burials from the time of Amenhotep II onward.[60] Foundation deposits naming the latter's mother, Queen Meryetre, were found outside tomb KV42, close to Thutmose III's KV34, but her original ownership of this sepulcher has been a matter of debate.[61] The walls of KV42's burial chamber had been plastered and given a frieze of *kheker* motifs, clearly with the intention of adding a hand-drawn copy of the Book of *Amduat* (fig. 110). The tomb also contained an unfinished quartzite sarcophagus, of a size and design consistent with it being the earliest of the sequence of such containers known from kings' tombs of the Eighteenth Dynasty. Accordingly, it has been suggested that KV42 (or at least the sarcophagus) might originally have been made for Thutmose II, but not used and later taken over for Meryetre. However, the proportions of the *kheker* motifs have been shown to correspond closely with examples in Thutmose III's Deir el-Bahari temple, pointing to KV42 having been cut during his reign, and implying that Meryetre was the original owner.

In any case, Meryetre seems unlikely to have ever been buried here. The tomb was actually found containing material from the burial of Senetnay, wife of the Mayor of Thebes, Sennefer (TT96), and a woman named Baketre, dating to the time of Amenhotep II and Thutmose IV. It remains unclear whether these deposits were original, or the result of later caching.[62]

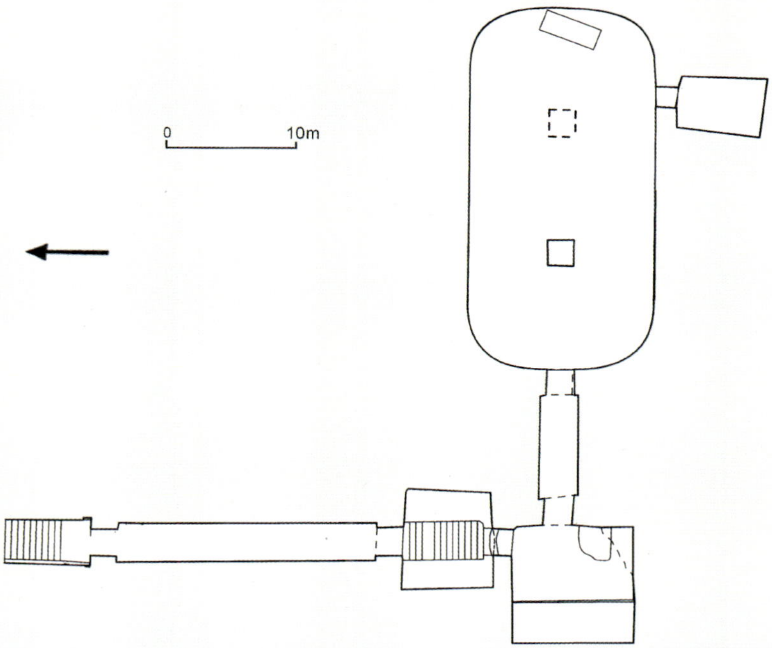

FIGURE 110 KV42, with the upper parts of the walls of its burial chamber decorated with *kheker* motifs, and containing an unfinished quartzite sarcophagus.

6 Legacy and Limbo

The passing of Thutmose III marked the end of an era. The five decades during which he and Hatshepsut had ruled Egypt had seen the consolidation of Egypt's status across a broad front. A mode of Egyptian kingship now existed that would be perpetuated for generations to come, ruling directly or indirectly a swath of territory that extended for some two thousand kilometers from north to south. This cultural–political complex would largely endure for nearly four centuries, and even after that, it is clear that later rulers' aspirations were heavily influenced by the Egyptian world that had been created by the Thutmosids, even if filtered through the lens of the later rule of the Ramesids, in particular of Rameses II. And when some later rulers wished to connect themselves specifically with the past, it was the Thutmosids that they wished to invoke (see pages 157, 160–61).

The Heirs of Thutmose III and Hatshepsut

In the immediate term, the inheritor of the legacy of Thutmose III and Hatshepsut was the eighteen-year-old Amenhotep II.[1] He certainly wished to perpetuate his father's status as a military leader, throwing himself into a series of campaigns into Syria-Palestine. These included the capture and execution of seven local rulers, six of whose corpses were hung from the walls of Thebes, with the seventh displayed on the walls of Napata. This kind of brutal display is not to be found in the surviving records of Thutmose III's campaigns. Amenhotep's self-presentation was also rather different. There was an emphasis on his personal strength and skills, in rowing, running, and chariot-driving, but especially as an archer (cf. fig. 57).[2]

FIGURE 111 Fragment of stela, with depiction of Thutmose III and a queen whose name has been overwritten by that of his mother Iset. The palimpsest name has been read both as that of Neferure and also that of Meryetre; from memorial temple of Thutmose III (Cairo CG34014).

There are indications of dissension within the royal family at the end of Amenhotep II's reign. No wife is named on any extant monument of the king's reign, although Tiaa, the mother of his son, Thutmose IV, is shown on a number of monuments of the latter's reign. Tiaa also had her name introduced into some existing reliefs of Amenhotep II, replacing that of his mother Meryetre.[3] There is also a possible case where the name of Meryetre was replaced by that of Thutmose III's mother, Iset (fig. 111),[4] although it is also possible that the overwritten name is actually that of Neferure (cf. pages 31–33). In addition, the monuments of a Prince Amenhotep (C), seemingly Amenhotep II's crown prince, have been mutilated. When combined with the fact that Thutmose IV ascribes his assumption of the throne to the divine intervention of the god Horemakhet, in his avatar of the Great Sphinx at Giza, the data would seem to imply a struggle for the throne at the end of Amenhotep II's reign.

Whether or not his accession was "regular," Thutmose IV seems to have been keen to link himself with his grandfather Thutmose III. His prenomen simply pluralized the *ḫpr*-element of the earlier king's cartouche (for Menkheper*ure*), while his Golden Falcon name also featured violence against the Nine Bows. The fourth Thutmose also erected the obelisk originally prepared for Thutmose III, but left alongside the Sacred Lake at Karnak throughout the reign of Amenhotep II (fig. 74 left). As noted above (page 98, fig. 74), this may have been left unerected owing to the cracking of its mate while yet in the quarry. Now, however, it was installed on its own as the fetish of a sun sanctuary at the eastern end of the Karnak complex, where it remained until its removal to Rome in the fourth century AD (page 165).[5]

Buildings and Memories

Buildings

As with all monuments linked to Amun, the structures erected and works of art produced under Thutmose III and Hatshepsut were attacked during the campaign against the god that was waged under Akhenaten. Restoration of mutilated images of the god began under Tutankhamun, and continued through Rameses II. The latter gave particular attention to Deir el-Bahari, where numerous examples of his standard restoration text can be seen (e.g., figs. 22, 103, 112). Extensive restorations had, of course, also been required at Karnak, where the heart of the complex had largely been the work of Thutmose III and Hatshepsut. It is likely that repairs were carried out here in advance of attention being given to such "secondary" locations as Deir el-Bahari. The memorial temple of Thutmose III was certainly functioning under Rameses II, as a High Priest of the king's cult is known from that time (Khonsu-Ta, buried in TT31),[6] when a mudbrick structure was added in the northeastern part of the complex.[7]

Natural phenomena also affected monuments of the era. A rock fall, probably triggered by an earthquake, destroyed Thutmose III's Deir el-Bahari temple around the beginning of the Twenty-first Dynasty, and probably also damaged that of Hatshepsut. The latter temple nevertheless remained functional, and during the eighth century BC became a burial place. Those interred there were mainly members of the priesthood of Montju, shaft tombs being cut under the floors of many parts of the temple.[8]

A further secondary use of the Deir el-Bahari temple of Hatshepsut came in Ptolemaic times. Under Ptolemy III, a structure of some kind was erected on the middle

FIGURE 112 Sunk-relief restoration text of Rameses II, contrasting with the original raised relief in the south colonnade of the First Court of the temple of Hatshepsut.

terrace, and major changes were made to the innermost room of the main Amun sanctuary under Ptolemy VIII.[9] This was converted to serve the cults of two deified mortals, Imhotep, architect of the Step Pyramid of Saqqara, and Amenhotep-son-of-Hapu, a celebrated official of Amenhotep III, together with the Greek goddess Hygieia.[10] As part of this work, a porch was added in front of the gate of the sanctuary (fig. 98 bottom). Finally, with the end of paganism, the temple became the site of a monastery of Saint Phoibammon from the sixth through thirteenth centuries AD (fig. 128 top).[11] This was part of a network of monastic institutions that grew up around the Theban necropolis. The funerary chapel of Hatshepsut became a church, with her mutilated false-door stela plastered over and adorned with a figure of Christ Pantokrator ("All-Ruler").[12]

Memories and mummies

As we have already seen (page 108), the attack on Hatshepsut's monuments at the end of Thutmose III's reign was distinctly patchy: while three-dimensional images were destroyed fairly comprehensively, many two-dimensional ones and their label texts remained legible to some degree. If the attempt had been intended to sever the link between Hatshepsut and Thutmose III, its futility would become apparent four centuries later.

Then, Panedjem I, High Priest of Amun at Karnak, and later king in southern Egypt,[13] decided to name two of his children Menkheperre and Maatkare. Neither name had hitherto been used as anything other than the prenomina of Thutmose III and Hatshepsut, and there seems little question that Panedjem wished to honor these two rulers together. This was perhaps partly in remembrance of the roles of Thutmose III and Hatshepsut in the building of the temple over which he presided. Indeed, the children would go on to become, respectively, High Priest and God's Wife of Amun at Karnak (fig. 113).[14] The names continued to be bestowed on children for a while after Panedjem's revival,[15] including on a daughter of Pasenkhanut II. She married the future Osorkon I, and became the mother of the High Priest Shoshenq Q.[16]

It is possible that Panedjem's choice of names reflected a wider interest in the Thutmosid kings on his part. In particular, he was actually buried in what had once been the outer coffin of Thutmose I, now extensively redecorated in the latest style for Panedjem, and with a brand-new inner coffin.[17] Thutmose's coffin presumably had become available after the king's mummy had been destroyed by plunderers in the tomb robberies that had begun in the late Twentieth Dynasty.

While it is likely that the initial penetration of the ancient royal tombs had been by criminal gangs (fig. 114), it seems that, once tombs had been opened, a process began of "official" recycling of the precious materials that lay within them. By the time of Panedjem's kingship, the state had become increasingly impoverished. This was, at least

FIGURE 113 Panedjem I and Thutmosids. Top: coffin of Thutmose I, as reworked for the burial of Panedjem himself. It has been twice stripped of its gilding and inlay: when appropriated for Panedjem, and then later in the Twenty-first Dynasty; from TT320 (NMEC CG61025). Bottom right: Panedjem's son and namesake of Thutmose III, the High Priest of Amun Menkheperre, as shown on a stela from Karnak (Cairo TR 3.12.24.2). Bottom left: Panedjem's daughter and namesake of Hatshepsut, the God's Wife of Amun, Maatkare, as shown on her Book of the Dead papyrus, from TT320 (Cairo CG40007).

in part, the result of the fracturing of international trade in the wake of the Bronze Age Collapse during the preceding century, combined with Egypt's loss of control of Nubia's gold mines and other southern resources. As a result, even though nominally "rescued" by the authorities, the royal mummies were then relieved of any remaining jewelry and any gilding left on such coffins as continued to house their original occupants. In the case of the surviving coffin of Thutmose III (fig. 109), it appears to have been initially stripped of its original, thick, gold sheeting, regilded more modestly (perhaps more than once), and then finally stripped down once more to the gesso and linen underlay.[18]

It is unknown when Thutmose's tomb was first disturbed. All that is certain is that the one surviving coffin, with the king's mummy within it,[19] found its way into tomb TT320, just to the south of Deir el-Bahari (fig. 127a). This sepulcher seems originally to have been the burial place of Queen Ahmes-Nefertiry, reused during the Twenty-first Dynasty for both the reburial of ancient mummies and the primary interment of the High Priest Panedjem II and his family.[20] The move of Thutmose III to the tomb can be placed no more exactly than some time between the middle of the Twenty-first Dynasty and the middle of the reign of Shoshenq I, founder of the Twenty-second Dynasty.[21]

The king's mummy[22] had by this time been badly damaged by robbers, with the head and all four limbs detached from the torso. An earlobe had been torn off along with an earring, and an ax or a knife had been employed to loosen the bracelets that had adhered tightly to the skin. As a result of the state of the body, ancient restorers had to resort to a splint to tie the right arm and hand together, and use four boat oars to hold the body rigid, three within the wrappings and one outside (fig. 127b–d). Of the mummy's original trappings, its inscribed shroud (page 149) was employed in the rewrapping, while two strings of carnelian, gold, and lapis lazuli survived within the innermost wrappings.

FIGURE 114 The sarcophagus of Thutmose III in KV34, as seen in the 1960s, with the lid still as left by tomb robbers.

FIGURE 115 Wooden box bearing the name of Hatshepsut and containing a mummified organ and a tooth; from TT320 (Cairo JE26250).

As far as the fate of the burial of Hatshepsut is concerned, we have very little evidence. There seems no reason to assume that her interment was desecrated as part of the attack on her monuments late in Thutmose III's reign, and her sarcophagus and canopic chest remain in excellent condition, with no sign of erasures. The only item bearing her name that was recovered from TT320 was a wooden box, perhaps intended for toiletries, found containing a mummified organ and a tooth (fig. 115). There is nothing to directly connect any of the contents with Hatshepsut.

However, a fragment of what would appear to be one of her coffins was found in the tomb of Rameses XI (fig. 95c), alongside various debris that suggest that items of royal funerary equipment were stripped for recycling there.[23] This would imply that Hatshepsut's burial was the subject of robbery/recycling alongside most other New Kingdom royal interments. However, no mummy of hers has been identified in either the TT320 cache, or the one established in the tomb of Amenhotep II (KV35). A number of mummies found in TT320 were anonymous, and five of these seem never to have been examined:[24] it is possible that Hatshepsut's body might be among these. Another proposed candidate for her remains will be discussed below (pages 201–202).

Thutmose III as Deity and Inspiration

During the later part of the New Kingdom, and into the Third Intermediate Period, a number of earlier kings were invoked as patrons of the Theban dead. Amenhotep I was the most popular of these, but others included Montjuhotep II of the Middle Kingdom, and Thutmose III. Amenhotep I was not infrequently substituted for Osiris on the floor of Twenty-first Dynasty coffin troughs, but examples also exist with Thutmose III playing the role (fig. 116).

The enduring prestige of Thutmose III is demonstrated in the eighth century BC by Pi(ankh)y, the Kushite king who also controlled the Thebaid, and who was ultimately suzerain of the rulers in the north of Egypt as well.[25] Although he would later employ other names instead, the Kushite monarch began his reign by appropriating Thutmose's titulary wholesale. The only change was to substitute "Napata" (Pi[ankh]y's home city) for "Thebes" in the Horus name. Thutmose III's probable status as the founder of Napata

FIGURE 116 The deified Thutmose III, as shown in the Twenty-first Dynasty coffin of Amenhotep (Vatican 22767).

and perhaps the cult of Amun at Gebel Barkal is likely to have further enhanced his status as a model for the Kushite king. It is instructive to note that the Year 47 stela of Thutmose III (fig. 82) was found in a part of the Barkal Amun temple built by Pi(ankh)y, close to stelae of that king, and must have been moved there by him, perhaps from some distance, possibly from Napata itself (cf. page 160).

FIGURE 117 Late Period sarcophagus of Hapimen, with its exterior decoration apparently copied from that of the sarcophagus of Thutmose III; found reused in the mosque of Ibn Tulun, Cairo (BM EA23).

Another area where Thutmose III served as a source of inspiration was in the design of the sarcophagus of a Twenty-sixth Dynasty nobleman, named Hapimen (fig. 117).[26] The combination of images and texts on the exterior of this piece are all-but-identical with those on Thutmose's sarcophagus, and quite unlike those found on contemporary pieces.[27] The implication can only be that the tomb of Thutmose III was accessible during the time of Hapimen (or not long before), allowing the king's sarcophagus to be copied. This is not necessarily as bizarre as would first appear, since it is clear that "archaeological" investigations of ancient monuments and the copying of their decoration by gridding (for often precise reproduction) went back to at least the late eighth century BC, and continued well into the seventh. One wonders whether the canopic chest of the king was removed at that time for reuse, as no trace of it has ever been found.

To the End of Antiquity

As we have already seen, the temple of Hatshepsut at Deir el-Bahari was still in use in Ptolemaic times, and had been partly repurposed. A number of the elements of the Karnak complex erected or decorated by Thutmose III and Hatshepsut underwent restoration under Ptolemy IV. In a number of cases where texts and images were recarved, the original composition was retained, but with the hieroglyphs and images very clearly

FIGURE 118 The inner gate of the temple of Ptah at Karnak, showing reliefs of Thutmose III recut in Ptolemaic times.

in Ptolemaic style (fig. 118). In some cases, this has left walls with a rather bizarre Eighteenth Dynasty/Ptolemaic mash-up of decoration.

As for what was known during the Ptolemaic Period about Thutmose III, Hatshepsut, and their time, our principal clue is provided by the Greek-language third-century BC work of the Egyptian priest Manetho.[28] Unfortunately, all that survives of this are later extracts and epitomes, and it is therefore unclear how accurately the now extant material reflects Manetho's original work. This is particularly important for the Eighteenth Dynasty, as there are significant discrepancies between the surviving extracts. All have also clearly become garbled in their transmission, especially at the very end of the dynasty.[29] The section from the beginning of the Eighteenth Dynasty down to an "Amenôphis," who can only be Amenhotep III, runs as follows:

Africanus		Eusebius		Josephus	
Amôs	—	Amôsis	25y	Tethmôsis	25y 4m
Khebrôs	13y	Khebrôn	13y	Khebrôn	13y
Amenôphthis	24y	Ammenôphis	21y	Amenôphis	20y 7m
Amensis	22y			Amesses (his sister)	21y 9m
Misaphris	13y	Miphrês	12y	Mêphrês	12y 9m
Misphragmuthôsis	26y	Misphragmuthôsis	26	Mêphramuthôsis	25y 10m
Tuthmôsis	9y	Tuthmôsis	9y	Thmôsis	9y 8m
Amenôphis	31y	Amenôphis	31y	Amenôphis	30y 10m

As far as the basic order is concerned, "Amenôphis/"Ammenôphthis" (who must be Amenhotep I) has slipped down a place, swapping with "Khebrôn/s," who is presumably Thutmose I. Given the gloss "his sister" in Josephus' version, "Amensis/Amesses" must be Hatshepsut, albeit a place too high. Thutmose II is presumably "Misaphris/Miphrês/Mêphrês" and the identity of Thutmose III concealed by "Misphragmuthôsis/Mêphramuthôsis." After him, the Manethonic sequence seems to jump to Thutmose IV ("T[ut]hmôsis"), omitting Amenhotep II entirely (who may have been accidentally merged with Amenhotep III, as the reign length seems to correspond to that of Amenhotep II).

Reign lengths in general seem to bear little resemblance to reality, with the exceptions of those for "Amôs/Amôsis/Tethmôsis" (Ahmose I), "Amenôphis/"Ammenôphthis" (Amenhotep I), and "T[ut]hmôsis" (Thutmose IV)—and "Amensis/Amesses" (Hatshepsut), if counting from the beginning of her regency, rather than the coregency. As far as the rest are concerned, little purpose seems to be served by trying to make sense of them,[30] other than by suggesting that by Ptolemaic times the period had become significantly misunderstood. This was exacerbated by weaving in Greek historiographic traditions and folk tales, which can be clearly discerned in the long-form renderings of Manetho that are to be found in the work of Josephus.[31]

In this latter source, which quotes Manetho in the broader context of writing Jewish history, there seems to be an attempt to make Thutmose III (aka "Misphragmuthôsis/Mêphramuthôsis") the pivotal figure, ascribing to him, rather than Ahmose I ("Amôs/Amôsis/Tethmôsis"), the expulsion of the Hyksos. This presumably reflected a continuity of Thutmose III's memory down to Roman times, seemingly to be manifested in (e.g.) the aforementioned Ptolemaic recarving of Thutmose's images and texts at Karnak, and mentions of Thutmose III in the Roman Period temples at Dendara[32] and Esna.[33]

During Roman times, at least two major monuments of Thutmose III found their way to Europe. We have already seen that two of the king's Heliopolitan obelisks were moved to Alexandria under Augustus (fig. 135). The "single" obelisk ultimately erected by Thutmose IV at Karnak (but manufactured under Thutmose III) was taken down by Constantine I and moved to Alexandria late in his reign, which ended in AD 337. It was then removed to Rome by Constantius II in AD 357, where it was re-erected in the Circus Maximus.[34]

One of the obelisks in front of Pylon VII at Karnak (or at least the top two-thirds of it) was also taken to Alexandria at some point, perhaps likewise by Constantine; in any case, it is known to have been there in AD 363. Plans were made by Constantius II to take it to Constantinople (Istanbul), but were frustrated by the emperor's death. It eventually made it to Constantinople at an unknown date, to be erected in the city's Hippodrome by Theodosius I in AD 390 (fig. 73 bottom left).

The Constantinople obelisk would remain standing down to modern times.[35] However, the Circus Maximus monument fell (or was pushed over) at some point after the fifth century AD, as were almost all of the numerous Egyptian obelisks brought to Rome during the Empire. Its three fragments were, however, retrieved in 1587, and re-erected outside Rome's Lateran Palace in 1588 (fig. 74 left).

7 Resurrection

Back in Egypt, if the knowledge of the time of Thutmose III and Hatshepsut had become sketchy by the Ptolemaic Period, the end of paganism and the consequent loss of the ability to read the hieroglyphic script around the end of the fourth century severed the last substantive links with the pharaonic era. Accordingly, for over a millennium and a half, any engagement with their time was through the lens of Manetho, and more generally through other writers in Greek, and works deriving from them. Some of the monarchs' remaining monuments had been repurposed for new sacred or profane purposes, but by medieval times all had become deserted ruins, slowly being swallowed up by their surroundings.

Although some local interest in such structures existed during medieval times,[1] it was not until the eighteenth century AD that European travelers made their first meaningful acquaintance with ancient Egyptian monuments.[2] One of the first such travelers to reach Thebes, and in 1737 make a detailed account of its ruins, was Richard Pococke* (1704–65).[3] From the point of view of the study of the monuments of the Thutmosid pharaohs, he made the first detailed plan of Karnak, which included the area around the granite sanctuary and the Festival Hall. He described the latter as "consisting of several small apartments, on each side of a spacious colonnade, as if for the officers of the temple."[4] Crossing the river, Pococke noted and summarily planned what he could see of the southern part of the Upper Terrace of Hatshepsut's Deir el-Bahari temple.[5]

> The . . . valley . . . seems to have been divided into four parts by walls or mounds, of which there are still remains . . . . The other three parts go towards some remains of buildings, as represented [in fig. 119 top]; the granite door A. leads to

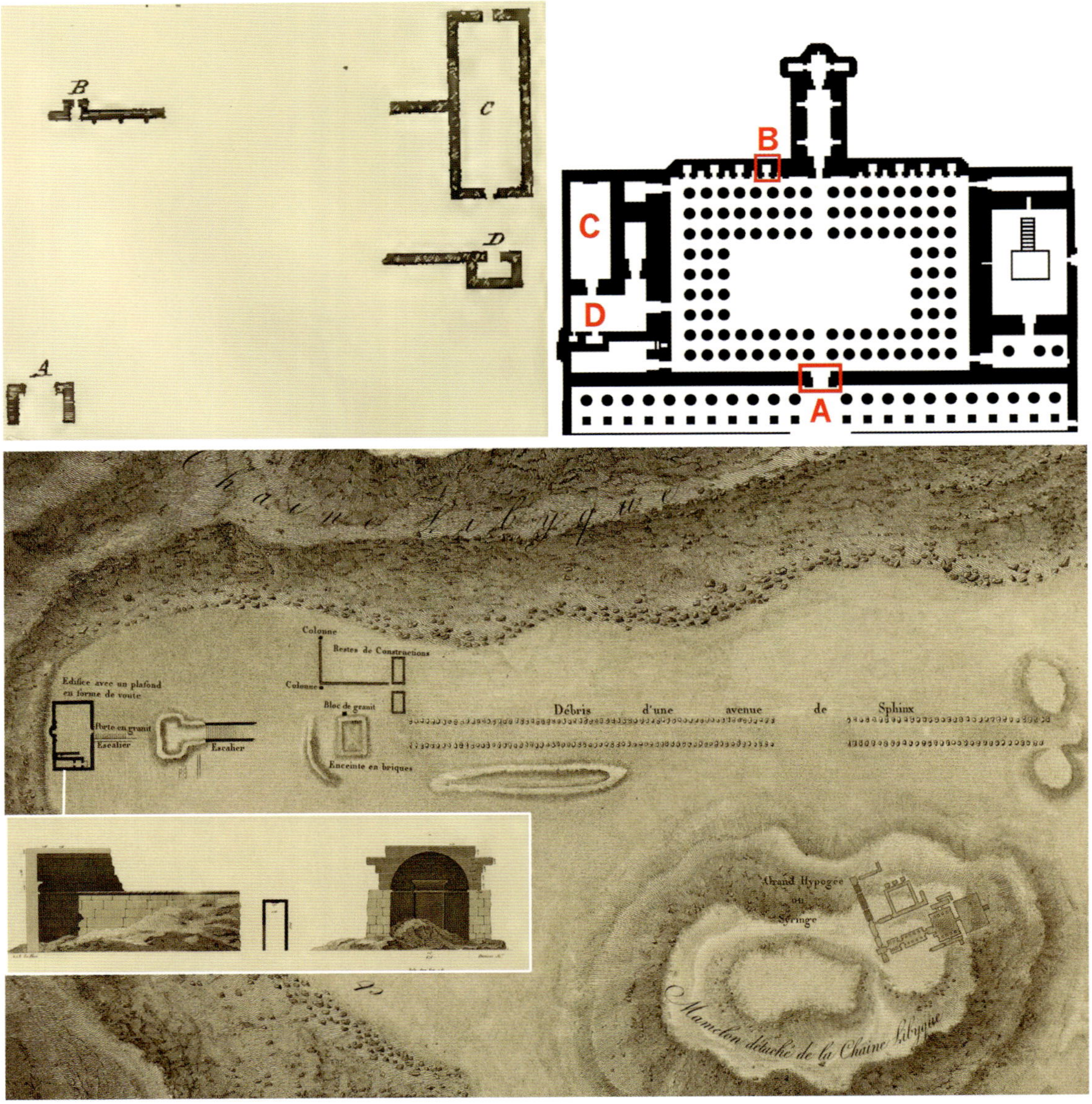

FIGURE 119 Top left: the southern part of the Upper Terrace at Deir el-Bahari, as planned by Richard Pococke. As printed, however, the image was reversed—a production error found in other plates in his book as well. The actual location of the elements is shown top right. Bottom: the plan of the temple area and the Asasif as made by the French expedition in 1798; the inset shows the funerary chapel of Hatshepsut. The tomb in the bottom right is that of Padamenopet (TT33), of the early Twenty-sixth Dynasty.

> the building B. which is all ruin'd, except a small part of the front. To the left is a room C. over which there is a well-turn'd arch, with a half round at the spring of it; the door at the north end has likewise a half round on each side of it, and is of granite. It appears to have been used as a Christian church, and the hieroglyphics have been cover'd over with plaster, which are in small columns, exquisitely well cut; Christ with a glory is painted on the plaster. As this was a church, it is probable the arch over this building is a Christian work.[6]

Pococke's "room C." was the funerary chapel of Hatshepsut, and "the door at the north end" was her false door (cf. page 157 for its decoration with a figure of Christ). "Building B." may have been one of the niches at the back of the Upper Terrace.

Rather more of the site was recorded in 1798 by Prosper Jollois* (1776–1842) and Édouard de Villiers du Terrage* (1780–1855), two of the team of *savants* attached to Napoleon Bonaparte's force that had invaded Egypt earlier that year. They planned (fig. 119 bottom) and described what was then visible of both the temple (including again the funerary chapel of Hatshepsut) and

> small piles of debris arranged in a regular and symmetrical way . . . . Only the habit of seeing these sorts of ruins could have made us judge what they once were, and an attentive examination has convinced us that it can only be remains of sphinx pedestals or similar rams to those that can still be seen almost whole at Karnak. All these debris are in very fine calcareous materials; their current state probably only comes from the composition of the stone, which would have been damaged by the atmosphere, and which would have been almost reduced to powder because, if they were the result of purposeful destruction one would certainly no longer see, in their arrangement, the regularity, symmetry and exact alignments they still present.[7]

Fragments of some seventy-four sandstone sphinxes (page 141) have subsequently been recovered.

Like Pococke, Jollois and de Villiers noted that much of the original decoration of the temple had been covered over with plaster during the conversion of the monument into a monastery in Coptic times. The team also examined the Small Temple at Medinet Habu, which later received attention from the various proto-Egyptologists who spent time at Thebes during the 1810s and 20s.[8]

Among them was Giovanni Belzoni* (1778–1823), who not only made a plan of Medinet Habu's Small Temple,[9] but may also have been responsible for the first clearance of the Amun sanctuary at Deir el-Bahari around 1817, since this element first appears in plans of the 1820s. Belzoni might also have been the person who removed Thutmose I's stela (page 138) from the temple, although it may rather have been done by Yanni d'Athanasi* (1798–1854) a few years later. In any case, the stela arrived at the Louvre Museum in Paris in 1826 as part of the second collection of Egyptian antiquities formed by the British Consul-General Henry Salt* (1780–1826), both Belzoni and Athanasi having acquired material on his behalf.

Around 1823–25, Henry Westcar* (1798–1868) visited Hatshepsut's temple, becoming apparently the first visitor to call it (in his diary) the "Northern Derr" (i.e., Deir—"monastery," fully in Arabic "Deir el-Bahari").[10] Like his predecessors, he noted the "doorway of granite in beautiful preservation is still standing; also an arched chamber [i.e., the chapel of Hatshepsut] of Egyptian workmanship, but it is formed of flat layers of stone hollowed out to that shape & not on our principle. Some of the rooms seem to be in the rock."

From a historiographic point of view, probably the most important of these visits were those to Deir el-Bahari by John Gardner Wilkinson* (1797–1875). Resident at Western Thebes (making his home in the tomb-chapel of Thutmose III's first vizier, Ametju [TT83: figs. 38, 59]) from 1821 to 1833, during 1827 he cleared the Amun chapel[11] and some walls. He then included the first detailed plan of the temple area in his great map of Thebes (fig. 120). Wilkinson also described the parts of the structure available to him,[12] remarking in addition on "granite androsphinxes and limestone columns of old style" along the side of the approach to the temple (fig. 120I), recognizing them as being "at least coeval with the founder of this structure."[13]

Like Jollois and de Villiers, he noted the "double row of sandstone sphinxes . . . their fragments, scattered on the site they once occupied, sufficiently mark[ing] their position, which is still more observable from the summit of the cliff" defining the causeway up to the temple. Wilkinson thought he had also identified a pair of obelisk bases in front of the point where it met the enclosure wall, equating these with supports for the obelisks depicted in the south colonnade of the first court (fig. 103, a scene that he was first to record), an error that endured for some time.

Jean-François Champollion* (1790–1832) and Ippolito Rosellini* (1800–43) visited in 1829, during their Franco-Tuscan expedition to Egypt. Champollion was able to identify the building as a temple dedicated to Amun, and also note the various restorations carried out down to the Ptolemaic Period. A detailed plan of the site (including the monastic elements, ignored by most later visitors) was made around 1832 by the expedition led by Robert Hay* (1799–1863).[14]

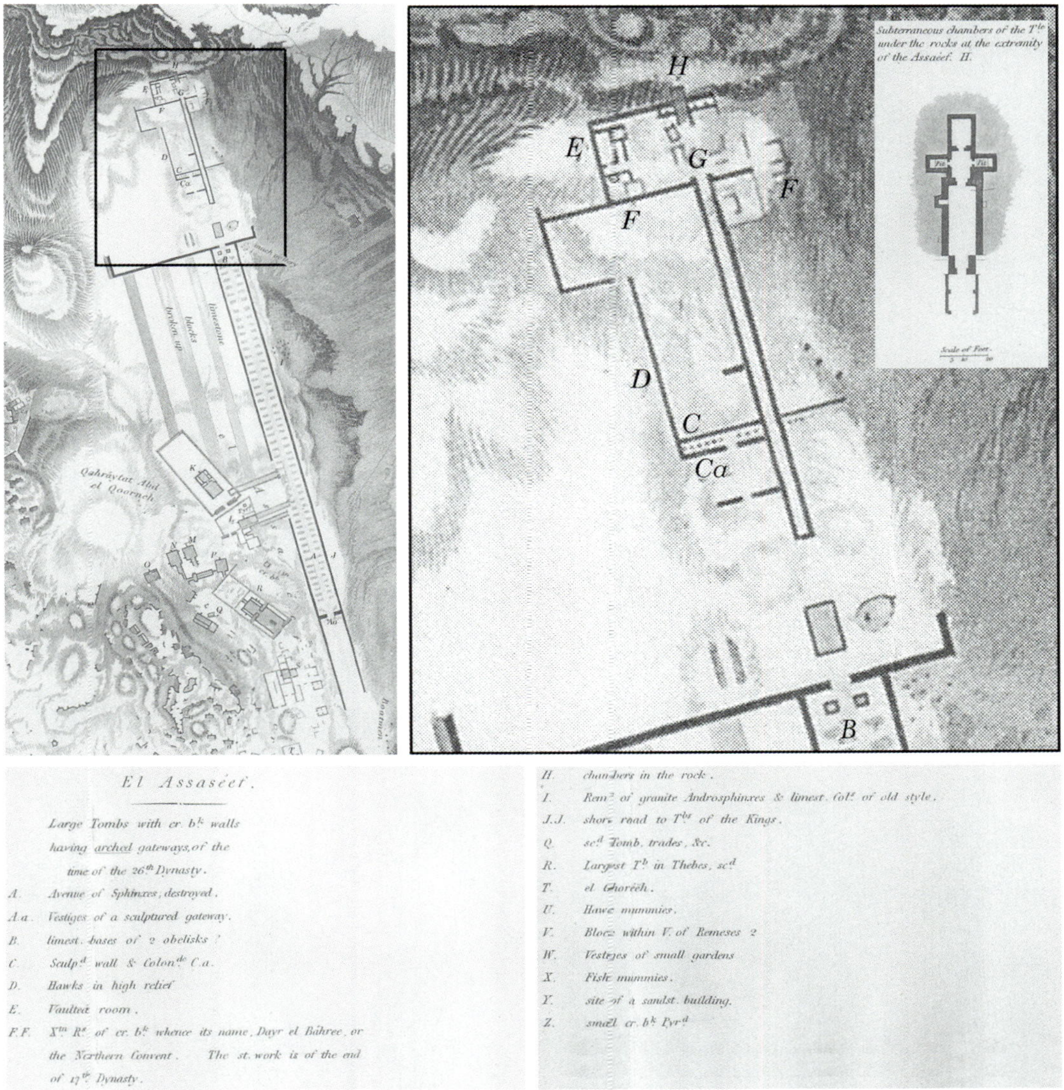

FIGURE 120 Deir el-Bahari, as planned by Gardner Wilkinson in his 1830 map of the Theban necropolis.

As a result of their observations, Champollion, Rosellini, and Wilkinson were able to establish preliminary hypotheses on the historical implications of what they could see on the standing monuments, not only at Deir el-Bahari, but also at Karnak and other sites in Upper Egypt.[15] These earliest attempts at reconstructing the history of ancient Egypt with the aid of actual ancient Egyptian sources focused on reconciling the emerging data from the as yet imperfectly understood hieroglyphs with the material

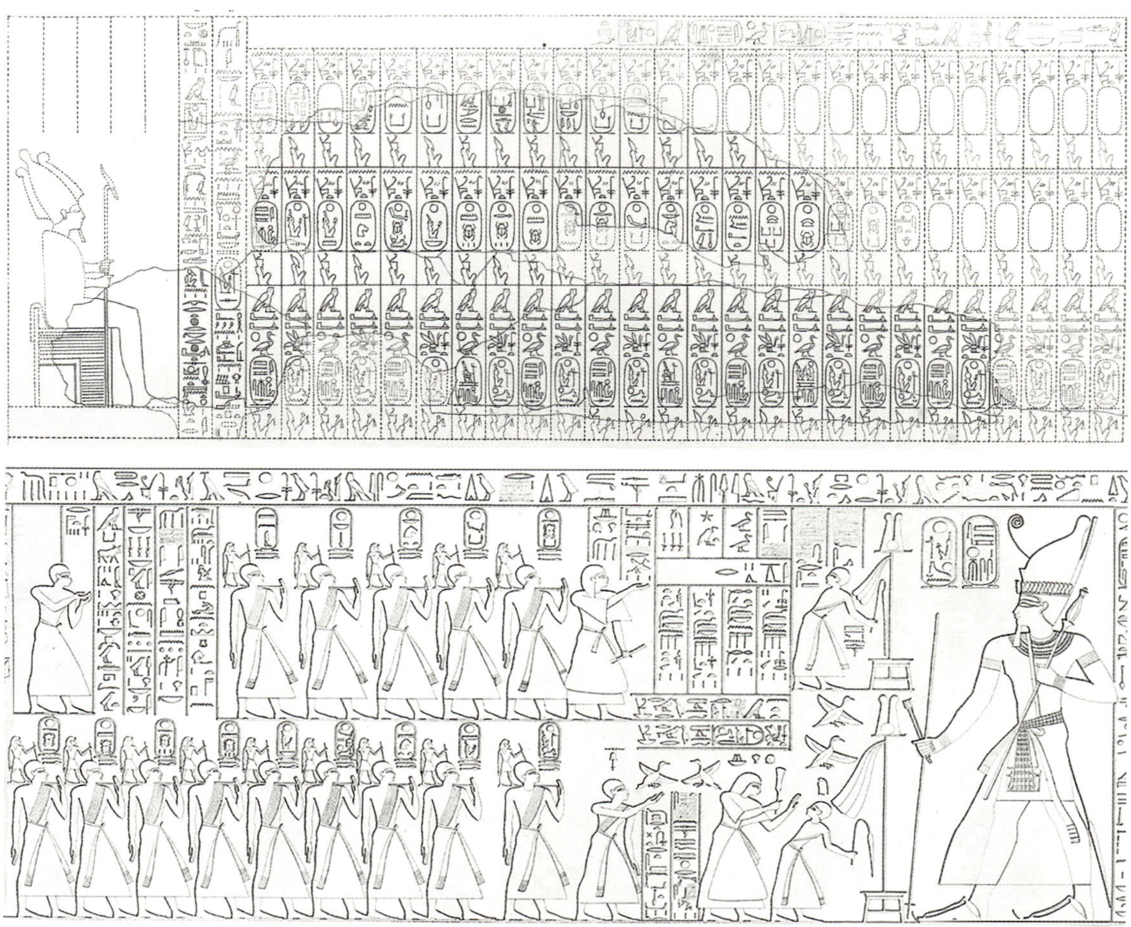

FIGURE 121 Top: the Abydos king list of Rameses II. Bottom: the Festival of Min relief of Rameses II at the Ramesseum, including Thutmose III among the procession of former kings' statues.

hitherto available—writers in Greek and Latin and the Old Testament. For the New Kingdom, the Manethonic lists were the key such documents, now to be integrated with hieroglyphic sources of contemporary monuments and the two lists of kings that were currently available. These were the chronological presentations of former monarchs found in the temple of Rameses II at Abydos in 1819 by W.J. Bankes* (1786–1855), and as part of the Min Festival tableau in the Ramesseum of the same king (fig. 121).

This reconciliation was hampered by the above-mentioned corruption of the Manethonic list for the Eighteenth Dynasty. This meant that Champollion, Rosellini, and Wilkinson all produced different solutions for working out which names (and thus reign lengths) should be equated with which.[16] Thus, Champollion plumped for Thutmose III being Manetho's "Misaphris/Miphrês/Mêphrês." He further considered him (on the basis of Thutmose III's occasional use of the epithet *mry-r'*) to be equivalent to a King "Mœris" who appears in Herodotus. Accordingly, Champollion henceforth used the name "Mœris" interchangeably with "Thouthmosis III" when referring to the king. Today "Mœris" is understood to be Amenemhat III of the Twelfth Dynasty. Wilkinson preferred to make Thutmose III the Manethonic "Touthmosis," with "Misaphris/Miphrês/Mephres" being Thutmose I, and "Misphragmouthôsis" Thutmose II. Champollion did not recognize the Thutmose II nomen as belonging with the prenomen Aakheperenre, instead pairing the latter with the name "Ammon-mai" (Meryamun), on the basis of his understanding of a stela in Turin.[17]

Nevertheless, the overarching sequence of kings, grounded in the Abydos list, was agreed between the three scholars. Rather, the major issues concerned the Manethonic "Amensis," glossed by Josephus as the "sister" (of "Amenôphis") and original monuments belonging to a ruler whose nomen was read as "Aménenthé" by Champollion and "Amunneitgori" by Wilkinson (i.e., Hatshepsut; these readings focused on her epithet "Khnemetamun"). This person was clearly linked in some way with the first three Kings Thutmose, but was absent from the Abydos and Ramesseum sequences.

Not yet willing to consider that "Aménenthé" might be the Manethonic "Amensis," Champollion equated the latter with the King's Sister Sitamun, whom he had found depicted linked with Amenhotep I in a Rameside relief in TT2 (Khabekhnet) at Deir el-Medina.[18] While the idea that the "missing" king "Aménenthé/Amunneitgori" might be a woman and thus "Amensis" was something that neither Champollion nor Wilkinson were yet willing to contemplate, both were fully aware that something was not quite right. The French scholar professed himself

> somewhat surprised at seeing here, as elsewhere throughout the temple, the celebrated Mœris, adorned with all the insignia of royalty, giving place to this Amenenthé, for whose name we may search the royal lists in vain, still more astonished was I to find on reading the inscriptions that wherever they referred to this bearded king in the usual dress of the Pharaohs, nouns and verbs were in the feminine, as though a queen were in question. I found the same peculiarity everywhere. Not only was there the prenomen of Amenenthe preceded by the title of sovereign ruler of the world, with the feminine affix, but also his own name immediately following on the title of "daughter of the Sun." Finally, in all the bas-reliefs representing the gods speaking to this king, he is addressed as a queen.[19]

In search of a solution, he proposed:

> 1° That *Thouthmosis I*st [Aakheperkare Thutmose] directly succeeded the great Aménéthph Ist [Djeserkare Amenhotep], the chief of the XVIIIth Dynasty, that of the *Diospolitans*;
> 2° That his son, *Thouthmosis II*nd [Aakheperenre Thutmose], occupied the throne after his death and died without children;
> 3° That his sister, *Amensé* [Sitamun], succeeded him as daughter of Thouthmosis Ist, and reigned for twenty years in sovereignty;
> 4° That this Queen had for her *first* husband a *Thouthmosis* [Aakheper⸢neb⸣re Thutmose-sitamun] who included in his own name that of the queen *Amensė* [Sitamun], his wife; that this *Thouthmosis* was the father of *Thouthmosis III* or Mœris, and governed in the name of *Amensé*;
> 5° That at the death of this *Thouthmosis*, the queen *Amensé* married in second marriage *Aménenthé* [Maatkare Hatshepsut-khnemetamun], who also governed in the name of *Amensé*, and was *regent* during the minority and the first years of *Thouthmosis III* or Mœris;
> 6° That *Thouthmosis III* [Menkheperre Thutmose-neferkheper], the Mœris of the Greeks, exercised the joint power with *Aménenthé*, who kept him under his tutelage for some years.
>
> We thus understand why the regent Aménenthé only appears in the bas-reliefs to receive the gracious words which the gods address to Queen Amensé, of whom he is only the representative; this explains the style of the dedications made by Aménenthé, himself speaking in the name of the queen, as well as the dedications of the same kind in which we read the name of Thouthmosis, first husband of Amensé, who at first played the same passive role, and was, like his successor Aménenthé, only a kind of figurehead of the royal power exercised by the queen.[20]

Wilkinson confessed himself mystified as to why Champollion had decided that "Queen Amense" was Sitamun, given that there was no evidence of her having ever been married to a king.

> I do not know on what authority the name of Amense is here brought forward by M[onseiur] C[hampollion]. There was a sister of Amunnoph I. of this name, whom I supposed to have been the queen Amesses of Manetho; but it seems that the wife of Thothmes I., queen Ames, has quite as good, perhaps a better claim.[21]

Wilkinson also pointed out that her alleged "first husband" was none other than Thutmose II. Champollion's error over this had arisen because he had failed to recognize that the  found at the end of the prenomen of the "first husband" had exactly the same reading as the 𓈖 at the end of that of Thutmose II: the sound *n*. Wilkinson's conclusion was, however, disputed by Champollion's collaborator Rosellini (who read Hatshepsut's name as "Amenenthi-thuot"), who generally supported his French colleague's reconstruction, proclaiming that "To prove the marriage between Amense and this Thutmes III [as Rosellini dubbed the "first husband"], a clearer argument could be wished for in vain."[22]

The English scholar was quite correct on this point, but was still baffled by the apparent mismatch of images and texts.

> Though the figure is of a man, the style of the name and grammatical construction of the hieroglyphics prove them to allude to a queen, whose name this ought to be; for if the regent had sufficient authority to introduce his *own* name and figure, why would he have used a feminine pronoun? Amense's "first husband" the unknown Thothmes to all appearances, is a non-entity; and how does M. C. prove him to be the father of Thothmes III.? or the husband of Amense?
>
> The best way to solve the difficulty (if it is to be done arbitrarily) would be, to suppose the ovals to belong to the queen, and affirm that the regent's figure is *alone* introduced and his name entirely *omitted*.[23]

The idea of an image of one individual accompanied by the name of a completely different person was, of course, quite bizarre. By 1837 Wilkinson finally felt able to recognize that the names and figures all belonged to the same person.

> Between [Thutmose I and II] appears to have intervened a queen, whom I have ventured to call Amun-neit-gori, and who has hitherto given rise to more doubts and questions than any other sovereign of this Dynasty. But whether she was only regent during the minority of Thothmes II. and III., or succeeded to the throne in right of Thothmes I., in whose honour she erected several monuments, is still uncertain, and some have doubted her being a queen.[24]

Edward Hincks* (1792–1866) was not yet ready to accept Wilkinson's view,[25] preferring the Champollion-Rosellini construct of five Kings Thutmose, but felt "quite satisfied that Queen Amenset, the sister of Amenoph I., was a distinct person from the queen who erected the Karnak obelisks.—I cannot venture to write down her name." The problem of the correct transliteration of Hatshepsut's name would endure for a while.

FIGURE 122 Block statue of the Viceroy of Nubia, Inebny, bearing the names and titles of Hatshepsut (erased) and "her brother" Thutmose III; from Henry Salt collection (BM EA1131).

Hincks was, however, now able to publish firm proof of the joint rule between Hatshepsut and Thutmose III by citing the block statue of Inebny (page 39), in the British Museum, that originally bore both of their names (fig. 122). A negative issue deriving from the texts on this statue, however, was the fact it calls Thutmose III the "brother" of Hatshepsut, leading to a long-standing assumption regarding their blood relationship. This would endure, largely unchallenged,[26] until 1892 (see page 194). This new "working hypothesis" was set out by Hincks (who had also now abandoned the "extra" Thutmose) in a paper read in February 1844 before the Royal Irish Academy in Dublin.

> Queen Amuneth [Hatshepsut], the successor of Thothmos II. . . . governed Egypt for about twenty-nine years, during which her brother, Thothmos III., appears to have had no share in the sovereignty. He possessed, however, the title of king, and appears along with his sister on most of her monuments, as on the great obelisk at Karnac, and on the propylon at El-Assassif [Deir el-Bahari]. It seems that the king was not satisfied with this state of things; and that on his attaining to the sole sovereignty he defaced the name of his sister in a variety of places. He sometimes left a blank space, as on the statue of Onevto [Inebny] in the British Museum . . . .
>
> In other instances, as on the propylon at El Assassif, he substituted either his own name, or that of his father, for that of his sister, adding a beard to the face of the latter . . . . The feminine pronoun remained unaltered, and its use in reference to a bearded figure completely mystified M. Champollion, leading him to adopt a theory respecting these royal cartouches . . . involving a tissue of absurdities.[27]

As to how Hatshepsut's name should be transcribed, in 1842 Samuel Birch* (1813–85) was calling her "Amoun-noum-he." His proposed reconstruction for the period suggested that Sitamun had assumed the prenomen "Re-mei-ka [Maatkare] on the death of her brother Amenophis I.; that she was allied in the sovereignty with his brothers Thothmes I. and II., and held the regency during the early part of the reign of Thothmes III., when she changed her name from Amense to that of Amoun-noum-he."[28]

Soon afterward, however, Birch had accepted the evidence of the statue of Inebny, stating that Hatshepsut "was regent after the death of her father till the middle of the reign of Thothmes III., and the regnal years are probably dated from the death of Thothmes I."[29] He had also now adopted a new transliteration of the female king's name ("Num-t-amen-Ha-asu"), and was able to cite the rock stela from Wadi Maghara (fig. 123) to show that the association between Thutmose III and Hatshepsut had endured into at least a Year 16. An image of this stela had been published by Léon de Laborde (1807–69) in 1830.

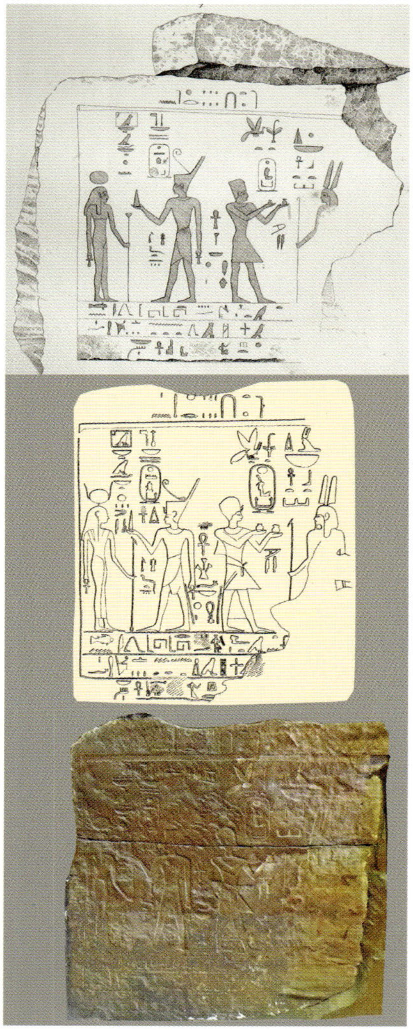

FIGURE 123 Year 16 Wadi Maghara inscription of Thutmose III and Hatshepsut, as drawn by Léon de Laborde in the 1820s, by Flinders Petrie's expedition during 1904–1905, and as in the Egyptian Museum, Cairo (CM JE45493).

A similar scheme had also been adopted in 1845 by Christian von Bunsen* (1791–1860), advised by Richard Lepsius* (1810–84), in his monumental work on Egyptian history.[30] This would essentially remain the standard view until the 1890s, as would the practice of referring to Hatshepsut as "Ha(t)asu," the other signs in her nomen being recognized as simply belonging to an epithet.

There were, however, some eccentric variations, in particular in the popular history first published by Samuel Sharpe* (1799–1881) in 1835, and reprinted with minimal changes into the 1870s.[31] Sharpe's conceptions thus influenced popular British views of the history of Egypt well after far sounder ideas had been presented elsewhere. He maintained that Egypt had remained split into northern and southern kingdoms down to the Eighteenth Dynasty, with the union of the two entities achieved by the marriage between Thutmose II and Hatshepsut, whom he calls "Amun-Nitocris" and sees as

> the last of the race of Memphite sovereigns, the twelfth or eleventh in succession from the builders of the great pyramids; and by her marriage with Thothmosis, Upper and Lower Egypt were brought under one sceptre.[32]

In calling Hatshepsut "Nitocris," and placing her only a dozen generations after the Fourth Dynasty Khufu and Khaefre, Sharpe equates her with the thus-named queen whom Manetho places at the end of the Sixth Dynasty (which for him ruled from Memphis in parallel with the Twelfth and early Eighteenth Dynasties at Thebes). As a result, Sharp goes further:

> Queen Nitocris, according to the historian Manetho, was the builder of the smallest of the three large pyramids near Memphis. The name of King Mecora, or Mencora, or Mencophra has been found on the wooden mummy case in its underground chamber. The same name has also been found in the fourth pyramid,[33] which was

> built beside it within the same enclosure and at the same time. The largest of these two was no doubt meant for the king, and the smaller for somebody of less importance, probably Queen Nitocris herself. The name of King Mecora, which was used only at Memphis, and never at Thebes, was probably meant for her second colleague on the throne, Thothmosis III., whose first name, as written in Thebes, was Mehora, Menhora, or Menhophra. The guttural sound, written H or Th in Thebes, was written K or Ch in Memphis. Or it might even mean herself, as her full name was Mykera Amun-Neithchori; and in her sculptures she is usually, though not always, dressed in man's clothes, to represent that she was a queen in her own right and not a queen consort . . . . At any rate, the agreement between the name in the pyramids and this queen's name, proves that Nitocris, who reigned at Thebes and was the last Memphite sovereign, was of the same family with the builder of the third and fourth pyramids. But she was probably the builder of them both, the smaller one for herself, and the larger one for the young King Thothmosis III.[34]

Aside from matters of the royal succession, contemporary calculations of the absolute dates of Old Testament events were combined with Josephus's extract from Manetho to place the Exodus during the first half of the Eighteenth Dynasty. As a result, Wilkinson proposed to place this event in the year 1491 BC, during the reign of Thutmose III.[35] While many later writers preferred to place the Exodus under Rameses II or Merenptah, the idea of Thutmose III as Pharaoh of the Exodus (or Oppression) was revived later in the nineteenth century, and still has adherents.[36]

Toward a Standard Reconstruction

In 1847, Birch published the first detailed discussion of the blocks upon which were carved the Year 29 to 41 Annals of Thutmose III, these having been removed by Henry Salt from Karnak and acquired by the Louvre in 1826.[37] In his work, Birch set the texts in the context of other military and tributary narratives and depictions available to him, and the resulting military and political geography of not only Syria-Palestine, but also Nubia.

Shortly before, the Prussian expedition to Egypt under Richard Lepsius had spent November 1844 to March 1845 at Luxor, planning and copying the principal monuments.[38] In addition, Lepsius identified a structure, noted by Wilkinson as "vestiges of a sandst[one] ruin surrounded by a cr[ude] brick, with towers in front," as a "peculiar temple . . . erected on the border of the desert by TUTHMOSIS III., [which] can now only be recognized by its ground plan, and by the remains of a brick pylon"[39]—his memorial temple. In noting the close alignment between the axis of the Deir el-Bahari temple and that of Karnak, Lepsius remarked that

FIGURE 124 The central area of Karnak, as seen between the 1860s and 1880s. The northern obelisk of Hatshepsut is on the right, and the upper part of its southern companion lies on the left (cf. fig. 46).

> [i]t was a Queen, NUMT AMEN, the elder sister of Tuthmosis III., who accomplished this bold plan of a structural connection between the two sides of the valley, the same who had erected the two greatest obelisks in front of the temple of Amun. She never appears on her monuments as a woman, but in male attire; we only find out her sex by the inscriptions. No doubt at that period it was illegal for woman to govern; for that reason, also, her brother, probably still a minor, appears at a later period as a ruler along with her. After her death her Shields [cartouches] were everywhere converted into Tuthmosis Shields, the feminine forms of speech in the inscription were changed, and her names were never adopted in the later lists along with the legitimate kings.[40]

The Prussian team brought much material back to Berlin, including the funerary stela of Senenmut from TT71 (fig. 39 top left inset), and various fragments of statuary found

FIGURE 125 Top: view from Karnak to Deir el-Bahari. Bottom: 1854 view from the granite gate of the Upper Terrace at Deir el-Bahari, looking east toward Karnak; the lower third is buried in debris. As with the front jambs (fig. 99), the Horus names of Hatshepsut have been left intact, while all the cartouches have been recut for Thutmose III. The pylon of TT34 (Montjuemhat) is visible to the right.

FIGURE 126 Richard Lepsius recovered a number of fragments of statues of Hatshepsut from the former quarry along the north side of the Deir el-Bahari causeway (seen in fig. 40 top), and brought them to Berlin. They included: (a) a head of a sphinx; (b) a head wearing a white crown (Berlin ÄM2279, both in granite); (d) the lower part of an indurated limestone seated statue (Berlin ÄM2306). The latter had been exposed for some time, being sketched in situ by Nestor l'Hôte* (1804–42) in 1838. Further parts of these statues were found in the same location by the Metropolitan Museum of Art expedition during the 1920s. As a result, the white-crowned head and the limestone statue were sent to New York to be reunited with their respective lower and upper parts (c and fig. 29c), while Berlin received in exchange the body of the sphinx, allowing the whole sculpture to be restored (e). It was also given one of a series of small kneeling statues discovered by the New York team (fig. 131).

lying on the surface at Deir el-Bahari (fig. 126). Among these were pieces that would later prove to match fragments found some seven decades later (see page 197).

The first extensive excavations at the Deir el-Bahari temple were begun in 1858 by Auguste Mariette* (1821–81), the first head of the Egyptian Antiquities Service; he continued the work in 1862 and 1866. However, much of the temple was left still encumbered, and nothing was done as far as the approach was concerned. It was from the north side of this that Prince Henrik of the Netherlands (1829–79, a son of King Willem II) obtained the torso of what turned out to be a statue of King Hatshepsut wearing female attire (fig. 29b), while representing his country at the opening of the Suez Canal in 1869. This was subsequently placed in Soestdijk Palace, near Utrecht, equipped with a plaster head, with a cast of the torso donated to the Museo Egizio in Turin.

Mariette's publication of his work came out in 1877. A decade earlier, however, Johannes Dümichen* (1833–94) had published the first study of the Punt reliefs,[41] and this may have encouraged the theft of a number of blocks from the temple during the following years (cf. fig. 33), which had certainly gone by the time that Mariette's book came out.[42] In a volume published at the end of his life in 1881, Mariette included a vase of unknown provenance that gave Hatshepsut's titles as the wife of a king, contributing to knowledge of her pre-kingly career.

The Mummy of Thutmose III Revealed

Almost simultaneously, tomb TT320, with the mummy of Thutmose III, was revealed to the world. The actual discovery of TT320 had been made by three brothers of a local family, Muhammed (d. 1926), Ahmed (d. 1918/19), and Husein Abd el-Rassul*, either by accident or as part of a systematic search for tombs to rob (stories vary).[43] Key members of the Abd el-Rassul family were reported as saying that the discovery had been made in the summer of 1871.

The Abd el-Rassuls had been selling off material from the tomb—principally deriving from the burials of the Twenty-first Dynasty—for a number of years before suspicion fell upon them; Muhammad finally confessed on 25 June 1881 in exchange for an amnesty. On 5 July, Émile Brugsch* (1842–1930), keeper of Cairo's Bulaq Museum, and at that time the most senior Antiquities Service official actually in the country (it was holiday season), arrived in Luxor with Ahmed Kamal* (1851–1923), the Museum's secretary–interpreter, and an inspector from Giza, Thadeos Matafian. Concerned for the security both of the tomb's contents and of himself and his colleagues, Brugsch began clearing of the tomb on the morning of the seventh and finished the following day. The coffins and their contents arrived at Bulaq by boat from Luxor on the twenty-first.

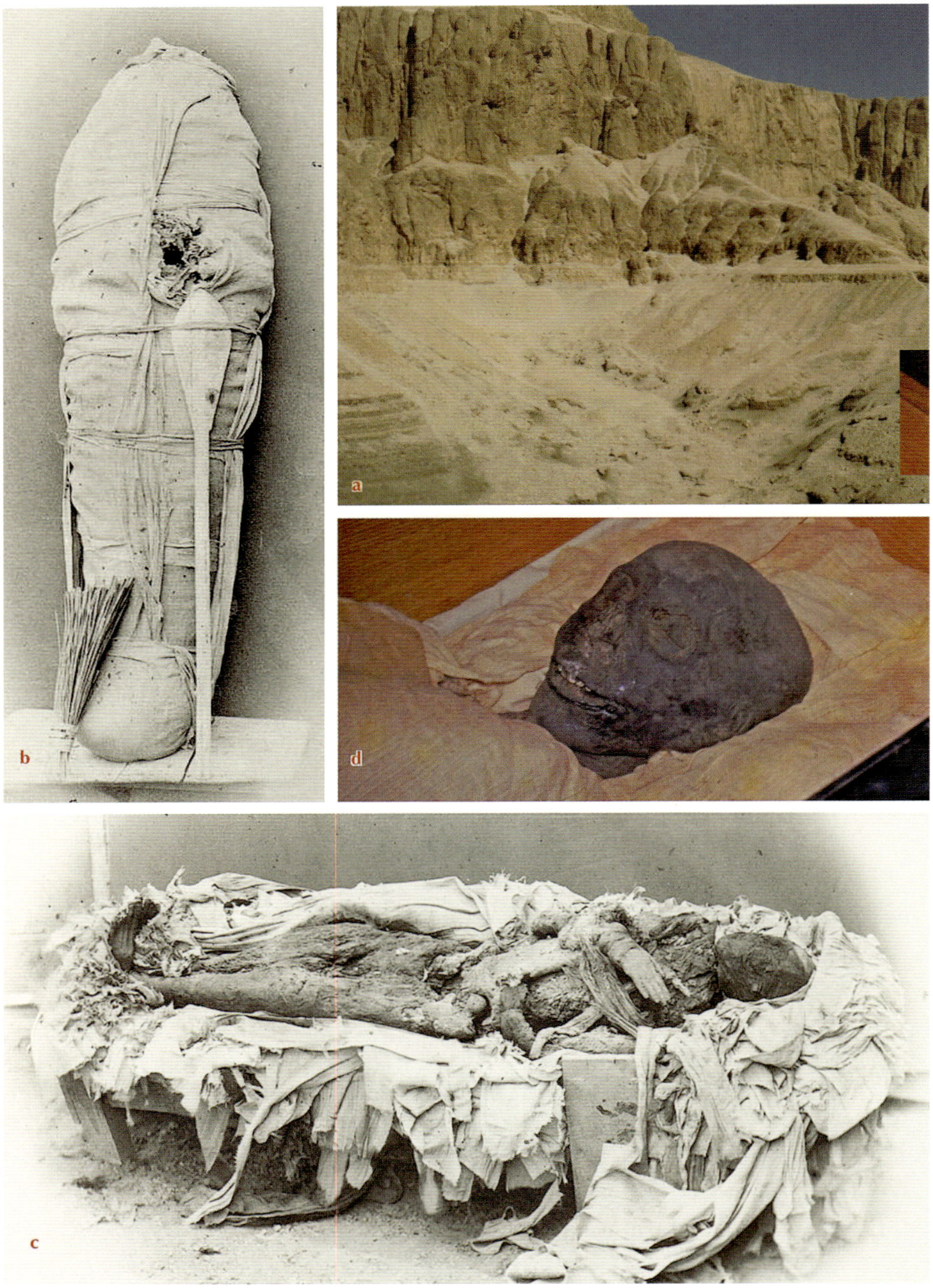

FIGURE 127 a. The location of TT320, where the mummy of Thutmose III was found. b. The wrapped mummy, showing an oar used by the restorers to stabilize the remains; the oar probably came from the original furnishings of Thutmose III's tomb. c. As revealed in 1881, the mummy proved to have been badly damaged. d. The well-preserved head of the king (NMEC CG61068), as seen in in the Egyptian Museum in 1962.

The mummy of Thutmose III was unwrapped by Brugsch immediately after its arrival in Cairo (fig. 127c), in the presence of Eugène Lefébure* (1838–1908), Urbain Bouriant* (1849–1903), and Victor Loret* (1859–1946) of the French Archaeological Mission in Cairo, but in the absence of the Director of the Service, Gaston Maspero* (1846–1916).[44] It was recorded that

> [t]he mummy had been probed by the Arabs. It carried attached to its exterior two small oars and a bunch of rushes. It was in such bad condition that it had to be opened: the mummy found inside was broken in three places, and measured 1.60 m in length. The shroud which enveloped it carried long hieroglyphic texts drawn in ink, Chapter XVII of the *Book of the Dead* and fragments of the *Litanies of the Sun*, on behalf of King Thutmos III, son of Queen Isi, whose name appears here for the first time.[45]

A further piece of data regarding the royal family had thus now become available.[46]

Until 1891, it was assumed that Thutmose I had been a son of Amenhotep I by a Queen Ahhotep II (who was much later shown *not* to have been a wife of his, and possibly not even to have existed).[47] Now, the publication, by Adolf Erman* (1854–1937), of the first known copy of Thutmose I's coronation decree (page 12) showed his mother to have been Seniseneb.[48] In the wake of this publication, and that of Ineni's autobiographical text (pages 14–15, 19) the next year,[49] Maspero revisited the whole question of the genealogy of the Thutmosids,[50] concluding that Thutmose III was indeed a son of Thutmose II, and Hatshepsut his aunt and stepmother.

The month of February 1893 saw the beginning of the first comprehensive campaign of clearance and restoration of the Deir el-Bahari temple by Edouard Naville* (1844–1926), working for the Egypt Exploration Fund, and would continue until 1899 (fig. 128). The whole temple was cleared and many displaced blocks returned to their original positions, with roofs added to some of the colonnades to protect the reliefs. The vast majority of wall surfaces were copied by a team led by Howard Carter* (1874–1939), which included one of his brothers, and Marguerite Naville, the dig director's wife, most using an innovative freehand facsimile method.[51] These were published in six royal folio volumes (examples of this work are to be found in our figs. 6, 22, 23, 33, 34, 100, 103).[52] Naville's publication introduced the spelling of "Hatshepsu" for the temple's creator, which has (with the addition of the feminine "*t*" at the end) subsequently become the standard way of referring to her.[53]

Naville returned to Deir el-Bahari in 1903 to excavate the Montjuhotep II temple. While he missed the main body of the Thutmose III temple (as did everyone else until

FIGURE 128 Top: the ruins of Deir el-Bahari in the early 1890s. Extensive remains of the Coptic monastery of Saint Phoibammon, built into the Upper Court and the northwestern part of the Second Court, and including a brick tower, are still visible (see also fig. 125 bottom). Inset: the chapel of Hatshepsut in 1869. Bottom: these remains were removed without record during 1893–99, when the temple was cleared and extensive restoration of the original structure carried out. Much of the work was done under the direction of Howard Carter, who is to be seen in the bottom right image.

FIGURE 129 The Hathor shrine of the Thutmose III temple, shortly after its discovery in 1905 (see also fig. 56), and as now displayed in Cairo (JE38574-5). The cow itself dates to the reign of Amenhotep II.

1962—see pages 198–99), he did reveal its all-but-perfect Hathor sanctuary during 1905–1906 (figs. 56 top, 129). Carter had now moved on, first to the Antiquities Service, and then to work for the Fifth Earl of Carnarvon* (1866–1923). During 1909–10, they uncovered remains of the valley temple of Hatshepsut's Deir el-Bahari monument.

The Tombs of Thutmose III and Hatshepsut Revealed

Thutmose III

Although Thutmose III's mummy had been known since 1881, the king's original burial place remained unknown until 1898. Then, Victor Loret, now Director of Antiquities, began excavations in the Valley of the Kings to try to locate some of the many "missing" royal tombs that he believed were still to be found there.[54] On 4 February 1898, he ordered the local inspector, Hassan Hosni, to begin digging test pits in the southern sector of the Valley. As Loret recounts,

> [on] 8 February, as nothing had yet been found . . . I left Thebes for Aswan, while the work continued without me . . . . On the 12th, I received in Aswan, from the inspector of Qurna, a telegram announcing a discovery. A letter from the same, which came shortly afterwards, informed me, thanks to some copied fragments of inscription, that the tomb found was that of Thoutmès III.
>
> I had, upon receipt of the telegram, telegraphed to the inspector of Qurna to close the tomb immediately and wait for my return to continue the work.

Accordingly, on the 21st, when I returned to Thebes, I had the clearing resumed and I was able to go and see the importance of the discovery.

It took several hours to open, under the lintel of the door, a passage through which a man could slide. The tomb of Thoutmès III is placed, at a distance of about 250 meters beyond that of Ramses III, in a sort of fracture in the mountain where the rocky walls, rising steeply, lead between them to a corridor barely one meter wide at its opening. The entrance to this corridor is located about eight or ten meters above the floor of the valley, and it is reached by climbing painfully up a very steep embankment formed by scree that rolls under the feet and forces the sufferer to take ten steps to climb one meter. Arrived at the top of the scree, we must be hoisted by the Arabs to climb a sheer wall about two meters high. We are then in the place, or at least in a narrow gorge leading to the place.

A black hole, very low, opens at the bottom of the cleft: it is the entrance to the tomb, it is the door, with its upper part cleared [fig. 130]. Intense heat and a strange smell come out of this hole as if a mysterious furnace. We enter it. Suddenly the floor, formed of hard and angular flakes of limestone, descends, forming a slope of forty-five degrees. We let ourselves slide on our backs, on our stomachs, as best we can. It is hard to hold on, either on the floor, on the moving blocks that slide with you, or on the roughness of the sloping ceiling, where the nails find it difficult to find a place to cling. After about twenty meters, a void.

A well, four times wider than the corridor, blocks the way. You have to cross this well, five or six meters deep and four or five meters wide. A ladder, barely long enough, is placed into it and, in the shadows, one reaches the bottom of the well, formed of fallen debris. To continue the journey, on the other side of the well, opposite from the opening through which one entered, there is another opening located at the same height . . . and one climbs with the help of a rope attached to a wall placed across the door and left by thieves in the past.

We are then in a vast room supported by two massive square pillars. You can stand there, light candles, and recognize a room cluttered with debris, among which a wooden statuette, still standing on its base, immediately catches the eye. The four walls are covered with paintings, in sober and severe tones, admirably preserved. In a corner of the floor of the room, a vast dark opening indicates that the tomb does not end there. You have to go down again, into this gaping hole, by a stairway as steep as that at the entrance, a stairway with worn steps cluttered with limestone chips. Finally, you can relax and find that you are at the entrance to a vast room, measuring about fifteen meters by nine, and supported by two quadrangular columns. The walls, decorated with line figures and cursive hieroglyphs, all in black and red on a gray background, seem to have been lined with a papyrus of monstrous dimensions. The corners of the hall are rounded, giving it the shape of a gigantic royal cartouche.

Debris clutter the ground: shards of limestone, broken vases, bones. Near a column, is a swan made of bitumined wood, headless and legless. To the right of the entrance, two statues still stand, similar to those in the first room. Finally, at the back, behind the second column, the open, empty sarcophagus rests on a calcite plinth, while beside it its lid lies on the ground [fig. 114]. I feel no disappointment in seeing the empty sarcophagus, the mummy of Thoutmès III having been found fifteen years ago in the royal hiding place of Deir-el-Bahri and being exhibited at the Museum since that date. Everywhere, on the walls, on the columns, the name and first name of Thoutmès III . . . .

FIGURE 130 The entrance to KV34, as discovered.

When I left Thebes [at the end of February], the tomb, almost entirely cleared away, presented a very different aspect from that which had so struck me on the first day. Instead of the slippery mound, a temporary staircase formed of solidly superimposed blocks. Instead of the two meters of steep rock that we had to climb hoisted by Arabs, a prosaic but practical wooden ladder. Instead of the perilous and involuntary descent, stairs and sloping corridors. Over the well, a bridge formed by two boards. Briefly, the tomb is now relatively easy to access and will require little work to make it available to tourists.[55]

The other segment of Thutmose III's funerary complex, his memorial temple, was cleared by Arthur Weigall* (1880–1934) a few years later.

In the early part of 1905, H.H. Djemil Pasha Toussoun[56] very generously offered to place at the disposal of the Service des Antiquités the sum of £400 which was to be spent in archaeological work at Thebes. Mr. Quibell . . . selected a site to the north of the Ramesseum which appeared to be that of an XVIIIth dynasty temple. Work was commenced there on April 15th, and a few days later, on his departure to Saḳḳâra, the direction of the work was handed over to me. About 150 men and boys were employed upon it, and the main part of the temple area

> was cleared in five weeks, the excavation being brought to a close on May 20th, at a total cost of L.E. 208.037 m.
>
> The site had been known to Egyptologists for some time. The ruined brick pylons standing at the edge of the cultivated land, and behind them an obvious courtyard enclosed by a brick wall, plainly indicated the existence of a temple; and a few trial pits sunk several years ago, which had exposed a block or two of limestone with the cartouches of Thoutmosis III inscribed upon them, showed the date of the place. Lepsius had already unearthed a few bricks from the site imprinted with the name of the temple, which reads  "Ra'-men-kheper endowed with life." Bricks with a similar inscription had been found at Medinet Habu, and others are said to have been found immediately to the south of the Ramesseum. This has led to a confusion of ideas as to the real site of the temple, but the present excavation has finally settled the question. The name 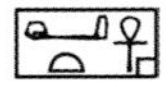 was found on many of the fragments of stelae, statuettes, etc., as well as upon the bricks unearthed in the work; and thus the presence of similarly inscribed bricks at Medinet Habu and elsewhere must be due to the fact that a surplus stock from the real temple was used for other buildings of Thoutmosis III.[57]

A program of re-excavation of the temple was begun by a Spanish team in 2008.[58]

The tombs of Hatshepsut

Although the tomb of Thutmose III had now been identified, that of Hatshepsut was seemingly still missing. In fact, KV20 had stood open since antiquity,[59] and had been mapped by both the French expedition (who penetrated twenty-six meters into the debris-choked tomb) and Belzoni. James Burton* (1788–1862) had penetrated as far as chamber C (see fig. 91), as had Lepsius, before dismissing the sepulcher as "a corridor uninscribed and undecorated."

It was finally identified and cleared by Howard Carter, funded by Theodore Davis* (1838–1915), beginning in early February 1903, and finished at the end of March 1904.

> The identification of the tomb arose largely from its contiguity to the tomb of Thoutmôsis IV, the finding in the rubbish at the entrance of his tomb of a blue scarab bearing the Queen's name, and the discovery in this foundation deposit of an usurped calcite saucer also bearing her name. With these evidences in mind, we thought it possible that the Queen's tomb might be in the neighbourhood of our work; therefore we concluded to make a thorough investigation of all the ground in the immediate vicinity, and to this end we had our workmen clear the ground of

all dirt and stones down to the hard rock, and continue the clearing to the mouth of the Napoleon tomb [KV20], and also sound the rock from time to time in order that no tomb which might have been vertically sunk should remain undiscovered. Shortly after this work was started our men came upon a spot directly before the door of the Napoleon tomb which yielded a hollow sound, and which, upon excavation, proved to be a small pit cut in the solid rock, which contained models of objects used in making the tomb, such as bronze tools, calcite vases, reed mats, magic symbols, bread, fringed mummycloth, napkins, etc., many of them bearing the cartouche of Hâtshopsîtu. Then we knew that the doorway, which had been standing open for thousands of years, and the corridor beyond, partly explored by a famous French general and a great archaeologist, and abandoned by both, was in fact the outer door of the corridor leading to the long sought for tomb of Queen Hâtshopsîtu. Subsequently I undertook the exploration of this corridor for the benefit of the Cairo Museum, under the direction of Mr. Howard Carter, the Inspector-General of the Service des Antiquités, who most kindly undertook the management of the work, for which I am under great obligations. The long, patient, tiresome, and dangerous work executed by Mr. Carter, the difficulties which he overcame, and the physical discomforts which he suffered, are not fairly described in his modest official report, as will be seen from the following details.

The corridor proved to be 213·25 metres long and 97·70 metres vertically deep, and the entire length was filled to the roof with small stones, which had either been put in by the builders, or had been carried in by the rains of centuries. In places these broken stones had by the action of the water become cemented together, and required the use of pickaxes to make a passage. In addition to this, the ceilings of the corridors and of the chambers, which were 8 metres long, 7 metres wide and 2 metres high, had in many cases fallen in; all of which had to be broken up to a size admitting of its transport on the heads of boys to the mouth of the tomb. At a point of the work Mr. Carter reached one of these chambers, and found it entirely filled with small stones and large blocks fallen from the ceiling. We decided that it could not be the burial chamber, and we also were satisfied that there must be somewhere in the chamber, a corridor leading below, and the question was, where to find it without clearing the entire chamber—the work of weeks, and our time limited. There being no certain solution of this situation, we agreed to toss a penny, with the understanding that if "heads" came up, we were to make for the right-hand corner. Fortunately it came "heads," and when we had tunneled through the debris to the designated corner, we found the mouth of the descending corridor.

Long before we reached this chamber the air had become so bad, and the heat so great, that the candles carried by the workmen melted, and would not give enough light to enable them to continue their work; consequently we were compelled to install electric lights, in the shape of hand wires, which could be extended to any length, with lamps attached as needed. For a time this enabled the work to progress, but as soon as we got down about 50 metres, the air became so foul that the men could not work. In addition to this, the bats of centuries had built innumerable nests on the ceilings of the corridors and chambers, and their excrement had become so dry that the least stir of the air filled the corridors with a fluffy black stuff, which choked the noses and mouths of the men, rendering it most difficult for them to breathe. To overcome these difficulties, we installed an air suction pump at the mouth of the tomb, to which was attached a zinc pipe, which before the burial chamber was reached extended about 213 metres. Not only had these obstacles to be overcome, but the serious danger of caving ceilings throughout the entire length of the corridors and chambers was a daily anxiety, and in some places required either bracing or taking down. Happily the work was so well watched and conducted that no accidents occurred, though many of the men and boys were temporarily overcome by the heat and bad air. Braving all these dangers and discomforts, Mr. Carter made two or three descents every week, and professed to enjoy it.

We all looked forward to the finding of the burial chamber, which we intended to enter formally, and where we expected to see the fruits of our labour: but our hopes were frustrated when we found this chamber also filled with small stones and fallen ceilings, through which we "entered" at the rate of 2 metres a day, and which required a month's work to clear entirely.

Subsequently all of the chambers and corridors were cleaned to the solid rock, and thoroughly tested by sounding and tapping, but without any result. To appreciate the difficulties of our work, it must be remembered that all the debris found in the tomb was carried on the heads of men and boys from the lowest chamber to the mouth of the tomb, a distance of 10 to 213 metres, including an ascent of 1 to 97 metres.[60]

Carter was also responsible for the identification and recording of Hatshepsut's tomb as regent, in October 1916. His own description of events runs as follows.

While on a short holiday at Luxor, I found myself involved quite unexpectedly in another piece of work. The absence of officials owing to the war, to say nothing of the general demoralization caused by the war itself, had naturally created a great revival of activity on the part of the local native tomb-robbers, and prospecting parties were out in all directions. News came into the village one afternoon that a find had been made in a lonely and unfrequented region on the western side of the mountain above The Valley of the Kings. Immediately a rival party of diggers armed themselves and made their way to the spot, and in the lively engagement that ensued the original party were beaten and driven off, vowing vengeance.

To avert further trouble the notables of the village came to me and asked me to take action. It was already late in the afternoon, so I hastily collected the few of my workmen who had escaped the Army Labour Levies, and with the necessary materials set out for the scene of action, an expedition involving a climb of more than 1,800 feet over the Qurna hills by moonlight. It was midnight when we arrived on the scene, and the guide pointed out to me the end of a rope which dangled sheer down the face of a cliff. Listening. we could hear the robbers actually at work, so I first severed their rope, thereby cutting off their means of escape, and then, making secure a good stout rope of my own, I lowered myself down the cliff. Shinning down a rope at midnight, into a nestful of industrious tomb-robbers, is a pastime that at least does not lack excitement. There were eight at work, and when I reached the bottom there was an awkward moment or two. I gave them the alternative of clearing out by means of my rope, or else of staying where they were without a rope at all, and eventually they saw reason and departed. The rest of the night I spent on the spot and, as soon as it was light enough, climbed down into the tomb again to make a thorough investigation.

The tomb was in a most remarkable situation ([fig. 88]). Its entrance was contrived in the bottom of a natural water-worn cleft, 130 feet from the top of the cliff, and 200 feet above the valley bed, and so cunningly concealed that neither from the top or the bottom could the slightest trace of it be seen. From the entrance a lateral passage ran straight into the face of the cliff, a distance of some 51 feet, after which it turned at right angles, and a short passage, cut on a sharp slope, led down into a chamber about 18 feet square. The whole place was full of rubbish from top to bottom, and through this rubbish the robbers had burrowed a tunnel over 90 feet long, just big enough for a man to crawl through.

It was an interesting discovery, and might turn out to be very important, so I determined to make a complete clearance. Twenty days it took, working night and day with relays of workmen, and an extraordinarily difficult job it proved. The method of gaining access to the tomb by means of a rope from the top was unsatisfactory, for it was not a very safe proceeding at best, and necessitated,

> moreover, a stiff climb from the valley. Obviously means of access from the valley-bottom would be preferable, and this we contrived by erecting sheers at the entrance to the tomb, so that by a running tackle we could pull ourselves up or let ourselves down. It was not a very comfortable operation even then, and I personally always made the descent in a net.
>
> Excitement among the workmen ruled high as the work progressed, for surely a place so well concealed must contain a wonderful treasure, and great was their disappointment when it proved that the tomb had neither been finished nor occupied. The only thing of value it contained was a large sarcophagus of crystalline sandstone, like the tomb, unfinished, with inscriptions which showed it to have been intended for Queen Hat·shep·sût. Presumably this masterful lady had had the tomb constructed for herself as wife of King Thothmes II. Later, when she seized the throne and ruled actually as a King, it was clearly necessary for her to have her tomb in The Valley like all the other kings—as a matter of fact I found it there myself in 1903—and the present tomb was abandoned. She would have been better advised to hold to her original plan. In this secret spot her mummy would have had a reasonable chance of avoiding disturbance: in The Valley it had none. A king she would be, and a king's fate she shared.[61]

The sarcophagus was removed from the tomb by Émile Baraize in 1921, who also discovered that the tomb was not unfinished after all, and that Carter had simply failed to clear the innermost chamber.[62] Carter's adventure at the tomb of Hatshepsut had been a consequence of the discovery of the nearby tomb of Menwi, Merti, and Menhet (page 150) by men from Qurna around the beginning of August 1916.[63] Almost everything in the tomb was removed by them, although a few items were recovered in an emergency Antiquities Service excavation led first by Ahmed Kamal, and then by Muhammed Shaban* (1866–1930). Most of the items removed by the plunderers were sold to Luxor antiquities dealers, and later purchased by the Metropolitan Museum of Art, many through Carter, but also via other routes. A few items were later deaccessioned and passed to other collections. The tomb was re-excavated and fully documented by the Metropolitan Museum of Art during November–December 1988.

The "Feud of the Thutmosids"

The 1892 publication of Ineni's autobiographical text, with its apparently clear statement of the royal succession following Thutmose I's death (Thutmose II, followed by his son Thutmose III, with Hatshepsut as regent), had seemingly settled the issue. However, four years later, Kurt Sethe* (1869–1934) issued a study in which he proposed a complicated set of coups and counter-coups that yielded the following succession after an initial "fall" of Thutmose I.[64]

1. Thutmose III reigns for a time alone.
2. Hatshepsut's party forces her upon Thutmose III as coregent.
3. About year 6 of Thutmose III, Thutmose I and II together gain the throne, for a brief coregency, but are not able to suppress Thutmose III, who, on the disappearance (probably death) of Thutmose I, regains the throne, and rules as coregent with Thutmose II, till the latter's death, which followed shortly, about year 8 of Thutmose III's reign (numbered from his first accession).
4. Thutmose III, with Hatshepsut now associated with him permanently, holds the throne, and they rule together at least twelve years more, till the death of the queen, when Thutmose III finally holds undivided possession. He numbered his years from his first accession, ruling at least thirty-four years more, until the year 54.

This was based on Sethe's assessment of the erasures of Hatshepsut's cartouches on her monuments, and their replacement by the names of, variously, Thutmose I, Thutmose II, or Thutmose III. Crucial to his view was the notion that such secondary cartouches could *only* have been inscribed by the king named.

Given Sethe's standing in Egyptology (he eventually became Professor at Berlin University), his reconstruction was embraced in whole or part by a number of colleagues. In particular, it looms large in the relevant chapter of the influential *History of Egypt* by James H. Breasted* (1865–1935).[65] Others, however, were less persuaded, implicitly or explicitly cherry-picking only discrete elements,[66] expressing skepticism,[67] or vigorously rejecting the idea altogether. Édouard Naville, the excavator of Hatshepsut's temple at Deir el-Bahari, was the leading exponent of the latter approach to Sethe's ideas.[68]

However, it was not until 1928 that Eduard Meyer* (1855–1930)[69] and Herbert Winlock* (1884–1950)—like Naville, a director of fieldwork at Deir el-Bahari (see next page)—independently published works refuting Sethe's theories. In introducing his own preferred narrative, Winlock remarked:

> For several years now, our excavations have been yielding facts on Hatshepsut's Temple at Deir el Bahri . . . . Unfortunately, as told in most of the recent histories, the tale of Hatshepsut is given a plot of over-ingenious complexity into which such impressions of Deir el Bahri as we are gaining would have to be strained to fit.[70]

Sethe hit back with a new book in 1932,[71] which significantly simplified his original scheme, but still insisted on Thutmose I and II returning to power after both had been successively deposed by Hatshepsut, with Thutmose III as her puppet. Thutmose II was then held to have ruled alone after the death of Thutmose I, before the throne passed again to Hatshepsut and Thutmose III together, and finally to the latter alone. However, the following year, William Edgerton* (1893–1970) published a systematic analysis of all the relevant material,[72] which demonstrated definitively the impossibility of Sethe's proposals in their entirety. Since then, the basic structure of the period has been stable as far as Egyptologists are concerned.

Thutmose III and Rosicrucianism

Various esoteric movements grew up in Europe during the seventeenth century AD. A number claimed (or came to claim) links back to ancient Egypt, one example being Freemasonry. This was also true of some strains of Rosicrucianism, especially the "Ancient and Mystical Order Rosæ Crucis" (AMORC), founded in the USA in 1915 by H. Spencer Lewis (1883–1939). The latter formulated an elaborate history of the philosophy, stretching it back to Eighteenth Dynasty Egypt.[73] In this origin story, Ahmose I is claimed to have been the "first Pharaoh who conducted in his private chambers" classes in "the more profound secrets of nature, science and art." It was Thutmose III, however, who is presented as the one "who organized the present form of the Rosaecrucian Order and outlined many of its rules and regulations." This was allegedly done at a meeting held "the week of March 28th to April 4th of 1489 B.C.," attended by "Twelve Brothers and Sisters," and "[a]t the close of his reign in 1447 there were thirty-nine Brothers and Sisters in the Order and the meetings, which had become regular and systematic, were held in one of the Halls of the Temple of Karnak, outside of which Thutmose III had erected two obelisks bearing a record of his achievements." In light of this, a scarab of Thutmose III became the pre-eminent symbol of AMORC, providing the king with a distinctly unusual additional strand of modern afterlife.

Re-excavating Deir el-Bahari

As already noted, Winlock's doubts as to the veracity of Sethe's theories, and important parts of Edgerton's evidence, came from new archaeological work at Deir el-Bahari. This project ran from 1911 to 1936, and embraced not only the temples of Hatshepsut and Montjuhotep II, but most of the Asasif in front of them as well, and discrete areas to the south. The latter included venturing up on to the Sheikh Abd el-Qurna hill to investigate and record the tomb-chapel of Senenmut (TT71). The two temples were re-examined, with ancient fill removed in places to go down to bedrock (e.g., to discover the remains

FIGURE 131 Small kneeling figure of Hatshepsut; from Deir el-Bahari (Berlin ÄM22283).

of the temple of Amenhotep I, under the Second Terrace of Hatshepsut). Some of this work was done in conjunction with an ongoing program of reconstruction and restoration of the Hatshepsut temple by the Antiquities Service, under the direction of Émile Baraize from 1925 onward.

Also cleared was the former quarry, from which Lepsius and others had removed odd fragments of sculpture (pages 180–83), with huge quantities of buried fragments now extracted. Many of the original pieces could be reconstructed, with some fragments matching material taken to Europe during the nineteenth century. A fruitful exchange program with the Ägyptisches Museum in Berlin resulted in a number of statues and sphinxes being reassembled (figs. 29c, 126, 131, 132). However, in the case of the fragment taken by Prince Henrik to the Netherlands, although this was transferred from the royal palace to the Rijksmuseum van Oudheden in Leiden, for many years it was only possible to swap casts to make two complete statues (fig. 29b).[74]

FIGURE 132 The principal Hatshepsut gallery (115) in the Metropolitan Museum of Art, New York, in 2015.

FIGURE 133 The sarcophagi of Hatshepsut and Thutmose III, as displayed in the Egyptian Museum in 2016 (JE47032, JE37678, JE52344).

One member of the Metropolitan team, William C. Hayes* (1903–63), made a significant contribution to the study of royal funerary monuments of the Thutmosid era by the publication of his doctoral dissertation on royal sarcophagi.[75] This work established the sequence of their manufacture, and made it clear that the quartzite sarcophagus of Thutmose I could only have been commissioned during the later reign of Thutmose III.

The next major work at Deir el-Bahari began in early 1962, when a Polish–Egyptian team began activities that are still underway at the time of writing. At the outset, the key original objective of the project was to continue the study and reconstruction of the temple of Hatshepsut, but before it was begun, the director, Kazimierz Michałowski* (1901–81),

> ordered the clearance of a huge heap of rocky debris outside the southwestern part of the third terrace of the great temple. Previous excavators had left the place unexplored and it had served them as a convenient spot for depositing garbage. Michałowski wanted to expose the southwestern part of the temple and

> in the process to check for architectural fragments for the reconstruction of the great temple. Unexpectedly, just two weeks after starting the clearance, early in 1962, partly preserved columns still standing on their bases were discovered and scattered among them were parts of broken statues and fragmentary polychrome reliefs. A hitherto unknown temple had been discovered.[76]

This proved to be the Deir el-Bahari temple of Thutmose III, and work here continued until 1967, followed by long years of study of the material recovered.[77] At the temple of Hatshepsut, restoration and study were largely concentrated on the Upper Terrace, allowing increasing amounts of it to be opened to the public over the years.

Hatshepsut, Queen of Sheba, and Other Stories

One of the most bizarre proposals regarding Hatshepsut was published in 1952. As part of his radical ideas about revising the chronology of the ancient world, Immanuel Velikovsky (1895–1979)[78] argued that Hatshepsut was none other than the biblical Queen of Sheba.[79] This proposal made her a contemporary of King Solomon of Israel in the tenth century BC, with Punt argued to be a term for Jerusalem(!). Not only this, but Qadesh was also asserted to be another name for this city. A further equation was of Thutmose III with Shishak, who is recorded in the Old Testament as having attacked Jerusalem.[80] Shishak is normally regarded as Shoshenq I of the Twenty-second Dynasty.[81] Although ignored by scholarship, Velikovsky's ideas have remained attractive to "alternative" writers, a book published in 2012 attempting to bolster the "Sheba theory" with alleged new evidence.[82] Another equation of Hatshepsut with a biblical character has been to make her the "Pharaoh's daughter" who plucked Moses from the Nile.[83]

A Question of Cancellation

Returning to the mainstream, by the 1960s, the concept of Thutmose III taking "revenge" on Hatshepsut as soon as the coregency was over had long become a central plank of analyses of the period. But then, in 1966, Charles Nims* (1906–88) undertook an analysis of the erasures of Hatshepsut's memorials at Karnak and realized that many could not have been carried out until after Year 42.[84] The key issue was that various architectural elements, whose inscriptions showed that they could not have been constructed before that year, lay over intact elements of Hatshepsut's decoration.

Although some of Nims's logic was tested—and in some cases found wanting—during the 1970s, the question was readdressed by Peter Dorman (b. 1945) in 1988.[85] He endorsed Nims's conclusions as to the dating of the proscription, but proposed some modifications to some of his views on the significance of some individual pieces of evidence. In addition to the data from central Karnak, where time limits could be placed by datable inscriptions, Dorman also noted that elsewhere at Karnak (e.g., on Pylon VIII) and at other sites (especially at Deir el-Bahari), Hatshepsut's decoration had been erased, but never replaced by new carvings, either under Thutmose III, or at any time later. This would support the view that the attacks came late in the reign of Thutmose III, perhaps not long before his death. The redating of Hatshepsut's proscription also impacted considerations regarding the erasure of the names and titles of a number of her associates, in particular Senenmut,[86] making it difficult to produce a coherent theory concerning these attacks (cf. pages 52–53, 108–11).

Mummy Matters

Following its removal from TT320, the mummy of Thutmose III remained in the Bulaq Museum until 1889. Then, it was moved, together with the rest of the museum collection, to a former palace in Giza, which opened on 12 January 1890.[87] This was regarded only as a temporary location for the institution, pending the 1902 completion of a purpose-built museum on what is today Midan Tahrir in Cairo. There, the royal mummies were placed in the western gallery at the rear of the upper floor of the new building.

In 1928, a general decision was taken to no longer display unwrapped mummies. Such bodies were accordingly either placed back in their coffins, which remained on display with their lids closed, or moved to a special room, access to which required ministerial permission. At this time, their original gallery (as of 2018 designated Gallery 7) was turned over to part of the newly arrived Tutankhamun collection.

From 1931 to 1936, the principal royal mummies were housed in the pharaonic-styled mausoleum commissioned to hold the body of the politician Saad Zaghlul (1859–1927), founder of the Wafd party, but then appropriated by a new anti-Wafd government to be a national pantheon.[88] With a return to power by the Wafd in May 1936, however, this decision was reversed, Zaghlul's body being reburied in the mausoleum, and the pharaohs evacuated to storerooms back at the museum.

The royal mummies were returned to display in 1945, in Gallery 52 in the southwest corner of the museum. Two decades later, in 1967, they were here the subject of X-ray examination by a mission from the Universities of Michigan and Alexandria. The mummies remained on view until 1981, when President Anwar Sadat (1918–81) ordered that the gallery be closed. It was not until 1994 that a number of kings, including Thutmose III, were conserved and partly rewrapped—but with their faces left exposed—before being moved to new high-specification cases in Gallery 56 at the opposite end of the south range of the museum. Gallery 52 was later refurbished to contain the later royal and high-priestly mummies. At the end of the 2000s, the mummy of Thutmose III was one of a number examined by computed tomography (CT).[89] This revealed something of the king's state of health at death (page 111).

The spaces employed for housing the royal mummies at the Egyptian Museum had always been regarded as suboptimal, and dedicated accommodation was included in the planning for the new National Museum of Egyptian Civilization (NMEC) in Fustat, in southern Cairo. Thutmose III and twenty-one other kings, plus four females, were transported from Tahrir Square to Fustat in a spectacular nighttime parade on 3 April 2021, with most of them, including Thutmose, put on display in the catacomb-like lower level of the museum on the eighteenth of that month.[90] Many of the mummies, including that of Thutmose III, were also now displayed alongside their coffins for the first time in well over a century.

The mummy of Hatshepsut?

Among the four mummies of women moved to Fustat in 2021 was a body found in KV60 in the Valley of the Kings by Howard Carter in the spring of 1903.[91] The tomb had contained a mummy in the coffin trough of what proved to be Hatshepsut's nurse, Sitre-In (page 12, above), another mummy lying on the floor, and some mummified geese. The geese were removed, and the tomb resealed. It was reopened by Edward Ayrton* (1882–1914) in early 1906, and the encoffined mummy removed to Cairo.

Apropos the mummy left behind, in 1966 Elizabeth Thomas* (1907–86) speculated whether Thutmose III might have "inter[red] Hatshepsut intrusively in this simple tomb below hers?"[92] It was once more revealed in the summer of 1989, when Donald Ryan re-excavated the tomb, finding that some coffin fragments, food offerings, and pottery also still remained in the tomb. Following on from Thomas's suggestion, in 2007 Zahi Hawass removed the mummy from the tomb, and had it CT-scanned, noting that one of the molars was missing, leaving a root behind.[93]

At the same time, the box bearing Hatshepsut's name in TT320 (fig. 115) was also scanned, and a tooth seen to be inside. It was announced in 2007 that the "shape and size of the tooth and root from the box corresponded exactly with the socket and root in the mummy's jaw."[94] On this basis, the mummy was proclaimed to be that of Hatshepsut, and the body moved into the royal mummies display in the Egyptian Museum, and then on to the NMEC in 2021, labeled confidently as her.

However, apart from the presence of her name on the box, there is no logical basis for linking the tooth (or the organ found in the box) with Hatshepsut. Indeed, back in 1889, Maspero opined that "the name of the god Amon has been scraped off, which seems to show that the casket was still in use at the time when the heretical kings proscribed the worship of the god. I do not believe, therefore, that the human remains here preserved for us belong to the queen of the XVIIIth Dynasty."[95] On the other hand, a century later, Nicholas Reeves felt that Maspero was wrong on the matter of the name of Amun having been attacked,[96] and proposed the box might have originally come from KV20.

Either way, the piece was certainly intended as a domestic container, probably for something of value. The presence of the organ roughly pushed into it, with resin dripping down the front, was certainly secondary, as must be that of the tooth, seemingly embedded in the same mass of resin. Any link between either item and Hatshepsut accordingly seems most unlikely. Maspero suggested that "advantage [was taken] of the resemblance in name between this princess and Queen Mâkerî [the God's Wife Maatkare] of the XXIst Dynasty, [as] another usurpation on behalf of the high priests of Amun and their contemporaries."[97] We have already commented on the interest shown by Maatkare's father, Panedjem I, in the Thutmosids and their funerary equipment (pages 157–58).

The notion that the tooth had come from the mouth of the KV60 mummy has also been questioned. This has been on the basis that not only has the type of the tooth been misidentified, but also that there is no gap in the mummy's jaw in the location where it would (as now correctly identified) have belonged.[98] The likelihood of the mummy being that of Hatshepsut was also reduced in 2007. That year, the fragments of the second coffin from KV60 were cleaned, to reveal that it had belonged to a singer, named Ty.[99] She would thus seem to be the leading candidate for the true identity of the alleged "Hatshepsut mummy."

Reputations

Although not "megastars" like Tutankhamun and Rameses II, Thutmose III's military renown and Hatshepsut's status as by far the most eminent of the tiny cohort of female pharaohs, along with their prominent standing monuments, have made them among the better-known pharaohs. Modern treatments of them have been heavily colored by contemporary views, in Thutmose III's case exemplified by his proclamation as the "Napoleon of ancient Egypt," with all of its implications, both positive and negative, depending on the prevailing views on imperialism and militarism.[100]

Stereotypes, whether regarding gender, race, or other attributes, have always played an important role in history writing, consciously or unconsciously, negatively or positively. Accordingly, assessments of the life motivations and activities of Hatshepsut have regularly been dependent on contemporary views on the role of women in society and politics.[101] In addition, the later career of Thutmose III and the "cancellation" of Hatshepsut contributed to the idea of a negative relationship between them, with Hatshepsut "suppressing" Thutmose, and implicitly thwarting his allegedly glorious destiny, bringing aboard the ageless trope of the "wicked stepmother," against whom Thutmose eventually has his "revenge." Layered onto this have been perceptions that her assumption and maintenance of power were in some way achieved in an underhand manner, through "devious politics,"[102] practiced by a "vain, ambitious, and unscrupulous woman,"[103] who had a "deviant personality," with a "pathological drive towards male impersonation."[104]

Like many judgmental tropes in Egyptian history,[105] important aspects of this negative image can be traced back to the 1877 edition (translated into English in 1879) of the influential history of Heinrich Brugsch. For example, he asserted, through a misunderstanding of the alterations to be seen among the names on the monuments of the period, that

> Thutmes II. ascended the vacant throne, not without exciting the jealousy of his energetic sister, Hashop. She had been the favourite of the late king and was superior to her brother both in courage and capacity, and she left nothing untried to bring the royal power into her own hands or under her control. It is difficult at this day to determine if she took only legitimate means to accomplish her ends; but we know the fact that she found a hostile reception, since, after the death of her elder brother, she, with the greatest diligence, erased his name from the monuments, a clear proof of the unfriendly feeling which existed between the brother and sister.[106]

The idea that a woman (even one "superior to her brother both in courage and capacity") was unlikely to be able to achieve great things without male help has fed into views on her relationship with Senenmut. Winlock characterized her reign as "a rule dominated by an architect,"[107] whom Hayes held to be a "canny politician and brilliant administrator,"[108] and Donald Redford called a potential "evil genius."[109] As already noted (pages ix, 43–44), another area where gender-based perceptions have played a role has been contrasting a "peaceful" Hatshepsut[110] with a "warlike" Thutmose III. Although data refuting this has been available since 1957,[111] this conception has remained part of the popular reputation of the female pharaoh.

More modern approaches have also had potential to undermine understandings, as explicitly or implicitly based on Western concepts that, while possessing validity in the context of society in Europe and North America during the past century, are problematic when applied to a more remote place and time.[112] Thus, Hatshepsut is sometimes presented in feminist discourse as a revolutionary, potentially intending to perpetuate female kingship in the person of Neferure (cf. pages 26, 31), yet could also be seen as someone keen to situate her rule within the context of tradition. Jacqueline Williamson concluded that "Hatshepsut wielded power and had complete agency, but used her position to serve the orthodox establishment of traditional Egyptian rule. Her exception to

FIGURE 134 Modern visualizations. Top left: cigarette card from around 1910. Top right and bottom: portraits of Hatshepsut and Thutmose III, as painted by Winifred Brunton* (1880–1959), and published during the 1920s. Based on statuary (and his mummy in Thutmose III's case), the light skin tones employed by Brunton reflect contemporary views as to the ancient Egyptians' racial affiliations.

tradition is indeed the exception that proved—and reinforced—the rule."[113] These wide variations in interpretation in many ways indicate that they in practice say far more about modern historiographical discourse than they do about the realities of the past.

At the opposite end of the spectrum from such "gendered" approaches has been David Brügger's attempt at an "objective" assessment of Hatshepsut's reign,[114] ostensibly omitting discussions of "her personal traits (e.g. gender, character, relationships or motives)" and "speculat[ions] on later attempts to erase her from historical records," by using a system of business-style benchmarking. This concluded that "[e]xamining Hatshepsut's action as king while ignoring personal traits and applying standards of her time leads to a recognition of her reign as eminently successful." However, in spite of having forsworn any mention of Hatshepsut's gender, Brügger finds it impossible to avoid finishing his article without commenting that she could be seen as an "uber king,"[115] "blending essential feminine and male roles constitutive of … divine kingship."

Hatshepsut has been an obvious target for novelists,[116] beginning in the mid-1970s with Irene Roberts's *Hatshepsut, Queen of the Nile*,[117] and Pauline Gedge's *Child of the Morning*,[118] both of which gave feminist-inspired positive depictions of Hatshepsut.[119] Since then, a number of other novels about her have appeared, aimed at both adults and children. Most work within the "classic" framework of a peace-loving Hatshepsut, a warlike Thutmose III, and an animus between them culminating in an attack on Hatshepsut's monuments directly after the end of the coregency. Some have also used the suggestion that the Exodus might have taken place under Thutmose III (page 179) to weave the story of Moses into their tales.[120] This fits into a broader pattern of writers trying to link personalities from ancient Egypt with figures and events from the Old Testament, for both ideological and commercial reasons.

Display

Objects belonging to Thutmose III and Hatshepsut have been in museums and collections since the earliest days of the acquisition of Egyptian antiquities. However, they have never achieved the "superstardom" of later rulers such as Tutankhamun, Rameses II, and Cleopatra VII. Indeed, Thutmose III's greatest monuments outside Egypt are rarely associated with his name, being, rather, universally known as "Cleopatra's Needles."[121]

As already noted, two of Thutmose III's Heliopolitan obelisks were moved to Alexandria under Emperor Augustus. One remained standing into modern times, but the other fell, although it continued to be visible, and was offered as a gift to the United Kingdom by Mehmet Ali in 1819. However, concerns as to the cost of transporting it from Egypt repeatedly stymied proposals, in 1832 and during the 1850s, to actually take up the offer. In spite of this failure to take possession of something that Britain already

FIGURE 135 Part of the former site of the Caesarium in Alexandria in early 1879, viewed from close to the site of Ramleh Station, looking west. One of the two obelisks had already been removed to London, and work would soon begin on taking down the remaining example, to be taken to New York.

owned, there were suggestions in 1830 that the United Kingdom also be granted the standing obelisk of Hatshepsut at Karnak. This was to be as "compensation" for the gifting that year of the obelisks in front of the temple of Luxor to France.[122] Since retrieving a prostrate obelisk from the water's edge of Egypt's principal port had hitherto been beyond the British, extracting Hatshepsut's monument from the heart of the Karnak temple was clearly never going to happen.

Only one Luxor obelisk was actually removed by the French, to Paris in 1833. It was seeing it in the Place de la Concorde that led General Sir James Alexander* (1803–85), in 1867—half a century since the fallen Alexandria obelisk had been gifted to the United Kingdom—to launch a campaign to finally bring it to London, and have the city match Paris in possessing such a monument. Alexander also noted the growing risk that the owner of the land on which the obelisk lay might break it up for building material. The campaign culminated in a meeting between the general, the British consul-general Edward Stanton* (1827–1907), and the now-Viceroy of Egypt, Ismail Pasha, in 1876, with the surgeon Erasmus Wilson* (1809–84) subsequently agreeing to defray the costs—some £10,000 (£1.5 million at 2023 prices).

Built into a prefabricated iron cylinder that was then equipped with keels, a deck, cabin, and rudder, as the "obelisk ship" *Cleopatra*, it was towed from Alexandria by the steamship *Olga* on 21 September 1877, but the tow broke in a storm in the Bay of Biscay on 14 October. *Cleopatra* was, however, eventually recovered, floating off the Spanish coast, and arrived on the Thames on 21 January 1878. After the forecourt of the British Museum and Parliament Square had been rejected as sites, the obelisk was erected on London's Victoria Embankment on 12 September 1878.

Bronze plaques giving the obelisk's history and original author were placed on the pedestal, whose Egyptian-style ornaments also received the prenomen of Thutmose III. The pedestal was flanked by sphinxes bearing the king's name, albeit modeled on an example of Thutmose IV.[123] However, the "needle" remains universally associated with Cleopatra, and few who pass it have any inkling that the piece has absolutely no connection with the Macedonian queen, but is actually a memorial of a king who ruled some 1,500 years earlier (fig. 135 top middle).

Two years after the London obelisk left Egypt, it was the turn of its Alexandrine companion. A decade earlier, at the opening of the Suez Canal, Ismail Pasha had hinted to an American journalist that he might cede an obelisk to the United States. However, it was the transportation of the London obelisk that led to a campaign to secure an obelisk for New York, which successfully elicited an offer from the railway entrepreneur William H. Vanderbilt (1821–85) to finance the project to the tune of more than $100,000 (equivalent to $2.8 million at 2023 prices).

FIGURE 136 Replica of the burial chamber of the tomb of Thutmose III, in Bolton Museum and Art Gallery.

Through the good offices of the US consul, the standing Alexandria obelisk was secured as a gift to the United States from the viceroy in May 1877. A team to carry out the removal arrived in Alexandria in October 1879 and, despite various disputes and interruptions, during the second half of May 1880 the monument was inserted into the hull of the steamship SS *Dessoug* in a floating dry dock (fig. 135 bottom). *Dessoug* departed Alexandria on 12 June 1880, and arrived in New York in early July 1880. The obelisk was erected on Greywacke Knoll, in Central Park, just behind the Metropolitan Museum of Art on 22 February 1881. It stands unadorned, with just a pair of small metal plaques to explain its origins and significance to passers-by.

During the latter part of the twentieth century, the large-scale traveling exhibition has become an important part of the museum world. As far as ancient Egypt is concerned, Tutankhamun and Rameses II have been the headliners of a number of such shows, although in some cases with the majority of objects not directly linked to them. In contrast, of Thutmose III and Hatshepsut, only the latter has been the subject of full-fledged exhibitions. First, there was a show in Warsaw during 1997–98, with objects borrowed from Berlin, Hannover, and Munich.[124] Second was the exhibition organized by the Metropolitan Museum of Art, the possessor of the finest Hatshepsut collection in the world, and shown during 2005–2006 in San Francisco, New York, and Fort Worth.[125]

As far as Thutmose III is concerned, the nearest thing has been displays centering on a facsimile of Thutmose III's burial chamber (produced by Factum Arte, which was also responsible for the replica of Tutankhamun's tomb, behind Howard Carter's house at Luxor). The exhibition toured twelve venues in the United States during 2002–2007, and included loans from the Egyptian Museum, Cairo, although only a handful of items were related to Thutmose himself, in particular two wooden figures from his tomb. A version of the exhibition opened in Madrid in 2004, with the replica also appearing in Edinburgh in 2005 and Basel in 2006, although in these latter cases the Cairo material was replaced by items from the Museum August Kestner, Hanover, and the Antikensammlung, Basel. One of the replica burial chambers became a permanent part of the Egyptian galleries of Bolton Museum, Lancashire, UK, in September 2018 (fig. 136).

Whatever lens is used to regard them, the view of Thutmose III and Hatshepsut as among the most significant of Egypt's ancient rulers is difficult to question. Historically, the fact that Hatshepsut was a woman has to a degree skewed the views taken of her by historians, for example the creation of a false dichotomy between the "peace-loving" Hatshepsut and the "warlike" Thutmose III, when both were clearly enthusiastic heirs to the minatory traditions of their dynasty. Artistically, the two pharaohs were responsible for commissioning some supreme works of architecture and art. Hatshepsut's temple at Deir el-Bahari and her indurated limestone statue (fig. 29c), and Thutmose III's Luxor Museum statue (fig. 83d), are difficult to better.

But perhaps the pharaohs' most enduring impact was on ancient perceptions of what it meant to be a king of Egypt. In many ways, the monarchy as bequeathed by the two pharaohs would be the one to which their successors aspired—albeit later filtered through the lens of its implementation by the Rameside kings. It was only with the traumas of the ninth and eighth centuries that eyes shifted back in time to the Old Kingdom as a point of inspiration for kingship.[126] Likewise, in art, the modes of royal representation established by Thutmose III and Hatshepsut would—except for the Amarna interlude—remain a baseline, albeit with an elaboration of narrative elements during late Eighteenth/early Nineteenth Dynasty times until the late Third Intermediate Period.

These aspects were doubtless enhanced by the fact that the two rulers were the creators of the core of the temple complex of Karnak. While, unlike those of Thutmose, almost all of Hatshepsut's images had been destroyed, much of Karnak's architectural conception was hers. And even though allegedly written out of history, enough of Hatshepsut's heritage remained known for a centuries-later Thutmosidphile ruler to resurrect one of her names to bestow on his eldest daughter—as well as to name one of his sons for Thutmose III. So, whatever Thutmose III had hoped to do by his attack on Hatshepsut's memory, some four centuries later "Menkheperre" and "Maatkare" were still seen to be inextricably linked—as they still are, three and a half millennia later after their deaths.

Chronology of Ancient Egypt

LE = Lower Egypt only; UE = Upper Egypt.
All dates prior to 690 BC are more or less uncertain.
Parentheses around a name and date indicate a co-ruler without independent reign

Early Dynastic Period

Dynasty 1		3050–2800 BC
Den		
Dynasty 2		2800–2660

Old Kingdom

Dynasty 3		2660–2600
Dynasty 4		2600–2470
Menkaure	2493–2475	
Dynasty 5		2470–2360
Dynasty 6		2360–2200
Pepy II	2270–2200	

First Intermediate Period

Dynasties 7/8		2200–2100
Dynasties 9/10 (LE)		2100–2000
Dynasty 11a (UE)		2080–2010

Middle Kingdom

Dynasty 11b		2010–1943
Montjuhotep II	2010–1955	
Dynasty 12		1943–1760
Senwosret III	1838–1797	
Amenemhat III	1825–1777	
Amenemhat IV	1777–1769	
Sobekneferu	1769–1765	
Dynasty 13		1765–1650

Second Intermediate Period

Dynasty 14 (LE)		1700–1650
Dynasty 15 (LE)		1650–1525
Apepy		
Dynasty 16 (UE)		1660–1585
Dynasty 17 (UE)		1585–1530
Inyotef V		
Inyotef VI		
Ahmose the Elder		
Taa	–1534	
Kamose	1534–1530	

New Kingdom

Dynasty 18		1530–1278
Ahmose I	1530–1506	
Amenhotep I	1506–1486	
Thutmose I	1486–1471	
Thutmose II	1471–1468	
Thutmose III	1468–1415	
(Hatshepsut	1462–1447)	
Amenhotep II	1415–1386	
Thutmose IV	1386–1377	
Amenhotep III	1377–1337	
Akhenaten	1337–1321	
(Neferneferuaten	1322–1318)	
Tutankhamun	1321–1312	
Ay	1312–1308	
Horemheb	1308–1278	

Dynasty 19		1278–1176
Rameses I	1278–1276	
Sethy I	1276–1265	
Rameses II	1265–1200	
Dynasty 20		1176–1078
Sethnakhte	1176–1173	
Rameses III	1173–1142	
Rameses XI	1110–1078	

Third Intermediate Period

Dynasty 21		1078–941
Panedjem I	1063–1041 (UE)	
Pasebkhanut I	1049–999	
Dynasty 22		943–666
Shoshenq I	943–922	
Osorkon I	922–872	
Dynasty 25		755–656
Pi(ankh)y	750–713	
Shabaka	705–690	
Taharqa	690–664	

Saite Period

Dynasty 26		664–525

Late Period

Dynasty 27 (Persians)		526–404
Dynasty 28		404–398
Dynasty 29		398–379
Dynasty 30		379–340
Dynasty 31 (Persians)		340–332

Hellenistic Period

Dynasty of Macedonia		332–310
Dynasty of Ptolemy		310–30
Ptolemy II	284–246	
Ptolemy III	246–221	
Ptolemy IV	221–204	

Roman Period	**30 BC–AD 395**
Augustus	30 BC–AD 14
Constantine I	306–337
Constantius II	337–361

Notes

Notes to Introduction

1 The prenomen was formerly believed to have belonged to a king named Taa (cf. Winlock 1924: 243–46), but a doorway found at Karnak during 2010/12 revealed the king's correct nomen (Biston-Moulin 2012; Thiers and Zignani 2013: 509–10).

2 Shaw 2009; Saleem and Hawass 2021.

3 Gardiner 1916; Habachi 1972; Van Siclen 2010.

4 For an overview of the reign of Ahmose I, see Harvey, in preparation.

5 Porter and Moss 1937: 182.

6 Porter and Moss 1937: 176–77.

Notes to Chapter 1

1 Dodson 2023: 24–25, 56.

2 Dodson 2019b: 8–9.

3 Assche 2010; Galán 2017.

4 He has been equated with a Prince Ahmose, a son of Taa, who certainly died young (Louvre statue E15682, Vandersleyen 2005), but given the ubiquity of the name Ahmose during this period there is no certainty over this. A mummy of a child found in TT320 (Cairo CG61064, Smith 1912: 22–25) was found in a coffin bearing a docket ("*p3i*") that has been read by some as "Sipairi" (Cairo CG61007, Daressy 1909: 9–10), but the coffin is certainly some decades later than the time of Sipairi (cf. Dodson 2006). In any case, while Ahmose-sipairi was depicted posthumously as a child, the standard iconography of royal sons during at least the Eighteenth Dynasty generally shows them as children, even if the context clearly indicates that they were fully grown by the time that the depiction was made.

5 Bennett 1994.

6 It should be noted, however, that Krauss 1992: 86 n. 4, has suggested that the piece may be a forgery.

7 https://www.livescience.com/59066-burial-chamber-of-princess-in-egypt-pyramid.html

8 For some of the Hatshepsut/Thutmose III era, see Bryan 2006: 98–99.

9 Porter and Moss 1972: 371; Roehrig 2002.

10 Porter and Moss 1952: 84, 141.

11 Porter and Moss 1952: 174–75.

12 Davies 2017.

13 Texts from Aswan and Sehel (Porter and Moss 1937: 248, 250).

14 Indeed, Bradbury ([1984–85]: 6–9) and Vandersleyen (1995: 257–59) have suggested that the "inverted waters" are actually the stretch of the Nubian Nile between the Dongola and Abu Hamed Reaches.

15 Porter and Moss 1960–64: 159.

16 For an overview of the evolution of the Karnak temples, see Blyth 2006.

17 There have been questions over the authenticity of a document bearing a Year 4 date (see fig. 9 inset, page 215 n. 6).

18 See discussions in Wente and Van Siclen 1976: 225–26; Krauss 1992: 86–87; on the irrelevance of an alleged "Year 11" in the autobiographical text of Nebwawy (BM EA1199) to any king's reign-length, see Frood 2003: 75–78.

19 A stela (Berlin ÄM15699) showing Hatshepsut, with Queen Ahmes and Thutmose II, has been argued to be a forgery (Goedicke and Krauss 1999).

20 Text from Aswan (Porter and Moss 1937: 245).

21 Or, perhaps more accurately, autobiographical self-presentation. Such texts are not "autobiographies" in the modern sense, but a much more formulaic kind of work, intended to highlight the deceased's position relative to the king and the gods.

22 For summaries of the arguments, see Hornung 2006: 200–201; Shirley 2014: 173 n. 1.

23 His exact age is unclear. Examination of his mummy has suggested between twenty-five and thirty-five, but the precise aging of premodern human remains can be problematic: see page 220 n. 64.

24 Long regarded, erroneously, as a brother of Senenmut (Roehrig and Dorman 1987).

25 Shirley 2014: 180–82.

26 NMEC CG61066 (G.E. Smith 1912: 28–31; Hawass and Saleem 2016: 52).

Notes to Chapter 2

1 Dodson 2016: 83–118.

2 See Dodson 2019a: 202–204.

3 For the evolution of royal representation between the death of Thutmose II and that of Hatshepsut, see Laboury 2014.

4 Caminos 1998a: 78–79.

5 Caminos 1998a: 79–84, pl. 42–43.

6 Larché 2016; 2020.

7 On Hatshepsut's building programs on the East Bank at Thebes, as both queen and king, see Iwaszczuk 2021a; 2021b.

8 Rumelhard Le Borgne 2018.

9 For overviews of the career of Senenmut, see Dorman 1988; Price, in preparation.

10 For detailed maps of this area, see thebanmappingproject.com/sites/default/files/plans/Map-WW.pdf.

11 On the latter, see Litherland 2018.

12 For a preliminary account, see Litherland 2023; my thanks go to Dr. Litherland for an advance copy of this paper, and other information on the find.

13 As noted in Dodson 2022b: 131.

14 Although its ownership has been questioned in Gabolde 1987: 73–75; Wente and Harris 1992: 9.

Notes to Chapter 3

1 Texts in the Chapelle Rouge at Karnak (page 53) and Northern Upper Portico at Deir el-Bahari (Karkowski 2015).

2 For a discussion of Hatshepsut's royal names, see Robins 1999a.

3 The later female pharaoh, Tawosret, did not have this problem, and affected a "Strong Bull" Horus name.

4 Oppenheim 2011; there is therefore no basis for the frequent suggestion that the sequence had been "invented" to justify

Hatshepsut's accession to kingship, and thus that its use by later kings might also conceal doubtful claims to the throne.

5 Megahed and Vymazalová 2011; 2015.

6 Brunner 1986.

7 Porter and Moss 1972: 507.

8 Porter and Moss 1972: 271.

9 Sethe 1906–1909: 257.

10 Cf. Barbotin 2004; O'Connor 2008; Taterka 2022a.

11 Gabolde 2009: 44.

12 Chicago-Field A173800 (Dorman 1988: 193[12]).

13 E.g., Pawlicki 2007; Szafrański 2007; cf. Bolshakov 2014.

14 Piccione 2003.

15 Dorman 1988: 78–79.

16 For many years it was accepted that Neferure had died before Year 16, but Dorman has demonstrated that this is not supported by any data (1988: 77–79).

17 Szafrański 2007.

18 The "Nitokris" listed by Manetho as ruling as a pharaoh at the end of the Sixth Dynasty seems to have been the result of a scribal misunderstanding (Ryholt 2000; but cf. Brose 2018).

19 Ryholt 1997: 2013–14; Callender 1998; Pignattari 2018: 12–25, 107–109, 209–14.

20 Dodson 2000; Pignattari 2018: 5–12.

21 Ryholt 1997: 209–12; Pignattari 2018: 5–33.

22 Dodson 2021: 32, with references.

23 Cf. Ćwiek 2007 on the implications of colors used for royal flesh tones.

24 See Laboury 2014.

25 Cf. Matić 2016.

26 For analyses, see V. Davies 2004; Sankiewicz 2015.

27 For overviews of the administration of the reigns of Hatshepsut and Thutmose III, see Bryan 2006 and Shirley 2014. The account of the officials of Hatshepsut, below, is largely derived from the second of these works.

28 Zivie 1984: 247; 2007: 140; for doubts, see Staring 2023: 242–43.

29 Personal communication, Piers Litherland, 10 July 2023.

30 On the viceroys, see also Bács 2014.

31 Bács 2020.

32 See Wachsmann 1987; cf. Matić 2014.

33 El Awady 2009: 155–86.

34 For discussions, see Kitchen 1971; Harvey 2003; Meeks 2003; Diego Espinel 2011: 59–120; Taterka 2019c.

35 All quotations are from the Punt tableaux at the Deir el-Bahari temple.

36 Taterka 2019b.

37 Cf. Roehrig 2005: 152–53[79].

38 Porter and Moss 1952: 347–66; Valbelle and Bonnet 1996.

39 Gardiner and Peet 1955: 74, 151–63.

40 As set out by Wilson 1951: 175; cf. Dorman's overview of such opinions (1988: 9–11), and Redford's comments on the issue (1967: 63–64); see also pages 43–44, below.

41 For discussion and references to all the material covered in this section, see Redford 1967: 57–64; Taterka 2017; on Nubia under Hatshepsut, see W.V. Davies 2005.

42 Who also appears in a record of an expedition to Sinai in Year 25 of Thutmose III (see page 38).

43 Habachi 1957; Gasse and Rondot 2007: 135, 482.

44 Dorman 1991: 34.

45 Taterka 2022b.

46 Uphill 1961, and sources listed in Dorman 1988: 174 n. 62.

47 Hornung and Staehelin 1974: 56, 64–65.

48 See Karkowski 2001.

49 Cf. Landgráfová and Navrátilová 2009; Navrátilová and Landgráfová 2015.

50 For comprehensive treatments of Senenmut, see Dorman 1988 and Price, in preparation.

51 Hayes 1957: 80–84.

52 Fazzini 2002: 69–70; Bryan 2014: 94, fig. 6.4.

53 Price, in preparation.
54 For Senenmut's funerary monuments, see Dorman 1991.
55 The corridors of TT353 are certainly high enough, and seem to be just wide enough, to take the sarcophagus. However, while it would fit neatly in the northern half of either of the outer chambers, it would not have fitted into the innermost one.
56 Hayes 1950: 21–23; Fisher 2015.
57 Cf. Ikram and Dodson 1998: 245–65.
58 Dodson and Griffin 2024.
59 For an overview, see Dorman 1988: 141–64; see now also Price, in preparation.
60 Cf. Price, in preparation.
61 Cf. Iwaszczuk 2021a: 46–47.
62 Barwik 2008.
63 Wallet-Lebrun 1994.
64 Burgos and Larché 2015; Iwaszczuk 2021a: 127–35.
65 Iwaszczuk 2021a: 133–34.
66 As shown by its foundation deposits (Mensan 2007).
67 Bryan 2005; Fazzini and Bryan 2021: 35–38; Iwaszczuk 2021a: 187–97.
68 Bryan 2014.
69 Porter and Moss 1972: 275–76; Iwaszczuk 2021a: 181–85.
70 Porter and Moss 1972: 276–77; Iwaszczuk 2021a: 201–205.
71 Iwaszczuk 2021a: 199, 205.
72 On the early history of the temple of Luxor, see Iwaszczuk 2021a: 207–13.
73 Iwaszczuk 2021a: 5–7.
74 Iwaszczuk 2021a: 11–13.
75 Iwaszczuk 2021a: 15–16.
76 Iwaszczuk 2021a: 17–30.
77 Iwaszczuk 2016a: 167–74.
78 Porter and Moss 1972: 460–75; Iwaszczuk 2016a: 175–80.
79 Iwaszczuk 2016a: 147–55.
80 Porter and Moss 1934: 163–64; Chappaz 2014.
81 Fakhry 1939.
82 Porter and Moss 1937: 144.
83 Mond and Myers 1940: 16–17, 21.
84 Porter and Moss 1937: 174; Van Siclen 1999.
85 Barsanti 1907: 236.
86 Porter and Moss 1939: 200; Gardiner 1946; Fairman and Grdseloff 1947; Goedicke 2004; Bickel and Chappaz 1988.
87 Kaiser et al. 1980; Kaiser 1993: 104–106.
88 Kaiser et al. 1995; Dreyer et al. 2002; 2005: 44–61.
89 Porter and Moss 1952: 41.
90 On Hatshepsut's work in Nubia, see Bonnet 2014 and Valbelle 2014.
91 Caminos 1998b; on Hatshepsut's presence in Nubia in general, see Valbelle 2006.
92 Caminos 1974.
93 Porter and Moss 1952: 126.
94 Gabolde 2011–12.
95 Budka 2015.
96 Khartoum 443 (Porter and Moss 1952: 165).
97 Bonnet and Valbelle 2018: 54–91.

Notes to Chapter 4

1 Porter and Moss 1972: 106[328].
2 Kitchen 1968–90: 2:323–36; 1993–2014: 2:162–76.
3 Leading to the long-standing, but erroneous, belief by many scholars that Rameses II was a coregent with his father Sethy I (for discussion, see Brand 2000: 312–32; 2023: 47–49, 61–63).
4 Named on offering table Cairo JE23034 (Porter and Moss 1937: 52).
5 Gitton 1984: 75–78.
6 Robins 1999b.
7 To use forms of their names taken directly from the hieroglyphs; the forms Manhata, Manuwai, and Maruta have also been proposed, based on the individuals' presumed ethnic affiliations (J.E. Hoch in Lilyquist 2003: 329–32).

8 D'Auria 1983; a number of other items may also be attributed to her.
9 Cairo CG1112 (Porter and Moss 1960–64: 785).
10 Giza stela, l. 8–10 (Porter and Moss 1972: 39–40).
11 An ink sketch shows a prince seated in front of his father, apparently being shown how to shoot. The tomb-chapel would seem to date to the general period of Thutmose III and Amenhotep II (Porter and Moss 1960–64: 255[5]).
12 For the officials of Thutmose III see Bryan 2006 and Shirley 2014: 239–44.
13 For material from his tomb, see Staring 2023: 107–109, 439[418].
14 See Gessler-Löhr 1995.
15 The first part of a stela from Armant (Mond and Myers 1940: pl. ciii) is dated to Year 22, but it is unclear whether the text in question dates to this year's narrative, or is related to a narrative dated to Year 29.
16 For an overview of Nubia under Thutmose III and his immediate predecessors, see Spalinger 2006.
17 Sethe 1906–1909: 814–15[222].
18 Leblanc 2008.
19 Dorman 1995; Bryan 2006: 108–109; Shirley 2014: 200 n. 94, 241 n. 227.
20 Louant 2000: 59–62.
21 For overviews, see Redford 2003; 2006.
22 Porter and Moss 1960–64: 144–46; Brack and Brack 1977.
23 Copies of the Annals are published in Sethe 1906–1909: 645–756, and Redford 2003; all translations on the following pages from texts in this corpus.
24 Probably at modern Tell Hebua.
25 For the topography of the area and the battle, see Nelson 1913; Spalinger 2021: 84–108.
26 For example Kamose, when arguing (on his stela K2—fig. 2) for the opening of hostilities against the Hyksos at the end of the Seventeenth Dynasty against his court, who are content with the status quo.
27 The day of a new moon, which has been used in calculating the absolute date of the battle.
28 For the question of the nature and functioning of the so-called Egyptian "empire" in Syria-Palestine, see Galán 2008; Zangani 2022.
29 For discussion, see Redford 2003: 38–40.
30 Well illustrated by the archives of Late Bronze Age diplomatic correspondence surviving from Tell el-Amarna in Egypt and Boğazkale in Anatolia.
31 Sethe 1906–1909: 890–97[268].
32 Bryan 2006: 103–107.
33 Preserved in pHarris 500 [pBM EA10060] (Peet 1925: 226–27).
34 Lilyquist 1988; Staring 2023: 103, 458–60[486].
35 But see Redford 2003: 82–83.
36 Murnane 1990.
37 Bietak, Marinatos, and Palivou 2007; when first discovered, they were believed to be of Hyksos date, leading to all kinds of speculations about the international dynamics of that era.
38 For an overview of Thutmose III's work at Karnak, see Blyth 2006: 68–92; Laskowski 2006.
39 Thiers 2020.
40 It has been suggested that this work might even have been begun under Hatshepsut, refuting the frequently expressed view that the sheathing of the lower parts of the obelisks was part of her "cancellation" (see Wallet-Lebrun 1982; but cf. Gabolde 2012).
41 Beaux 1990.
42 Originally proposed in Engelbach 1923: 27.
43 Porter and Moss 1972: 444–46; Loyrette 1992; Lecuyot and Loyrette 1995; 1996.

44 Porter and Moss 1972: 378–81; Lipińska 1977; 2005; Dolińska 2010; 2012; 2014; 2015.

45 A view that it was dedicated to the Royal Ka finds no support in the surviving decoration; on the whole question of the Royal Ka (an idea developed in Bell 1985), see Winnermann 2023.

46 This was finished under Amenhotep II, as the cult image bears his name, and, although the decoration names only Thutmose III as king, Princess Meryetamun is called "King's Sister," appropriate only during Amenhotep's reign.

47 Bedier 1994.

48 Porter and Moss 1934: 63; Radwan 1981; Collombert 2008–10; Dietze 2020.

49 Porter and Moss 1934: 60–61; El-Banna 1981.

50 Staring 2023: 280–81; office bearers in memorial temples of Amenhotep II and Horemheb were also buried at Saqqara, while such a sanctuary of Rameses II "in the House of Ptah" is definitely attested in texts.

51 Pouls Wegner 2001; Laskowski 2009.

52 Mond and Myers 1940: 3, 11–17, 24–28.

53 Vercoutter 1952; Barguet 1952: 81–105.

54 Pierrat et al. 1995: 440; 1996: 506–507.

55 Van Siclen 1999; Laskowki 2001.

56 Porter and Moss 1952: 65–73.

57 Bonnet and Valbelle 2018: 92–118.

58 For an overview, see Laboury 1998; 2006.

59 For an overview, see Dorman 2005.

60 For a recent discussion of the varying treatments of Hatshepsut's monuments, see Wong 2023.

61 Van Siclen 1989.

62 E.g., those noted in Dorman 2005: 269.

63 Laboury 2006: 265–66.

64 Estimates of age derived from X-ray and CAT scans have been "35:0–40:00" and "40+" years respectively (Harris and Wente 1980: 210–11[47]; Hawass and Saleem 2016: 53)—clearly of little help given that the king reigned for fifty-four years. The problem of "under-aging" is not, however, unique to this mummy: a considerable number of other kings have been assessed with impossible, or at best unlikely, ages at death (cf. Robins 1981). That the problem of aging non-recent human remains concerns not just those of ancient Egyptians has been made clear by studies carried out on over a thousand sets of eighteenth- to nineteenth-century AD human remains recovered from the crypts of Christ Church, Spitalfields, in London (Reeve and Adams 1993; Molleson and Cox 1993). Of these, nearly half were of individuals whose age at death was indicated by coffin plates but, when assessed against the conventional anatomical criteria then used in archaeology for aging skeletal remains, less than 30 percent of the sample was correctly placed within five years of the real age, and only 50 percent within ten years. Among cases of under-aging, individuals who were known certainly to have died in their late eighties, or their nineties, appeared according to the anatomical criteria to be in their sixties, or in one case late fifties! While the methodology of these determinations has been questioned, and thus the reality of these actual discrepancies (Dabbs and Rose 2018), it remains the case that historic age determinations of premodern remains have delivered ages inconsistent with actual ones.

65 Hawass and Saleem 2016: 53, fig. 17. CT scans (page 201) also revealed that the king's brain had not been removed during the mummification process.

66 For full discussions, see Murnane 1977: 57; Manuelian 1987: 1–40, 57–58; 2006.

67 Sethe 1906–1909: 895–96[37–39].

68 Stela MFA 25.632 (Leprohon 1991: 150–63).
69 E.g., Redford 1965.
70 Cf. Manuelian 1987: 39–40.
71 As argued in Taterka 2019a, who also deals with other alleged evidence, concluding that none provides corroboration for the putative coregency.
72 For the latter, see Johnson 2018; Dodson 2020: 75–77.
73 See page 218 n. 3.
74 Cf. Dodson 2014b.
75 Excluding here the dates of allied lines that exist in the Karnak Nile level texts of the Theban civil war of the late ninth century BC (for which see Dodson 2019a: 122–24). It should be noted that even the Twelfth Dynasty double dates have been questioned (Obsomer 1995: 35–145).
76 Most set out in Murnane's seminal work of 1977.

Notes to Chapter 5

1 Winlock 1924; Polz and Seiler 2003; Polz 2010.
2 Dodson 2010; 2013; 2022b: 120–21, 127–28.
3 For references and discussion, see Dodson 2022b: 121–26.
4 Polz 2007: 211–29.
5 Porter and Moss 1960–64: 591; Iwaszczuk 2016a: 195–98.
6 Hayes 1935.
7 Porter and Moss 1960–64: 546–47; Iwaszczuk 2016a: 199–209.
8 Currelly and Weigall 1904: pl. xlix.
9 Usefully summarized and described by Hornung 1999, with references.
10 Porter and Moss 1960–64: 125; Dziobek 1994: 42–47.
11 Manuelian and Loeben 1993.
12 Porter and Moss 1960–64: 557–59; Piacentini and Orsenigo 2004: 195–96, 285–86.
13 Hayes 1935: 53, 109–11.
14 Romer 1974; or even Thutmose II (Roehrig 2007: 122).
15 Dodson 2022a: 109.
16 None of the surviving blocks from the lining of the chamber preserves a royal name—although such are not in any case a regular feature of Eighteenth Dynasty *Amduats*; exceptionally, Thutmose III and Queen Meryetre appear (only) in the 4th Hour in KV34.
17 Romer 1974: 123–24.
18 Dodson 2022b: 129.
19 Dodson 1994: 49–50, 118[27], 154–55[27].
20 Dodson 1994: 37–47.
21 Porter and Moss 1960–64: 547.
22 Luxor Museum (Ciccarello and Romer 1979: 4; figs. 8, 9).
23 Porter and Moss 1972: 343; Arnold 1980: 67. For a proposal that the House-of-Amenhotep-of-the-Garden might have been a cult place of Amenhotep I within the temple of Montjuhotep II, see Niwiński 2017: however, this seems impossible to reconcile with the pAbbott itinerary, which places the monuments of Amenhotep I and Montjuhotep II at opposite ends of the commissioners' tour of inspection.
24 Porter and Moss 1972: 368–69; Roehrig (ed.) 2005: 141–46; Iwaszczuk 2016b: 10–20.
25 I.e., completely the opposite of Winlock's initial interpretation of the deposits as marking out an "original" smaller temple for Hatshepsut, as shown in Winlock 1942: endpapers, and (erroneously) as the temple of Amenhotep I in Porter and Moss 1972: pls. xxxiv–xxxv.
26 It is interesting to note that this alignment is shared with the fieldstone wall that had preceded the definitive layout of the

Montjuhotep II temple (Arnold 1980: 8–9, 40, 45). This may suggest a recurring perception of a "natural" orientation, following the line of the bedrock on the northern side of the Deir el-Bahari bay, contrasting with that definitively adopted by Montjuhotep, Hatshepsut, and, later, Thutmose III, presumably to secure an uninterrupted processional route from the east.

27 Cf. Arnold 1980: pl. 38.

28 Winlock 1942: 103–104.

29 Porter and Moss 1972: 343, 425; Iwaszczuk 2016a: 43–48. The transfer of the statues may have been accompanied by restoration works in the Montjuhotep temple by Hatshepsut, as attested by a number of small inscribed objects (e.g., Dodson 1989).

30 Van Siclen 1980.

31 Porter and Moss 1972: 340–77, 423–24; Weeks 2001: 66–75; Iwaszczuk 2016a: 49–135; 2016b:. 24–255.

32 Haeny 1997; Ullmann 2002; Białostocka 2016.

33 Porter and Moss 1937: 92.

34 Pawlicki 2017.

35 Barwik 2010.

36 Karkowski 2003.

37 Stupko-Lubczyńska 2016.

38 Barwik 2021.

39 Martinez 2007a; 2007b.

40 Iwaszczuk 2016a: 137–45; 2016b: 256–50.

41 Iwaszczuk 2021c.

42 Karkowski 2016.

43 Smilgin 2009.

44 Ćwiek 2014: 71, 91.

45 Ćwiek 2014.

46 Porter and Moss 1972: 426–29; Seco Álvarez and Radwan 2010; Seco Álvarez et al. 2010; Seco Álvarez 2012; Iwaszczuk 2016a: 157–65; http://thutmosisiiitempleproject.org.

47 Cf. Staring 2023: 280–81.

48 Porter and Moss 1960–64: 551–54; Thomas 1966: 77; Romer 1975; Piacentini and Orsenigo 2004: 3–52.

49 Dodson 2022b: 118–28.

50 Harvey, in preparation.

51 They would, however, appear in the royal tomb at Amarna (TA26).

52 On the closing of doors in Valley of the Kings tombs, see Roehrig 1995.

53 Brown 2020–21; Cooney 2024: 194–202.

54 Initially depicting the dead person as a human-headed *(ba)* bird, but later debased into much more schematic arrangements (cf. Dodson 1998).

55 Extant examples made for kings (or fragments thereof) comprise those of Inyotef V (Louvre E3019), Inyotef VI (BM EA6652), Taa (Cairo CG61001), Ahmose I (Cairo CG61002), Thutmose I (Cairo CG61025), Amenhotep III (fragment from WV22), Tutankhamun (Cairo JE60670, JE60671, and GEM7590), Sethnakhte (Cairo CG61039), and Pasebkhanut I (Cairo JE85912).

56 Cairo CG40001+JE26203*bis*+MFA 60.1472+former Amherst Collection (Porter and Moss 1960–64: 660–61).

57 Litherland 2014; 2018.

58 Lilyquist 2003.

59 Litherland 2014: 34–37.

60 KV39, a multi-phase tomb, intended for plural burials, is datable to Amenhotep II by its foundation deposits (Rose 2000; Buckley 2005; Buckley, Buckley, and Cooke 2005; Dodson 2003: 188–89). The large KV33 belonged to Tiaa, mother of Thutmose IV (Jenni, Dorn, and Paulin-Grothe 2021), while shaft tombs KV40 and KV64 held multiple burials of the reign of Amenhotep III (Bickel 2021).

61 Porter and Moss 1960–64: 559; Thomas 1966: 78–80; Hornung 1975; Reeves

1990: 24–25; El-Bialy 1999; Eaton-Krauss 1999; 2012; Preys 2011: 333–37; Dodson 2022b: 131–33; Irsay-Nagy 2023.

62 Eaton-Krauss 1999: 122–23, 127.

Notes to Chapter 6

1 For his reign, see Manuelian 1987, with a summary in Dodson 2014a: 9–21.

2 Manuelian 1987: 192–99.

3 Bryan 1991: 98–99; Van Siclen 1995.

4 Piccione 2003: 94–97.

5 Porter and Moss 1952: 409; Iversen 1968–72: 1:55–64; Bryan 1991: 176–79. While nothing of any sanctuary of Thutmose IV has been identified other than the base for the obelisk, it may have been the core of one of Akhenaten's Karnak Aten monuments, and was later incorporated into Rameses II's Re-Horakhty chapel.

6 Porter and Moss 1960–64: 47–49.

7 Seco Álvarez 2017.

8 Sheikholeslami 2003.

9 Karkowski and Winnicki 1983.

10 Laskowska-Kusztal 1984.

11 Godlewski 1986.

12 Godlewski 1986: 36–39.

13 Dodson 2019a: 24–52.

14 Dodson 2019a: 52–57, 64–65.

15 Three Menkheperres and two Maatkares are among the coffin owners listed in Niwiński 1988.

16 Dodson 2009: 60–64.

17 Cairo CG61025 (Cooney 2024: 293–303). The mummy long identified as that of Thutmose I (CG61056) is most certainly not his (Hawass and Saleem 2016: 47–51). Key issues are: that the person is far too young; that his arms are in the wrong position for a king of the period (crossed arms were introduced for Amenhotep I); that the original identification was purely on the basis of gross facial morphology; and that the mummy was found in a coffin that had once belonged to Thutmose I, but had long since been taken over and reworked for Panedjem I (see pages 157–58).

18 Cooney 2024: 199–207.

19 In contrast to some of the royal mummies, its identification seems solid, since its wrappings included an original shroud of the king (cf. Laboury 1997).

20 Aston 2013; 2015.

21 For a recent discussion, see Aston 2021.

22 NMEC CG61068 (G.E. Smith 1912: 32–36; Hawass and Saleem 2016: 53–55).

23 Reeves 1990: 123.

24 Maspero 1889: 282; Reeves 1990: 200[14–18], 207[13–17].

25 Dodson 2023: 27–40.

26 Now BM EA23 (Porter and Moss 1934: 72; Hayes 1935: 153–54 n. 42).

27 Hayes 1935: 153–54 n. 42.

28 Waddell 1940.

29 Cf. Dodson 2020: 104–105; 2022a: 134–35.

30 Although many have tried: e.g., Redford 1986: 242–47.

31 Cf. Dillery 1999.

32 Porter and Moss 1939: 90[127, 129].

33 Porter and Moss 1939: 115.

34 Iversen 1968–72: 1:55–64.

35 Iversen 1968–72: 2:9–33.

Notes to Chapter 7

1 El-Daly 2005.

2 For an overview, see Bednarski, Dodson, and Ikram 2020.

3 Pococke 1743–45: 1:90–110.

4 Pococke 1743–45: 1:96.

5 For a history of the exploration of the Deir el-Bahari temple, see Godlewski 1986: 13–20.

6 Pococke 1743–45: 1:100.

7 *Description* 1809–26: Ant 2:341–42; English translation by author.

8 Porter and Moss 1972: 460–61.

9 Bristol City Museum & Art Gallery H4547.
10 Schmidt 2011: 136.
11 Which may have previously been investigated by Salt: see Wilkinson 1828: 77 n. 2; 1835: 98 n†.
12 Wilkinson 1835: 90–99.
13 Wilkinson 1835: 98.
14 Godlewski 1986: 14–15, 23, 24.
15 Champollion 1909; Rosellini 1832–33; Wilkinson 1828; 1830a.
16 Cf. Harvey, in preparation, on the issues with the beginning of the dynasty.
17 Not now identifiable (see Champollion 1824: 26–27).
18 Now Berlin ÄM1625 (Porter and Moss 1960–64: 7).
19 Champollion 1909: 329–30; English translation by author.
20 Champollion 1909: 329–32; English translation by author.
21 Wilkinson 1835: 97 n*.
22 Rosellini 1832–33: 226–27; English translation by author.
23 Wilkinson 1835: 97 nn†‡.
24 Wilkinson 1837: 52.
25 Hincks 1839: 194–95.
26 Heinrich Brugsch (1859: 93) was one of few who regarded the point as still open, but recanted, and was confident that Thutmose III and Hatshepsut were siblings in H. Brugsch 1877: 371; 1879: 1:296–98 (see Maspero 1892: 175–76).
27 Hincks 1846: 105–106.
28 Arundale, Bonomi, and Birch [1842]: 77–79.
29 Birch 1847a: 221 n. 11.
30 Bunsen 1845: 79.
31 First under the title *The Early History of Egypt, from the Old Testament, Herodotus, Manetho, and the hieroglyphical inscription* (London: Moxon, 1836), and later as *The History of Egypt from the earliest times till the conquest by the Arabs* A.D. *640*.
32 Sharpe 1876: 42.
33 Queen's pyramid GIIIb, which contained a quarry mark naming Menkaure on the ceiling of the burial chamber (Porter and Moss 1974–81: 35).
34 Sharpe 1876: 46–47.
35 Wilkinson 1835: 510.
36 See Bimson 1981, who reviews the question in detail, before concluding that the Exodus should be indeed be dated around 1470. It may be noted that Bimson's overview of the historiography of the issue (1981: 13–17) fails to note Wilkinson's authorship of the idea of placing the Exodus under Thutmose III, rather attributing it Eugène Lefébure. Others have argued for the Exodus narrative being inspired by the expulsion of the Hyksos by Ahmose I (e.g., Di Lenardo 2016; Vandersleyen 2016), or even that the event should be placed as far back as the Thirteenth Dynasty (Rohl 1995: 251–325).
37 Birch 1847b.
38 Lepsius 1853: 243–74.
39 Lepsius 1853: 256.
40 Lepsius 1853: 256.
41 Dümichen 1868.
42 See Millet 1962.
43 For the story of the discovery of TT320 and a discussion of the many issues involved, see Bickerstaffe 2010; Aston 2021.
44 It is generally stated that the mummy was subsequently rewrapped, and unwrapped again, "officially," in 1886, but it has not been possible to locate any contemporary material confirming this.
45 E. Brugsch and Maspero 1881: 13.
46 Maspero 1882: 132–33[xxviii].
47 On the Ahhotep question, see Betrò 2022.
48 Cairo CG34006 (Erman 1891; Porter and Moss 1952: 141).
49 Bouriant 1892; the publication of the decoration of the tomb appeared six years later (Boussac 1898).

50 Maspero 1892: 170–82.
51 For the techniques used see James 1997.
52 Naville 1895–1908.
53 Variations have essentially concerned how to represent vowels (e.g., Maspero's "Hatshopsîtu") and whether or not to include the terminal *t* (e.g., Alan Gardiner's "Ḥatshepsowe").
54 For Loret's work in the Valley, see Piacentini and Orsenigo 2004.
55 Loret 1898: 91–96; English translation by author.
56 Brother-in-law of Khedive Abbas II Helmy.
57 Weigall 1906: 121–22.
58 Seco Álvarez 2012.
59 For a summary of its pre-1903 modern history, see Davis 1906: xi–xii.
60 Davis 1906: xi–xiv.
61 Carter and Mace 1923: 79–82.
62 Baraize 1921.
63 For full documentation, see Lilyquist 2003.
64 Sethe 1896, as summarized in Breasted 1906: 2:53–54.
65 Breasted 1905: 266–71; also in his contribution to the *Cambridge Ancient History* (1924: 60–61).
66 E.g., Petrie 1896: 54, who allows a short coregency between Thutmose I and II, and a longer one between the latter and Hatshepsut.
67 Hall 1913: 286–88.
68 Naville 1897; 1899.
69 Meyer 1928: 20–31.
70 Winlock 1928: 46.
71 Sethe 1932.
72 Edgerton 1933.
73 Lewis 1915.
74 Winlock 1942: 169–72; in 1998, the fragments of the latter piece were finally rejoined, the complete statue now splitting its time between New York and Leiden
75 Hayes 1935.
76 Lipińska 2007: 107.
77 Lipińska 2007; 1977.
78 For whom and whose ideas, see Bauer 1985.
79 Velikovsky 1952: 103–41.
80 Velikovsky 1952: 142–77.
81 See (e.g.) Dodson 2019a: 88–89, 186–87; it may be noted that more recent authors have attempted to deny this equation, turning him into either Rameses II or Rameses III (see James and van der Veen 2015 for the debate).
82 Scott 2012.
83 Williams 2012.
84 Nims 1966.
85 Dorman 1988: 46–65.
86 Dorman 1988: 141–64.
87 For more detail on the modern history of the royal mummies, see Ikram 2017 and Dodson 2019b: 144–49.
88 Coury 1992.
89 Hawass and Saleem 2016: 179–91.
90 Of the kings, Amenhotep III was not put on display, presumably owing to the severely damaged state of his head.
91 Porter and Moss 1960–64: 587; Ryan 1989; 1990; 2010: 384–85.
92 Thomas 1966: 138.
93 Hawass 2007.
94 Hawass 2007: 24.
95 Maspero 1889: 584[6].
96 Reeves 1990: 28 n. 25.
97 Reeves 1990: 28 n. 25.
98 Thimes 2008; for an attempted rebuttal, see Hawass and Saleem 2016: 60. The terms of the latter, however, as pointed out in Bickerstaffe n.d.: 2–4, undermine the original claim for an "exact correspondence" between the tooth and the gap in the jaw.
99 Ryan 2010: 384–85.
100 This has extended to his alleged short stature, although this has been overstated, as the oft-quoted height of 1.615 meters (5ft

3½in, derived from Smith 1912: 34) omits the feet. Hawass and Saleem (2016: 53) give his height as 1.67 meters (5ft 5¾in).

101 For an overview, see Keller 2005.

102 Winlock 1942: 147.

103 Hayes 1953: 82.

104 Margetts 1951: 559, 561.

105 Another being the racially tinged negativity attached to the Nubian kings of the Twenty-fifth Dynasty (see Dodson 2023: 155–56).

106 H. Brugsch 1879: 1:298.

107 Winlock 1942: 142.

108 Hayes 1959: 106.

109 Redford 1967: 85.

110 Although not necessarily by choice, H. Brugsch implying that her Punt expedition was to sublimate her being "[un]able to emulate a man by heroic deeds in the turmoil of battle" (1879: 1:313).

111 Habachi 1957.

112 See discussion in Williamson 2022.

113 Williamson 2022: 127.

114 Brügger 2022.

115 Citing the concept as developed in Gundlach 1998: 15.

116 And also dramatists: in 1920, British theater producer and amateur Egyptologist Terence Gray (1898–1986; Cornwell 2004) published a never-performed drama on Hatshepsut's career (Gray 1920). Gray later devised another dramatic presentation of ancient Egypt, and wrote the introduction to Brunton 1925.

117 Roberts 1976.

118 Gedge 1977.

119 Cf. Mosleth King 2023.

120 E.g., Collins 2016; R.S. Smith 2020.

121 For their histories, see Iversen 1968–72: 2:90–147; D'Alton 1994; Elliott 2022.

122 Elliott 2022: 76.

123 Durham N379 (Malek 1999: 50[800-624-800]).

124 Lipińska, Dolińska, and Aksamit 1997.

125 Roehrig (ed.) 2005.

126 Dodson 2021: 129–30.

Bibliography

Abbreviations for Periodicals

A&L	*Ägypten und Levante*
ASAE	*Annales du Service des Antiquités de l'Égypte*
BES	*Bulletin of the Egyptological Seminar*
BIÉ	*Bulletin de l'Institut Égyptien*
BIFAO	*Bulletin de l'Institut français d'Archéologie orientale du Caire*
BMMA	*Bulletin of the Metropolitan Museum of Art*
BSEG	*Bulletin de la Société d'Égyptologie de Genève*
BSFE	*Bulletin de la Société Française d'Égyptologie*
CdE	*Chronique d'Egypte*
CRIPEL	*Cahiers de Recherches de l'Institut de Papyrologie et d'Égyptologie de Lille*
E&T	*Études et Travaux*
EEFAR	*Egypt Exploration Fund Archaeological Report*
EgArch	*Egyptian Archaeology: Bulletin of the Egypt Exploration Society*
ENiM	*Équipe Égypte Nilotique et Méditerranéenne*
GM	*Göttinger Miszellen*
JAEA	*Journal of Ancient Egyptian Architecture*
JARCE	*Journal of the American Research Center in Egypt*
JEA	*Journal of Egyptian Archaeology*
JEgH	*Journal of Egyptian History*
JNES	*Journal of Near Eastern Studies*
JSSEA	*Journal of the Society for the Study of Egyptian Antiquities*
MDAIK	*Mitteilungen des Deutschen Archäologischen Instituts, Kairo*
MMJ	*Metropolitan Museum Journal*
NARCE	*Newsletter of the American Research Center in Egypt*
PAM	*Polish Archaeology in the Mediterranean*
PSBA	*Proceedings of the Society for Biblical Archaeology*
RdE	*Revue d'Égyptologie*
RecTrav	*Recueil de travaux relatifs à la philologie et à l'archéologie égyptiennes et assyriennes*
SAK	*Studien zur Altägyptischen Kultur*
ZÄS	*Zeitschrift für Ägyptische Sprache und Altertumskunde*

Arnold, D. 1980. *The Temple of Mentuhotep at Deir el-Bahari*. New York: Metropolitan Museum of Art.

Arundale, F., J. Bonomi, and S. Birch. [1842]. *Gallery of Antiquities Selected from the British Museum*. London: Weale.

Assche, B. van. 2010. "Ahmose Sapair: Discussing the Identity of a Deified Prince." *JSSEA* 37: 113–21.

Aston, D.A. 2013. "TT 320 and the *k3y* of Queen Inhapi: A Reconsideration Based on Ceramic Evidence." *GM* 236: 16–17.

———. 2015. "TT 358, TT 320 and KV 39: Three Early Eighteenth Dynasty Queen's Tombs in the Vicinity of Deir el-Bahari." *PAM* 24/2: 15–42.

———. 2021. "The Royal Cache: A History of TT 320." In *Bab el-Gasus in Context: Rediscovering the Tomb of the Priests of Amun*, edited by R. Sousa, A. Amenta, and K.M. Cooney, 31–68. Rome: "L'Erma" di Bretschneider.

El Awady, T. 2009. *Abusir XVI: Sahure—The Pyramid Causeway: History and Decoration Program in the Old Kingdom*. Prague: Czech Institute of Egyptology.

Bács, T. 2014. "Overseers of Southern Foreign Lands and Thebes in the Reign of Hatshepsut." In *Creativity and Innovation in the Reign of Hatshepsut: Papers from the Theban Workshop 2010*, edited by J.M. Galán, B.M. Bryan, and P.F. Dorman, 411–26. Chicago: Oriental Institute.

———. 2020. "A Theban Tomb-temple: The Mortuary Chapel of the High Priest Hapuseneb (TT 67)." In *11. Ägyptologische Tempeltagung: The Discourse between Tomb and Temple. Prague, May 24–27, 2017*, edited by F. Coppens and H. Vymazalová, 11–39. Wiesbaden: Harrassowitz.

El-Banna, E. 1981. "L'obélisque de Sésostris I à Héliopolis a-t-il été déplacé?" *RdE* 33: 3–9.

Baraize, É. 1921. "Rapport sur l'enlèvement et le transport du sarcophage de la reine Hatchopsitou." *ASAE* 21: 175–82.

Barbotin, C. 2004. "Pount et la naissance divine." *CRIPEL* 24: 9–14.

Barguet, P. 1952. "Tôd: Rapport de fouilles de la saison février–avril 1950." *BIFAO* 51: 80–110.

Barsanti, A. 1907. "Rapport sur la découverte à Edfou des ruines d'un temple ramesside." *ASAE* 8: 233–36.

Barwik, M. 2008. "Ahmose—a Mayor of Thebes of the Early Tuthmoside Period." *GM* 216: 13–16.

———. 2010. "Sanctuary of the Hatshepsut Temple at Deir el-Bahari." In *8. Ägyptologische Tempeltagung: Interconnections between Temples, Warschau, 22.–25. September 2008*, edited by M. Dolińska and H. Beinlich, 1–12. Wiesbaden: Harrassowitz.

———. 2021. *The Royal Mortuary Cult Complex in the Temple of Hatshepsut at Deir el-Bahari*. Vol. 1, *The Chapel of Tuthmosis I*. Louvain: Peeters.

Bauer, H.H. 1985. *Beyond Velikovsky: The History of a Public Controversy*. Champaign: University of Illinois Press.

Beaux, N. 1990. *Le cabinet de curiosités de Thoutmosis III: Plantes et animaux du "Jardin botanique" de Karnak*. Leuven: Peeters.

Bedier, S. 1994. "Ein Stiftungsdekret Thutmosis' III. aus Buto." In *Aspekte spätägyptischer Kultur: Festschrift für Erich Winter zum 65. Geburtstag*, edited by M. Minas and J. Zeidler, 35–50. Mainz: Philipp von Zabern.

Bednarski, A., A. Dodson, and S. Ikram. 2020. "The Prehistory of Egyptology." In *A History of World Egyptology*, edited by A. Bednarski, A. Dodson, and S. Ikram, 8–24. Cambridge: Cambridge University Press.

Bell, L. 1985. "Luxor Temple and the Cult of the Royal Ka." *JNES* 44: 251–94.

Bennett, C. 1994. "Thutmosis I and Ahmes-Sapaïr." *GM* 141: 35–37.

Betrò, M. 2022. "The Identity of Ahhotep and the Textual Sources." In *The Treasure of the Egyptian Queen Ahhotep and International*

Relations at the Turn of the Middle Bronze Age (1600–1500 BCE), edited by G. Miniaci and P. Lacovara, 131–52. London: Golden House.

Białostocka, Olga. 2016. *Temples of Millions of Years in Light of Older Architectural Models: Hatshepsut's ḏsr-ḏsrw as the Temple of Rebirth of the Divine k3*. Warsaw: Institute of Mediterranean and Oriental Cultures Polish Academy of Sciences/Polish Centre of Mediterranean Archaeology.

El-Bialy, M. 1999. "Récentes recherches effectuées dans la tombe no. 42 de la Vallée des Rois." *Memnonia* 10: 161–78.

Bickel, S., ed. 2021. *Räuber—Priester—Königskinder: die Gräber KV 40 und KV 64 im Tal der Könige*. Basel and Frankfurt am Mein: Librum.

Bickel, S., and J.-L. Chappaz. 1988. "Missions épigraphiques du fonds de l'Égyptologie de Genève au Speos Artemidos." *BSEG* 12: 9–24.

Bickerstaffe, D. 2010. "The History of the Discovery of the Cache." In *The Royal Cache TT 320: A Re-examination*, edited by E. Graefe and G. Belova, 13–36. Cairo: Supreme Council of Antiquities Press.

———. n.d. "The Royal Mummies of Ancient Egypt: Additional Notes and Updates in the Light of Recent Widely-publicised Work." https://www.academia.edu/37989560/The_Royal_Mummies_of_Ancient_Egypt

Bierbrier, M.L., ed. 2019. *Who Was Who in Egyptology*. 5th ed. London: Egypt Exploration Society.

Bietak, M., N. Marinatos, and C. Palivou. 2007. *Taureador scenes in Tell el-Dab'a (Avaris) and Knossos*. Vienna: Verlag der Österreichischen Akademie der Wissenschaften.

Bimson, J.J. 1981. *Redating the Exodus and Conquest*. 2nd ed. Sheffield: Almond Press.

Birch, S. 1847a. "Observations on the Hieroglyphical Inscription of the Obelisk of the Atmeidan at Constantinople." *Transactions of the Royal Society of Literature of the United Kingdom* ser. 2, 2: 218–28.

———. 1847b. "Observations on the Statistical Tablet of Karnak." *Transactions of the Royal Society of Literature of the United Kingdom* ser. 2, 2: 317–73.

Biston-Moulin, S. 2012. "Le roi Sénakht-en-Rê Ahmes de la XVIIe dynastie." *ENiM* 5: 61–71.

Blyth, E. 2006. *Karnak: Evolution of a Temple*. London: Routledge.

Bolshakov, V.A. 2014. "The King's Daughter Neferura: Eventual Heiress of Hatshepsut?" *CdE* 89/178: 261–63.

Bonnet, C. 2014. "An Unusual Architecture of Hatshepsut in Nubia." In *Creativity and Innovation in the Reign of Hatshepsut: Papers from the Theban Workshop 2010*, edited by J.M. Galán, B.M. Bryan, and P.F. Dorman, 427–35. Chicago: Oriental Institute.

Bonnet, C., and D. Valbelle. 2018. *Les temples égyptiens de Panébès "Le jujubier": à Doukki Gel–Soudan*. Paris: Khéops.

Bouriant, U. 1892. "Une stèle du tombeau d'Anna." *RecTrav* 12: 105–107.

Boussac, H. 1898. *Le tombeau d'Anna (XVIIIe dynastie)*. Paris: Semaine des Constructeurs.

Brack, A., and A. Brack. 1977. *Das Grab des Tjanuni: Theben Nr. 74*. Mainz: Zabern.

Bradbury, L. [1984–85]. "The Tombos Inscription: A New Interpretation." *Serapis* 8: 1–20.

Brand, Peter J. 2000. *The Monuments of Seti I: Epigraphic, Historical and Art Historical Analysis*. Leiden: Brill.

——— 2023. *Ramesses II, Egypt's Ultimate Pharaoh*. Columbus, GA: Lockwood Press.

Breasted, J.H. 1905. *A History of Egypt: From the Earliest Times to the Persian Conquest*. New York: Charles Scribner's Sons.

——— 1906. *Ancient Records of Egypt*. 5 vols. Chicago: University of Chicago Press.

——— 1924. "The Foundation and Expansion of the Egyptian Empire." In *Cambridge*

Ancient History, vol. 2, *The Egyptian and Hittite Empires to c. 1000* B.C., edited by J.B. Bury, S.A. Cook, and F.E. Adcock, 40–66. Cambridge: Cambridge University Press.

Brose, M. 2018. "Neue Fragen zur (Nicht-) Existenz der Königin Nitokris." *GM* 254: 37–52.

Brown, N. 2020–21. "Raise Me Up and Repel My Weariness! A Study of the Coffin of Thutmose III (CG 61014)." *MDAIK* 76–77: 11–35.

Brügger, D. 2022. "Re-assessing Hatshepsut as King." *GM* 266: 49–60.

Brugsch, E., and G. Maspero. 1881–87. *La trouvaille de Deir-el-Bahari*. Vol. 2. Cairo: Imprimerie française F. Mourès & Co.

Brugsch, H. 1859. *Histoire d'Égypte dès les premiers temps de son existence jusqu'à nos jours*. Leipzig: Hinrichs.

———. 1877. *Geschichte Ägyptens unter den Pharaonen*. Leipzig: Hinrichs.

———. 1879. *A History of Egypt under the Pharaohs, Derived Entirely from the Monuments*. Translated by H.D. Seymour. Edited by P. Smith. 2 vols. London: John Murray.

Brunner, H. 1986. *Die Geburt des Gottkönigs: Studien zur Überlieferung eines Altägytpischen Mythos*. Wiesbaden: Harrassowitz.

Brunton, W., ed. 1925. *Kings and Queens of Ancient Egypt*. London: Hodder and Stoughton.

Bryan, B.M. 1991. *The Reign of Thutmose IV*. Baltimore: Johns Hopkins University Press.

———. 2005. "The Temple of Mut: New Evidence on Hatshepsut's Building Activity." In *Hatshepsut: From Queen to Pharaoh*, edited by C.H. Roehrig, 181–83. New York: Metropolitan Museum of Art; New Haven, CT: Yale University Press.

———. 2006. "Administration in the Reign of Thutmose III." In *Thutmose III: A New Biography*, edited by E.H. Cline and D. O'Connor, 69–122. Ann Arbor: University of Michigan Press.

———. 2014. "Hatshepsut and Cultic Revelries in the New Kingdom." In *Creativity and Innovation in the Reign of Hatshepsut: Papers from the Theban Workshop 2010*, edited by J.M. Galán, B.M. Bryan, and P.F. Dorman, 93–123. Chicago: Oriental Institute.

Buckley, I.M. 2005. "Excavations at Theban Tomb KV 39." In *Current Research in Egyptology*, edited by A. Cooke and F. Simpson, 2:21–28. Oxford: Archaeopress.

Buckley, I.M., P. Buckley, and A. Cooke. 2005. "Fieldwork in Theban Tomb KV 39: The 2002 Season." *JEA* 91: 71–82.

Budka, J. 2015. "The Pharaonic Town on Sai Island and Its Role in the Urban Landscape of New Kingdom Kush." *Sudan & Nubia* 19: 40–53.

Bunsen, C.C.J. von. 1845. *Aegyptens Stelle in der Weltgeschichte*. Vol. 3, *Das mittlere und neue Reich*. Hamburg: Friedrich Perthes.

Burgos, F., and F. Larché. 2015. *La chapelle Rouge: le sanctuaire de barque d'Hatshepsout*. 2 vols. Paris: Soleb.

Callender, V.G. 1998. "Materials for the Reign of Sebekneferu." In *Proceedings of the Seventh International Congress of Egyptologists, Cambridge, 3–9 September 1995*, edited by C.J. Eyre, 227–36. Leuven: Peeters.

Caminos, R.A. 1974. *The New-Kingdom Temples of Buhen*. 2 vols. London: Egypt Exploration Society.

———. 1998a. *Semna-Kumma*. Vol. 1, *The Temple of Semna*. London: Egypt Exploration Society.

———. 1998b. *Semna-Kumma*. Vol. 2, *The Temple of Kumma*. London: Egypt Exploration Society.

Carter, H. 1917. "A Tomb Prepared for Queen Hatshepsuit and Other Recent Discoveries at Thebes." *JEA* 4: 107–18.

Carter, H., and A.C. Mace. 1923. *The Tomb of Tut·ankh·Amen*. Vol. 1. London: Cassell.

Champollion, J.-F. 1824. *Lettres à M. le duc de Blacas d'Aulps, Premier Gentilhomme de la Chambre, Pair de France, etc., relatives au Musée Royal Égyptien de Turin*. Paris: Didot.

———. 1845. *Monuments de l'Égypte et de la Nubie*. Vol. 2. Paris: Firmin Didot.

———. 1909. *Lettres de Champollion le Jeune*, edited by H. Hartleben. Paris: Ernest Leroux.

Chappaz, J.-L. 2014. "Remarques sur l'architecture du Spéos Artémedoros." In *Creativity and Innovation in the Reign of Hatshepsut: Papers from the Theban Workshop 2010*, edited by J.M. Galán, B.M. Bryan, and P.F. Dorman, 157–71. Chicago: Oriental Institute.

Ciccarello, M., and J. Romer. 1979. *A Preliminary Report of the Recent Work in the Tombs of Ramesses X and XI in the Valley of the Kings*. New York: The Brooklyn Museum Theban Expedition.

Collins, W.G. 2016. *Prince of the Nile: Moses, Son of Princess Hatshepsut*. n.p.: CreateSpace Independent Publishing Platform.

Collombert, P. 2008–10. "Les stèles d'enceinte de Thoutmosis III à Héliopolis." *BSEG* 28: 5–13.

Cooney, K. 2024. *Recycling for Death: Coffin Reuse in Ancient Egypt and the Theban Royal Caches*. Cairo: American University in Cairo Press.

Cornwell, P. 2004. *Only by Failure: The Many Faces of the Impossible Life of Terence Gray*. Cromer: Salt Publishing.

Coury, R.M. 1992. "The Politics of the Funereal: The Tomb of Saad Zaghlul." *JARCE* 29: 191–200.

Currelly, C.T., and A.E.P. Weigall. 1904. *Abydos*. Vol. 3. London: Egypt Exploration Society.

Ćwiek, A. 2007. "Red, Yellow, and Pink: Ideology of Skin Hues at Deir el-Bahari." *Fontes Archaeologici Posnanienses* 43: 23–50.

———. 2014. "Old and Middle Kingdom Tradition in the Temple of Hatshepsut at Deir el-Bahari." *E&T* 27: 61–93.

Dabbs, G.R., and J.C. Rose. 2018. "The S-word Addressed: Estimating Age from Human Skeletal Remains." *JARCE* 54: 41–44.

D'Alton, M. 1994. *The New York Obelisk: or, How Cleopatra's Needle came to New York and What Happened When It Got Here*. New York: Metropolitan Museum of Art.

El-Daly, O. 2005. *Egyptology: The Missing Millennium: Ancient Egypt in Medieval Arabic Writings*. London: UCL Press.

Daressy, G. 1909. *Cercueils des cachettes royales*. Cairo: Institut français d'archéologie orientale.

D'Auria, S. 1983. "The Princess Beketamun." *JEA* 69: 161–62.

Davies, N. de G. 1935. "The Egyptian Expedition 1934–1935: The Work of the Graphic Branch of the Expedition." *BMMA* 30/2: 46–57.

Davies, V. 2004. "Hatshepsut's Use of Tuthmosis III in Her Program of Legitimation." *JARCE* 41: 55–66.

Davies, W.V. 2005. "Egypt and Nubia: Conflict with the Kingdom of Kush." In *Hatshepsut: From Queen to Pharaoh*, edited by C.H. Roehrig, 49–56. New York: Metropolitan Museum of Art; New Haven, CT: Yale University Press.

———. 2017. "Nubia in the New Kingdom: The Egyptians at Kurgus." In *Nubia in the New Kingdom: Lived Experience, Pharaonic Control and Indigenous Traditions*, edited by N. Spencer, A. Stevens, and M. Binder, 65–105. Leuven: Peeters.

Davis, T.M., ed. 1906. *The Tomb of Hâtshopsîtû*. London: Archibald Constable.

De Morgan, J. 1894. *Catalogue des monuments et inscriptions de l'Égypte antique. Première série. Haute Égypte, tome premièr: De la frontière de Nubie à Kom Ombo*. Vienna: Adolphe Holzhausen.

Description de l'Égypte: ou, recueil des observations et des recherches qui ont été faites en Égypte pendant l'expédition de l'armée française. 1809–26. 20 vols. Paris: Imprimerie Impériale.

Diego Espinel, A. 2011. *Abriendo los caminos de Punt: Contactos entre Egipto y el ámbito afroárabe durante la Edad del Bronce (ca. 3000 a.C.–1065 a.C.)*. Barcelona: Bellaterra.

Dietze, K. 2020. "Das Korpus der Mauerstelen Thutmosis' III. und die innere Umfassungsmauer im Tempel von Heliopolis." In *Heliopolis: Kultzentrum unter Kairo*, edited by A. Ashmawy, K. Dietze, and D. Raue, 37–56. Heidelberg: Propylaeum.

Di Lenardo, A. 2016. *Israeliti & Hyksos: ipotesi sul II Periodo Intermedio d'Egitto e la sua cronologia*. Patti: Kimerik.

Dillery, J. 1999. "The First Egyptian Narrative History: Manetho and Greek Historiography." *Zeitschrift für Papyrologie und Epigraphik* 127: 93–116.

Dodson, A. 1989. "Hatshepsut and 'Her Father' Mentuhotpe II." *JEA* 75: 224–26.

———. 1994. *The Canopic Equipment of the Kings of Egypt*. London: Kegan Paul International.

———. 1998. "A Funerary Mask in Durham and Mummy Adornment in the Late Second Intermediate Period and Early Eighteenth Dynasty." *JEA* 84: 93–99.

———. 2000. "The Intact Pyramid Burial at Hawara of 12th Dynasty Princess Neferuptah." *Kmt* 11/4: 40–47.

———. 2003. "The Burial of Members of the Royal Family during the Eighteenth Dynasty." In *Egyptology at the Dawn of the Twenty-first Century: Proceedings of the Eighth International Congress of Egyptologists, Cairo, 2000*, edited by Z. Hawass and L. Pinch Brock, 2:187–93. Cairo: American University in Cairo Press.

———. 2006. Review of Vandersleyen 2005. *Biblioteca Orientalis* 63/5–6: 516–19.

———. 2009. "The Prophet of Amun Iuput and His Distinguished Ancestors." *JEA* 95: 51–66.

———. 2010. "The Burials of Ahmose I." In *Thebes and Beyond: Studies in Honour of Kent R. Weeks*, edited by Z. Hawass and S. Ikram, 25–33. Cairo: Conseil Suprême des Antiquités.

———. 2013. "On the Burials and Reburials of Ahmose I and Amenhotep I." *GM* 238: 19–24.

———. 2014a. *Amarna Sunrise: Egypt from Golden Age to Age of Heresy*. Cairo: American University in Cairo Press.

———. 2014b. "The Coregency Conundrum." *Kmt* 25/2: 28–35.

———. 2016. *Poisoned Legacy: The Fall of the Nineteenth Egyptian Dynasty*. 2nd ed. Cairo: American University in Cairo Press.

———. 2019a. *Afterglow of Empire: Egypt from the Fall of the New Kingdom to the Saite Renaissance*. 2nd ed. Cairo: American University in Cairo Press.

———. 2019b. *Sethy I, King of Egypt: His Life and Afterlife*. Cairo: American University in Cairo Press.

———. 2020. *Nefertiti, Queen and Pharaoh of Egypt: Her Life and Afterlife.* Cairo: American University in Cairo Press.

———. 2021. *The First Pharaohs: Their Lives and Afterlives.* Cairo: American University in Cairo Press.

———. 2022a. *Tutankhamun, King of Egypt: His Life and Afterlife.* Cairo: American University in Cairo Press.

———. 2022b. "The Genesis of the New Kingdom Royal Necropoleis." In *The Star Who Appears in Thebes: Studies in Honour of Jiro Kondo*, edited by N. Kawai and B.G. Davies, 117–36. Wallasey: Abercromby Press.

———. 2023. *The Nubian Pharaohs of Egypt: Their Lives and Afterlives.* Cairo: American University in Cairo Press.

Dodson, A., and K. Griffin. 2024. "The Sarcophagus and Stone Coffin of Amenhotep-son-of-Hapu." In *From Objects to Histories: Studies in Honour of John H. Taylor*, edited by N. Strudwick and D.A. Aston. Wallasey: Abercromby Press.

Dolińska, M. 2010. "Temple of Tuthmosis III at Deir el-Bahari after 30 Years of Research." In *8. Ägyptologische Tempeltagung: Interconnections between Temples, Warschau, 22.–25. September 2008*, edited by M. Dolińska and H. Beinlich, 57–66. Wiesbaden: Harrassowitz.

———. 2012. "Temple of Tuthmosis III in Deir el-Bahari in 2008 and 2009: Work in the Stores and Field." *PAM* 21: 261–67.

———. 2014. "Temple of Tuthmosis III at Deir el-Bahari, Seasons 2010–2011." *PAM* 23: 211–20.

———. 2015. "Deir el-Bahari, Temple of Tuthmosis III: Campaigns 2012–2013." *PAM* 24: 257–64.

Dorman, P.F. 1988. *The Monuments of Senenmut: Problems in Historical Methodology*. London: Kegan Paul International.

———. 1991. *The Tombs of Senenmut*. New York: Metropolitan Museum of Art.

———. 1995. "Two Tombs and One Owner." In *Thebanische Beamtennekropolen: neue Perspektiven archäologischer Forschung. Internationales Symposion, Heidelberg, 9.–13.6.1993*, edited by J. Assmann, E. Dziobek, H. Guksch, and F. Kampp, 140–54. Heidelberg: Heidelberger Orientverlag.

———. 2005. "The Proscription of Hatshepsut." In *Hatshepsut: From Queen to Pharaoh*, edited by C.H. Roehrig, 267–69. New York: Metropolitan Museum of Art; New Haven, CT: Yale University Press.

Dreyer, G., M. Bommas, J. Budka, R. Duttenhöfer, C. Jeuthe, J. Jones, P. Kopp, H. Kroll, E. Laskowska-Kusztal, R. Pasternak, B. von Pilgrim, C. von Pilgrim, D. Raue, S. Schaten, S.J. Seidlmayer, and C. Ubertini. 2005. "Stadt und Tempel von Elephantine: 31./32. Grabungsbericht." *MDAIK* 61: 13–138.

Dreyer, G., H.W. Fischer-Elfert, C. Heitz, A. Klammt, My. Krutzsch, C. von Pilgrim, D. Raue, S. Schönenberger, and Ch. Ubertini. 2002. "Stadt und Tempel von Elephantine: 28./29./30. Grabungsbericht." *MDAIK* 58: 157–225.

Dümichen, J. 1868. *Die Flotte einer ägyptischen Königin aus dem XVII. Jahrhundert vor unserer Zeitrechnung und altägyptisches Militair im festlichen Aufzuge auf einem Monumente aus derselben Zeit abgebildet*. Leipzig: Hinrichs.

———. 1871. *Photographische Resultate einer auf Befehl Sr. Majestät des Kaisers von Deutschland, Königs von Preussen Wilhelm I. nach Aegypten entsendeten archäologischen Expedition*. Berlin: Christmann.

Dziobek, E. 1994. *Die Gräber des Vezirs User-Amun: Theben Nr. 61 und 131*. Mainz: Philipp von Zabern.

Eaton-Krauss, M. 1999. "The Fate of Sennefer and Senetnay at Karnak Temple and in the Valley of the Kings." *JEA* 85: 113–29.

———. 2012. "Who Commissioned KV 42 and for Whom?" *GM* 234: 53–60.

Edgerton, W.F. 1933. *The Thutmosid Succession*. Chicago: University of Chicago Press.

Elliott, C. 2022. *Needles from the Nile: Obelisks and the Past as Property*. Liverpool: Liverpool University Press.

Engelbach, R. 1923. *The Problem of the Obelisks: From a Study of the Unfinished Obelisk at Aswan*. London: T. Fisher Unwin; New York: George H. Doran.

Erman, A. 1891. "Rundschreiben Thutmosis' I. an die Behörden mit der Anzeige seines Regierungsantrittes." *ZÄS* 29: 116–19.

Fairman, H.W., and B. Grdseloff. 1947. "Texts of Hatshepsut and Sethos I inside Speos Artemidos." *JEA* 33: 12–33.

Fakhry, A. 1939. "A New Speos from the Reign of Hatshepsut and Thutmosis III at Beni-Hasan." *ASAE* 39: 709–23.

Fazzini, R.A. 2002. "Some Aspects of the Precinct of the Goddess Mut in the New Kingdom." In *Leaving No Stones Unturned:*

Essays on the Ancient Near East and Egypt in Honor of Donald P. Hansen, edited by E. Ehrenberg, 63–76. Winona Lake, IN: Eisenbrauns.

Fazzini, R.A., and B.M. Bryan. 2021. *The Precinct of Mut at South Karnak: An Archaeological Guide*. Cairo: American University in Cairo Press.

Fisher, M. 2015. "A Recently Discovered Fragment of Senenmut's Sarcophagus." *BES* 19: 263–76.

Frood, E. 2003. "Ritual Function and Priestly Narrative: The Stelae of the High Priest of Osiris, Nebwawy." *JEA* 89: 59–81.

Gabolde, L. 1987. "La chronologie du règne de Thoutmosis II, ses conséquences sur la datation des momies royales et leurs répercutions sur l'histoire du développement de la Vallée des Rois." *SAK* 14: 61–81.

———. 2009. *Monuments décorés en bas relief aux noms de Thoutmosis II et Hatchepsout à Karnak*. Cairo: Institut français d'archéologie orientale.

———. 2011–12. "Réexamen des jalons de la présence da le XVIIIe dynastie naissante à Saï." *Cahiers de Recherches de l'Institut de Papyrologie et d'Égyptologie de Lille* 29: 15–137.

———. 2012. "Le parvis et la porte du IVe pylône à Karnak: Considérations sur une chapelle des obélisques." In *"Parcourir l'éternité": Hommage à Jean Yoyotte*, edited by C. Zivie-Coche and I. Guermeur, 1:459–65. Turnhout: Brepols.

Galán Allue, J.M. 2008. "Notes on Egyptian Imperialism ca. 1480–1430 BC (Hatshepsut–Amenhotep II)." In *La guerra e i suoi riflessi nelle società antiche: atti del Convegno del dottorato di orientalistica, Università di Pisa, 2–27 giugno 2007*, edited by G. Miniaci and M. Russo, 13–24. Pisa: ETS.

———. 2017. "Ahmose(-Sapair) in Dra Abu el-Naga North." *JEA* 103: 179–201.

Gardiner, A.H. 1916. "The Defeat of the Hyksos by Kamōse: The Carnarvon Tablet, no. 1." *JEA* 3: 95–110.

———. 1946. "Davies's Copy of the Great Speos Artemidos Inscription." *JEA* 32: 43–56.

Gardiner, A.H., and T.E. Peet. 1917. *The Inscriptions of Sinai*. Vol. 1, *Introduction and Plates*. London: Egypt Exploration Fund.

———. 1955. *The Inscriptions of Sinai*. Vol. 2, *Translations and Commentary*. London: Egypt Exploration Society.

Gasse, A., and V. Rondot. 2007. *Les inscriptions de Séhel*. Cairo: Institut français d'archéologie orientale.

Gedge, P. 1977. *Child of the Morning: A Novel*. London: Raven Books.

Gessler-Löhr, B. 1995. "Bemerkungen zur Nekropole des Neuen Reiches von Saqqara vor der Amarna-Zeit, I: Gräber der Wesire von Unterägypten." In *Gedenkschrift für Winfried Barta:* ḥtp dj ḥzj, edited by D. Kessler and R. Schulz, 133–57. Frankfurt am Main: Lang.

Gitton, M. 1984. *Les divines épouses de la 18e dynastie*. Paris: Les Belles Lettres.

Godlewski, W. 1986. *Le monastère de St Phoibammon*. Warsaw: Éditions scientifiques de Pologne.

Goedicke, H. 2004. *The Speos Artemidos Inscription of Hatshepsut and Related Discussions*. Oakville, CT: HALGO.

Goedicke, C., and R. Krauss. 1999. "Der Denkstein Berlin ÄGM 15699—eine Ägyptologen-Fälschung." *Jahrbuch Preussischer Kulturbesitz* 35: 203–20.

Gray, T. 1920. *The Life of the King of the South & North Kamari'a, Daughter of the Sun, Hatshepsut: A Pageant of Court Life in Old Egypt in the Early 18th Dynasty, Reconstructed from the Monuments. A Chapter of Egyptian History in Dramatic Form*. Cambridge: W. Heffer & Sons.

Gundlach, R. 1998. *Der Pharao und sein Staat: die Grundlegung der ägyptischen Königsideologie im 4. und 3. Jahrtausend*. Darmstadt: Wissenschaftliche Buchgesellschaft.

Habachi, L. 1957. "Two Graffiti at Sehēl from the Reign of Queen Hatshepsut." *JNES* 16: 88–104.

———. 1972. *The Second Stela of Kamose and His Struggle against the Hyksos Ruler and His Capital*. Glückstadt: Augustin.

Haeny, G. 1997. "New Kingdom 'Mortuary Temples' and 'Mansions of Millions of Years.'" In *Temples of Ancient Egypt*, edited by B.E. Shafer, 86–126. Ithaca, NY: Cornell University Press.

Hall, H.R. 1913. *Ancient History of the Near East from the Earliest Times to the Battle of Salamis*. London: Methuen.

Harris, J.E., and E.F. Wente, eds. 1980. *An X-Ray Atlas of the Pharaohs*. Chicago: University of Chicago Press.

Harvey, S.P. 2003. "Interpreting Punt: Geographic, Cultural and Artistic Landscapes." In *Mysterious Lands*, edited by D. O'Connor and S. Quirke, 81–91. London: UCL Press.

———. In preparation. *Ahmose I, King of Egypt: His Life and Afterlife*. Cairo: American University in Cairo Press.

Hawass, Z. 2007. "The Scientific Search for Hatshepsut's Mummy." *Kmt* 18/3: 20–25.

Hawass, Z., and S.N. Saleem. 2016. *Scanning the Pharaohs: CT Imaging of the New Kingdom Royal Mummies*. Cairo: American University in Cairo Press.

Hayes, W.C. 1935. *Royal Sarcophagi of the XVIII Dynasty*. Princeton, NJ: Princeton University Press.

———. 1950. "The Sarcophagus of Sennemūt." *JEA* 36: 19–23.

———. 1953. *The Scepter of Egypt: A Background for the Study of the Egyptian Antiquities in the Metropolitan Museum of Art*. Vol. 1, *From the Earliest Times to the End of the Middle Kingdom*. New York: Metropolitan Museum of Art.

———. 1957. "Varia from the Time of Hatshepsut." *MDAIK* 15: 78–90.

———. 1959. *The Scepter of Egypt: A Background for the Study of the Egyptian Antiquities in the Metropolitan Museum of Art*. Vol. 2, *The Hyksos Period and the New Kingdom (1675–1080 BC)*. New York: Metropolitan Museum of Art.

Hincks, E. 1839. "On the Years and Cycles Used by the Ancient Egyptians." *Transactions of the Royal Irish Academy* 18, polite literature: 153–98.

———. 1846. "On the Defacement of Divine and Royal Names on Egyptian Monuments." *Transactions of the Royal Irish Academy* 21, polite literature: 105–13.

Hornung, E. 1975. "Das Grab Thutmosis' II." *RdE* 27: 125–31.

———. 1999. *The Ancient Egyptian Books of the Afterlife*. Translated by D. Lorton. Ithaca, NY: Cornell University Press.

———. 2006. "The New Kingdom." In *Ancient Egyptian Chronology*, edited by E. Hornung, R. Krauss, and D.A. Warburton, 197–217. Leiden: Brill.

Hornung, E., and E. Staehelin. 1974. *Studien zum Sedfest*. Geneva: Éditions de Belles-Lettres.

Ikram, S. 2017. "From Thebes to Cairo: The Journey, Study, and Display of Egypt's Royal Mummies, Past, Present and Future." In *Volume in onore di M. Capasso*, edited by P. Davoli, 867–83. Lecce: University of Lecce.

Ikram, S., and A. Dodson. 1998. *The Mummy in Ancient Egypt: Equipping the Dead for Eternity*. London: Thames and Hudson.

Irsay-Nagy, B.J. 2023. "The Burial of Thutmosis II: Questions." In *ICE XII: Proceedings of the Twelfth International Congress of Egyptologists, 3rd–8th November 2019, Cairo, Egypt*, edited by O. el-Aguizy and B. Kasparian, 1:173–82. Cairo: Institut français d'archéologie orientale.

Iversen, E. 1968–72. *Obelisks in Exile*. 2 vols. Copenhagen: G.E.C. Gad.

Iwaszczuk, J. 2016a. *Sacred Landscape of Thebes during the Reign of Hatshepsut: Royal*

Construction Projects. Vol. 1, *Topography of the West Bank*. Warsaw: Institute of Mediterranean and Oriental Cultures, Polish Academy of Sciences; Wiesbaden: Harrassowitz.

———. 2016b. *Sacred Landscape of Thebes during the Reign of Hatshepsut: Royal Construction Projects*. Vol. 2, *Topographical Bibliography of the West Bank*. Warsaw: Institute of Mediterranean and Oriental Cultures, Polish Academy of Sciences; Wiesbaden: Harrassowitz.

———. 2021a. *Sacred Landscape of Thebes during the Reign of Hatshepsut: Royal Construction Projects*. Vol. 3: *Topography of the East Bank*. Warsaw: Institute of Mediterranean and Oriental Cultures, Polish Academy of Sciences; Wiesbaden: Harrassowitz.

———. 2021b. *Sacred Landscape of Thebes during the Reign of Hatshepsut: Royal Construction Projects*. Vol. 4, *Topographical Bibliography of the East Bank*. Warsaw: Institute of Mediterranean and Oriental Cultures, Polish Academy of Sciences (IMOC PAS/IKŚiO PAN); Wiesbaden: Harrassowitz.

———. 2021c. "Battle Scenes from the Temple of Thutmose I in Qurna." *A&L* 31: 148–62.

James, P., and P.G. van der Veen, eds. 2015. *Solomon and Shishak: Current Perspectives from Archaeology, Epigraphy, History and Chronology—Proceedings of the Third BICANE Colloquium held at Sidney Sussex College, Cambridge 26–27 March, 2011*. Oxford: BAR Publishing.

James, T.G.H. 1997. "'The Very Best Artist.'" In *Chief of Seers: Egyptian Studies in Memory of Cyril Aldred*, edited by E. Goring, N. Reeves, and J. Ruffle, 164–74. London: Kegan Paul International.

Jenni, H., A. Dorn, and E. Paulin-Grothe. 2021. *Das Grab der Königin Tiaa im Tal der Könige (KV 32)*. Basel and Frankfurt am Main: Librum.

Johnson, W.R. 2018. "Fresh Evidence for an Akhenaten/Nefertiti Coregency: A Talatat Block from Hermopolis with a New Join." *Kmt* 29/1: 71–76.

Kaiser, W. 1993. "Hatchepsout à Eléphantine." *Les dossiers d'archéologie* 187: 102–109.

Kaiser, W., P. Becker, M. Bommas, F. Hoffmann, H. Jaritz, S. Müntel, J.-P. Pätznick, and M. Ziermann. 1995. "Stadt und Tempel von Elephantine: 21./22. Grabungsbericht." *MDAIK* 51: 99–187.

Kaiser, W., G. Dreyer, P. Grossmann, W. Mayer, and S. Seidlmayer. 1980. "Stadt und Tempel von Elephantine: achter Grabungsbericht." *MDAIK* 36: 245–91.

Karkowski, J. 2001. "Pharaoh in the Heb-Sed Robe in Hatshepsut's Temple at Deir el-Bahari." *É&T* 19: 81–112.

———. 2003. *The Temple of Hatshepsut: The Solar Complex*. Warsaw: Éditions Neriton.

———. 2015. "Le texte oraculaire." In *La chapelle Rouge d'Hatshepsout*, by F. Burgos and F. Larché, 2:153–54. Paris: Soleb.

———. 2016. "'A Temple Comes to Being': A Few Comments on the Temple Foundation Ritual." *E&T* 29: 111–23.

Karkowski, J., and J.K. Winnicki. 1983. "Amenhotep, Son of Hapu, and Imhotep at Deir el-Bahari: Some Reconsiderations." *MDAIK* 39: 93–105.

Keller, C.A. 2005. "Hatshepsut's Reputation of History." In *Hatshepsut: From Queen to Pharaoh*, edited by C.H. Roehrig, 294–97. New York: Metropolitan Museum of Art; New Haven, CT: Yale University Press.

Kitchen, K.A. 1968–90. *Ramesside Inscriptions: Historical and Biographical*. 8 vols. Oxford: Blackwell.

———. 1971. "Punt and How to Get There." *Orientalia* 40: 184–207.

———. 1993–2014. *Ramesside Inscriptions: Translated and Annotated. Translations*. 7 vols. Oxford: Blackwell.

Krauss, R. 1992. "Das Kalendarium des Papyrus Ebers und seine chronologische Verwertbarkeit." *Ä&L* 3: 75–96.

Laborde, L. de, and L.M.A. Linant de Bellefonds. 1830. *Voyage de l'Arabie Pétrée*. Paris: Giard.

Laboury, D. 1997. "A propos de l'authenticité de la momie attribuée à Thoutmosis III (CG 61068)." *GM* 156: 73–79.

———. 1998. *La statuaire de Thoutmosis III: essai d'interprétation d'un portrait royal dans son contexte historique*. Liège: C.I.P.L.

———. 2006. "Royal Portrait and Ideology: Evolution and Significance of the Statuary of Thutmose III." In *Thutmose III: A New Biography*, edited by E.H. Cline and D. O'Connor, 260–91. Ann Arbor: University of Michigan Press.

———. 2014. "How and Why Did Hatshepsut Invent the Image of Her Royal Power?" In *Creativity and Innovation in the Reign of Hatshepsut: Papers from the Theban Workshop 2010*, edited by J.M. Galán, B.M. Bryan, and P.F. Dorman, 49–91. Chicago: Oriental Institute.

Lacau, P. 1909. *Stèles du Nouvel Empire*. Cairo: Institut français d'archéologie orientale.

Landgráfová, R., and H. Navrátilová. 2009. *Sex and the Golden Goddess*. Vol. 1, *Ancient Egyptian Love Songs in Context*. Prague: [Czech Institute of Egyptology].

Larché, F. 2016. "Les constructions axiales thoutmosides devant le 4e pylône de Karnak." *JAEA* 1: 71–80.

———. 2020. *La restitution des constructions en calcaire aux trois noms de Thoutmosis II, Hatshepsout et Thoutmosis III à Karnak*. Paris: Editions Soleb.

Laskowska-Kusztal, E. 1984. *Le sanctuaire ptolémaïque de Deir el-Bahari*. Warsaw: Éditions scientifiques de Pologne.

Laskowski, P. 2001. "A Note on the Building Activity of Thutmosis III in Elkab." In *Proceedings of the First Central European Conference of Young Egyptologists: Egypt 1999: Perspectives of Research, Warsaw 7–9 June 1999*, edited by J. Popielska-Grzybowska, 81–84. Warsaw: Institute of Archaeology, Warsaw University.

———. 2006. "Monumental Architecture and the Royal Building Program of Thutmose III." In *Thutmose III: A New Biography*, edited by E.H. Cline and D. O'Connor, 183–259. Ann Arbor: University of Michigan Press.

———. 2009. "The Building Activity of Thutmose III in Abydos." In *Proceedings of the Third Central European Conference of Young Egyptologists: Egypt 2004: Perspectives of Research: Warsaw 12–14 May 2004*, edited by J. Popielska-Grzybowska, O. Białostocka, and J. Iwaszczuk, 119–22. Pułtusk: Pułtusk Academy of Humanities.

Leblanc, C. 2008. "Nehy, prince et premier rapporteur du roi: deux nouveaux documents relatifs au vice-roi de Nubie, sous le règne de Thoutmosis III." *Memnonia* 19: 103–12.

Lecuyot, G., and A.-M. Loyrette. 1995. "La chapelle de Ouadjmès: rapport préliminaire—I." *Memnonia* 6: 85–93.

———. 1996. "La chapelle de Ouadjmès: rapport préliminaire—II." *Memnonia* 7: 111–22.

Leprohon, R.J. 1991. *Stelae*. Vol. 2, *The New Kingdom to the Coptic Period*. Boston: Museum of Fine Arts.

Lepsius, C.R. 1842. *Auswahl der wichtigsten Urkunden des aegyptischen Alterthums: theils zum Erstenmale, theils nach den Denkmaelern berichtigt, herausgegeben und erlaeutert*. Leipzig: Georg Wigand.

———. 1849–59. *Denkmaeler aus Aegypten und Aethiopien*. 6 vols. Berlin and Leipzig: Nicolaische Buchhandlung.

———. 1853. *Letters from Egypt, Ethiopia, and the Peninsula of Sinai*. Translated by L. and Jo.B. Horner. London: Bohn.

Lewis, H.S. 1915. "The Authentic and Complete History of the Ancient and Mystical Order

Rosæ Crucis." *The American Rosæ Crucis* I/1: 3–13.

Lilyquist, C. 1988. "The Gold Bowl Naming General Djehuty: A Study of Objects and Early Egyptology." *MMJ* 23: 5–68.

———. 2003. *The Tomb of Three Foreign Wives of Tuthmosis III*. New Haven, CT: Yale University Press.

Lipińska, J. 1977. *The Temple of Tuthmosis III: Architecture*. Warsaw: PWN/Éditions Scientifiques de Pologne.

———. 2005. "The Temple of Thutmose III at Deir el-Bahri." In *Hatshepsut: From Queen to Pharaoh*, edited by C.H. Roehrig, 285–88. New York: Metropolitan Museum of Art; New Haven, CT: Yale University Press.

———. 2007. "Deir el-Bahari—Temple of Tuthmosis III." In *Seventy Years of Polish Archaeology in Egypt*, edited by E. Laskowska-Kusztal, 105–14. Warsaw: PCMA UW.

Lipińska, J., M. Dolińska, and J. Aksamit, eds. 1997. *Geheimnisvolle Königin Hatschepsut: Ägyptische Kunst des 15. Jahrhunderts v. Chr.* Warsaw: Nationalmuseum in Warschau.

Litherland, P. 2014. *The Western Wadis of the Theban Necropolis: A Re-examination of the Western Wadis of the Theban Necropolis by the Joint-mission of the Cambridge Expedition to the Valley of the Kings and the New Kingdom Research Foundation, 2013–2014*. London: New Kingdom Research Foundation.

———. 2018. *The Shaft Tombs of Wadi Bairiya*. Vol. 1, *Preliminary Report on the Clearance Work on the WB1 Site by the Joint-venture Mission of the New Kingdom Research Foundation with the Ministry of Antiquities*. n.p.: New Kingdom Research Foundation.

———. 2023. "Has the Tomb of Thutmose II Been Found?" *EgArch* 63: 28–31.

Loret, V. 1898. "Le tombeau de Thoutmès III à Biban el-Molouk." *BIÉ* 3rd ser. 9: 91–97.

Louant, E. 2000. *Comment Pouiemrê triompha de la mort: Analyse du programme iconographique de la tombe thébaine no. 39*. Leuven: Peeters.

Loyrette, A.-M. 1992. "Les monuments du prince Oudjmès." *Memnonia* 3: 131–40.

Malek, J. 1999. *Topographical Bibliography of Ancient Egyptian Hieroglyphic Texts, Statues, Reliefs and Paintings*. Vol. 8, *Objects of Provenance Not Known*. Part 1, *Royal Statues, Private Statues (Predynastic to Dynasty XVII)*. Oxford: Griffith Institute.

Manuelian, P. Der. 1987. *Studies in the Reign of Amenophis II*. Hildesheim: Gerstenberg Verlag.

———. 2006. "The End of the Reign and the Accession of Amenhotep II." In *Thutmose III: A New Biography*, edited by E.H. Cline and D. O'Connor, 416–22. Ann Arbor: University of Michigan Press.

Manuelian, P. Der, and C.E. Loeben. 1993. "New Light on the Recarved Sarcophagus of Hatshepsut and Thutmose I in the Museum of Fine Arts, Boston." *JEA* 79: 121–55.

Margetts, E.L. 1951. "The Masculine Character of Hatshepsut, Queen of Egypt." *Bulletin of the History of Medicine* 25: 559–62.

Mariette, A. 1877. *Deir el-Bahari: documents topographiques, historiques et ethnographiques, recueillis dans ce temple*. 2 vols. Leipzig: Hinrichs.

Martinez, P. 2007a. "Seti I and the Ghosts of What Had Been: A Reappraisal of Qurna Temple and Its History." *Kmt* 18/1: 36–46.

———. 2007b. "Par des portails anépigraphes: un réexamen des développements architecturaux du début de l'époque ramesside à Thèbes Ouest." *CdÉ* 83: 41–74.

Maspero, G. 1882. "Notes sur quelques points de grammaire et d'histoire." *ZÄS* 20: 120–35.

———. 1889. *Les momies royales de Déir el-Baharî*. Paris: Ernest Leroux.

———. 1892. "Notes au jour le jour–IV." *PSBA* 14: 170–204.

Matić, U. 2014. "'Minoans,' *kftjw* and the 'Islands in the Middle of *w3ḏ wr*': Beyond Ethnicity." *Ä&L* 24: 277–94.

———. 2016. "(De)queering Hatshepsut: Binary Bind in Archaeology of Egypt and Kingship the Corporeal." *Journal of Archaeological Method and Theory* 23: 810–31.

Meeks, D. 2003. "Locating Punt." In *Mysterious Lands*, edited by D. O'Connor and S. Quirke, 53–80. London: UCL Press.

Megahed, M., and H. Vymazalová. 2011. "Ancient Egyptian Royal Circumcision from the Pyramid Complex of Djedkare." *Anthropologie* 49: 155–64.

———. 2015. "The South-Saqqara Circumcision Scene: A Fragment of an Old Kingdom Birth-legend?" In *Royal versus Divine Authority: Acquisition, Legitimization and Renewal of Power, Prague, June 26–28, 2013. 7. Symposion zur ägyptischen Königsideologie/7th Symposium on Egyptian Royal Ideology*, edited by F. Coppens, J. Janák, and H. Vymazalová, 275–87. Wiesbaden: Harrassowitz.

Mensan, R. 2007. "Tuthmosid Foundation Deposits at Karnak." *EgArch* 30: 21–25.

Meyer, E. 1928. *Geschichte des Altertums*. Vol. 2, part 1, *Die Zeit der ägyptischen Großmacht*. 2nd ed. Stuttgart and Berlin: Cotta.

Millet, N.B. 1962. "A Fragment of the Hatshepsut Punt Relief." *JARCE* 1: 55–57.

Molleson, T., and M. Cox. 1993. *The Spitalfields Project*. Vol. 2, *The Anthropology: The Middling Sort*. York: Council for British Archaeology.

Mond, R., and O.H. Myers. 1940. *Temples of Armant: A Preliminary Survey*. 2 vols. London: Egypt Exploration Society.

Mosleth King, M. 2023. "Pauline Gedge's Hatshepsut: *Child of the Morning*." In *How Pharaohs Became Media Stars: Ancient Egypt and Popular Culture*, edited by A.I. Fernández Pichel, 61–72. Oxford: Archaeopress.

Murnane, W.J. 1977. *Ancient Egyptian Coregencies*. Chicago: Oriental Institute.

———. 1990. *The Road to Kadesh: A Historical Interpretation of the Battle Reliefs of King Sety I at Karnak*. 2nd ed. Chicago: Oriental Institute.

Naville, É. 1894. *The Temple of Deir el Bahari: Its Plan, Its Founders, and Its First Explorers. Introductory Memoir.* London: Egypt Exploration Fund.

———. 1895–1908. *The Temple of Deir el Bahari*. 6 vols. London: Egypt Exploration Fund.

———. 1896. "Transport of Obelisks: As Illustrated by a Bas-relief in the Temple of Deir el Bahari." *EEFAR* 1895–96: 6–13.

———. 1897. "La succession des Thoutmès d'après un mémoire récent." *ZÄS* 35: 30–67.

———. 1899. "Un dernier mot sur la succession des Thoutmès." *ZÄS* 37: 48–55.

Navrátilová, H., and R. Landgráfová, eds. 2015. *Sex and the Golden Goddess*. Vol. 2, *World of the Love Songs.* Prague: Faculty of Arts, Charles University.

Nelson, H.H. 1913. *The Battle of Megiddo*. Chicago: University of Chicago Libraries.

Nims, C. 1966. "The Date of the Dishonoring of Hatshepsut." *ZÄS* 93: 97–100.

Niwiński, A. 1988. *21st Dynasty Coffins from Thebes: Chronological and Typological Studies*. Mainz: Philipp von Zabern.

———. 2017. "The Mystery of the 'High Place' from the Abbott Papyrus Revealed? The Results of the Works of the Polish Cliff Mission at Deir el-Bahari 1999–2014." In *Proceedings of the XI International Congress of Egyptologists, Florence Egyptian Museum, Florence, 23–30 August 2015*, edited by G. Rosati and M.C. Guidotti, 457–61. Oxford: Archeopress.

Obsomer, C. 1995. *Sésostris Ier: étude chronologique et historique du règne*. Brussels: Connaissance de l'Egypte Ancienne.

O'Connor, D. 2008. "The Middle Colonnade at Deir el-Bahari: Compositional Integrity and 'Intertextuality' in Egyptian Art." In *Beyond the Horizon: Studies in Egyptian Art, Archaeology and History in Honour of Barry J. Kemp*, edited by S. Ikram and A. Dodson, 2:325–37. Cairo: Supreme Council of Antiquities.

Oppenheim, A. 2011. "The Early Life of Pharaoh: Divine Birth and Adolescence Scenes in the Causeway of Senwosret III at Dahshur." In *Abusir and Saqqara in the Year 2010*, edited by M. Bárta, F. Coppens, and J. Krejčí, 1:171–88. Prague: Czech Institute of Egyptology.

Pawlicki, F. 2007. "Princess Neferure in the Temple of Queen Hatshepsut at Deir el-Bahari: Failed Heiress to the Pharaoh's Throne?" *É&T* 21: 109–27.

———. 2017. *The Main Sanctuary of Amun-Re in the Temple of Hatshepsut at Deir el-Bahari*. Warsaw: Polish Center of Mediterranean Archaeology.

Peet, T.E. 1925. "The Legend of the Capture of Joppa and the Story of the Foredoomed Prince: Being a Translation of the Verso of Papyrus Harris 500." *JEA* 11: 225–29.

Petrie, W.M.F. 1896. *A History of Egypt during the XVIIth and XVIIIth Dynasties.* London: Methuen.

Piacentini, P., and C. Orsenigo, eds. 2004. *La Valle dei Re riscoperta: i giornali di scavo di Victor Loret, 1898–1899 e altri inediti*. Vetrine del sapere 1. Milan: Skira/Università degli Studi di Milano.

Piccione, P.A. 2003. "The Women of Thutmose III in the Stelae of the Egyptian Museum." *JSSEA* 30: 91–102.

Pierrat, G., M. Etienne, and S. Guichard. 1996. "Fouilles récentes du Musée du Louvre à Tôd." In *Atti VI Congresso internazionale di Egittologia*, 505–11. Turin.

Pierrat, G., M. Étienne, D. Leconte, C. Barbotin, J.-P. Adam, and S. Guichard. 1995. "Fouilles du musée du Louvre à Tôd 1988–1991." *Cahiers de Karnak* 10: 405–503.

Pignattari, S. 2018. *Amenemhat IV and the End of the Twelfth Dynasty: Between the End and the Beginning*. Oxford: BAR Publishing.

Pococke, R. 1743–45. *A Description of the East and Some Other Countries*. 3 vols. London: Bowyer.

Polz, D. 2007. *Der Beginn des Neuen Reiches: zur Vorgeschichte einer Zeitenwende*. Berlin: De Gruyter.

———. 2010. "New Archaeological Data from Dra' Abu el-Naga and Their Historical Implications." In *The Second Intermediate Period (Thirteenth–Seventeenth Dynasties): Current Research, Future Prospects*, edited by M. Marée, 343–53. Leuven: Peeters.

Polz, D., and A. Seiler. 2003. *Die Pyramidenanlage des Königs Nub-Cheper-Re Intef in Dra' Abu el-Naga: ein Vorbericht*. Mainz: Philipp von Zabern.

Porter, B., and R.B. Moss. 1934. *Topographical Bibliography of Ancient Egyptian Hieroglyphic Texts, Reliefs and Paintings*. Vol. 4, *Lower and Middle Egypt*. Oxford: Clarendon Press.

———. 1937. *Topographical Bibliography of Ancient Egyptian Hieroglyphic Texts, Reliefs and Paintings*. Vol. 5, *Upper Egypt: Sites*. Oxford: Clarendon Press.

———. 1939. *Topographical Bibliography of Ancient Egyptian Hieroglyphic Texts, Reliefs and Paintings*. Vol. 6, *Upper Egypt: Chief Temples (excl. Thebes)*. Oxford: Clarendon Press.

———. 1952. *Topographical Bibliography of Ancient Egyptian Hieroglyphic Texts, Reliefs and Paintings*. Vol. 7, *Nubia, Deserts, and Outside Egypt*. Oxford: Clarendon Press.

———. 1960–64. *Topographical Bibliography of Ancient Egyptian Hieroglyphic Texts, Reliefs and Paintings*. Vol. 1, *The Theban Necropolis*. 2nd ed. Oxford: Clarendon Press.

———. 1972. *Topographical Bibliography of Ancient Egyptian Hieroglyphic Texts, Reliefs and Paintings*. Vol. 2, *Theban Temples*. 2nd ed. Oxford: Clarendon Press.

———. 1974–81. *Topographical Bibliography of Ancient Egyptian Hieroglyphic Texts, Reliefs and Paintings*. Vol. 3, *Memphis*. 2nd ed. by J. Málek. Oxford: Clarendon Press/Griffith Institute.

Pouls Wegner, M.-A. 2001. "The Chapel of Thutmose III: New Kingdom Pilgrims and Patrons at Abydos." *Archaeology* 54/4: 58–59.

Preys, R. 2011. "Les tombes non-royales de la Vallée des Rois." *SAK* 40: 315–38.

Price, C. In preparation. *Senenmut: His Life and Afterlife*. Cairo: American University in Cairo Press.

Radwan, A. 1969. *Die Darstellungen des regierenden Königs und seiner Familienangehörigen in den Privatgräbern der 18. Dynastie*. Berlin: Hessling.

———. 1981. "Zwei Stelen aus dem 47. Jahre Thutmosis' III." *MDAIK* 37: 403–407.

Ratié, S. 1979. *La Reine Hatchepsout: sources et problèmes*. Leiden: Brill.

Redford, D.B. 1965. "The Coregency of Tuthmosis III and Amenophis II." *JEA* 51: 107–22.

———. 1967. *History and Chronology of the Eighteenth Dynasty of Egypt: Seven Studies*. Toronto: University of Toronto Press.

———. 1986. *Pharaonic King-Lists, Annals and Day-Books*. Mississauga: Benben Publications.

———. 2003. *The Wars in Syria and Palestine of Thutmose III*. Leiden: Brill.

———. 2006. "The Northern Wars of Thutmose III." In *Thutmose III: A New Biography*, edited by E.H. Cline and D. O'Connor, 325–43. Ann Arbor: University of Michigan Press.

Reeve, J., and M. Adams. 1993. *The Spitalfields Project*. Vol. 1, *The Archaeology: Across the Styx*. York: Council for British Archaeology.

Reeves, C.N. 1990. *Valley of the Kings: The Decline of a Royal Necropolis*. London: Kegan Paul International.

Roberts, I. 1976. *Hatshepsut, Queen of the Nile*. London: Robert Hale.

Robins, G. 1981. "The Value of the Estimated Ages of the Royal Mummies at Death as Historical Evidence." *GM* 45: 63–68.

———. 1999a. "The Names of Hatshepsut as King." *JEA* 85: 103–12.

———. 1999b. "An Unusual Statue of a Royal Mother-in-law and Grandmother." In *Studies on Ancient Egypt in Honour of H.S. Smith*, edited by A. Leahy and W.J. Tait, 255–59. London: Egypt Exploration Society.

Roehrig, C.H. 1995. "Gates to the Underworld: The Appearance of Wooden Doors in the Royal Tombs in the Valley of the Kings." In *Valley of the Sun Kings: New Explorations in the Tombs of the Pharaohs. Papers from the University of Arizona International Conference on the Valley of the Kings*, edited by R.H. Wilkinson, 82–107. Tucson: University of Arizona Egyptian Expedition.

———. 2002. "The Statue of the Royal Nurse Sitre with Her Nursling Maatkare Hatshepsut." In *Egyptian Museum Collections around the World*, edited by M. Eldamaty and M. Trad, 1003–10. Cairo: Supreme Council of Antiquities.

———, ed. 2005. *Hatshepsut: From Queen to Pharaoh*. New York: Metropolitan Museum of Art.

———. 2006. "The Building Activities of Thutmose III in the Valley of the Kings." In *Thutmose III: A New Biography*, edited by E.H. Cline and D. O'Connor, 238–59. Ann Arbor: University of Michigan Press.

———. 2007. "Chamber Ja in Royal Tombs in the Valley of the Kings." In *Sacred Space and Sacred Function in Ancient Thebes*, edited by P.F. Dorman and B.M. Bryan, 117–38. Chicago: Oriental Institute of the University of Chicago.

Roehrig, C.H., and P.F. Dorman. 1987. "Senimen and Senenmut: A Question of Brothers." *Varia Aegyptiaca* 3/2: 127–34.

Rohl, D.M. 1995. *A Test of Time*. Vol. 1, *The Bible: From Myth to History*. London: Century.

Romer, J. 1974. "Tuthmosis I and the Bibân El-Molûk: Some Problems of Attribution." *JEA* 60: 119–33.

———. 1975. "The Tomb of Tuthmosis III." *MDAIK* 31: 315–48.

Rose, J. 2000. *Tomb KV39 in the Valley of the Kings: A Double Archaeological Enigma*. Bristol: Western Academic and Specialist Press.

Rosellini, I. 1832–33. *I monumenti dell'Egitto e della Nubia: disegnati dalla Spedizione Scientifico-Letteraria Toscana in Egitto*. Vol. 1, *Monumenti Storici*. 2 vols. Pisa: Nicoló Capurro.

Rumelhard Le Borgne, G. 2018. "Hatchepsout devient roi (I): relecture du graffito 181 bis de Jacques de Morgan à Assouan." *Memnonia* 29: 153–66.

Ryan, D.P. 1989. "The Pacific Lutheran University Valley of the Kings Project: A Synopsis of the First (1989) Season." *NARCE* 146: 8–10.

———. 1990. "Field Report: Who Is Buried in KV60?" *Kmt* 1/1: 34–39, 58–59, 64.

———. 2010. "Pacific Lutheran University Valley of the Kings Project: Work Conducted during the 2007 Field Season." *ASAE* 84: 383–88.

Ryholt, K.S.B. 1997. *The Political Situation in Egypt during the Second Intermediate Period c. 1800–1550* BC. Copenhagen: Museum Tusculanum Press.

———. 2000. "The Late Old Kingdom in the Turin King-list and the Identity of Nitocris." *ZÄS* 127: 87–100.

Saleem, S.N., and Z. Hawass. 2021. "Computed Tomography Study of the Mummy of King Seqenenre Taa II: New Insights into His Violent Death." *Frontiers in Medicine* 8/637527. DOI: 10.3389/fmed.2021.637527.

Sankiewicz, M. 2015. "The Iconography of Co-rule at Deir el-Bahari: Hatshepsut and Tuthmosis III in the Statue Room of the Main Sanctuary of Amun." *PAM* 24/2: 161–68.

Schmidt, H.C. 2011. *Westcar on the Nile: A Journey through Egypt in the 1820s*. Wiesbaden: Reichert.

Scott, E. 2012. *Hatshepsut: Queen of Sheba*. New York: Algora Publishing.

Seco Álvarez, M. 2012. "Últimos descubrimientos en el proyecto de excavación, restauración y puesta en valor del templo funerario de Tutmosis III en la orilla oeste de Luxor." In *Novos trabalhos de Egiptologia Ibérica: IV Congresso Ibérico de Egiptologia*, edited by L.M. de Araújo and J. das Candeias Sales, 2:1065–75. Lisbon: Instituto Oriental e Centro de História da Facultade de Letras da Universidade de Lisboa.

———. 2017. "Complejo ramésida en el templo de millones de años de Tutmosis III." In *Actas V Congreso Ibérico de Egiptología: Cuenca 9–12 de marzo 2015*, edited by L. Burgos Bernal, A. Pérez Largacha, and Inmaculada Vivas Sainz, 999–1011. Cuenca: Ediciones de la Universidad Castilla-La Mancha.

Seco Àlvarez, M., and A. Radwan. 2010. "Egyptian–Spanish Project at the Temple of Thutmosis III in Luxor West Bank: Results of Two Seasons." In *Les temples de millions d'années et le pouvoir royal à Thèbes au Nouvel Empire: sciences et nouvelles technologies appliquées à l'archéologie*, edited by C. Leblanc and G. Zaki, 59–71. Cairo: Dar el-Kutub.

Seco Álvarez, M., et al. 2010. "First Season of the Egyptian–Spanish Project at the Funerary Temple of Thutmosis III in Luxor." *ASAE* 84: 27–61.

Sethe, K. 1896. *Die Thronwirren unter den Nachfolgern Königs Thutmosis' I., ihr Verlauf und ihre Bedeutung. Die Prinzenliste von Medinet Habu und die Reihenfolge der ersten Könige der zwanzigsten Dynastie*. Leipzig: Hinrichs.

———. 1906–1909. *Urkunden der 18. Dynastie*. 4 vols. Urkunden des Ägyptischen. Leipzig: Hinrichs.

———. 1932. *Das Hatschepsut-Problem: noch einmal untersucht*. Berlin: Verlag der Akademie der Wissenschaften.

Sharpe S. 1876. *The History of Egypt from the Earliest Times till the Conquest by the Arabs A.D. 640*. 6th ed. London: George Bell.

Shaw, G.J. 2009. "The Death of King Seqenenre Tao." *JEA* 45: 159–76.

Sheikholeslami, C.M. 2003. "The Burials of Priests of Montu at Deir el-Bahari in the Theban Necropolis." In *The Theban Necropolis: Past, Present and Future*, edited by N. Strudwick and J.H. Taylor, 131–37. London: British Museum Press.

Shirley, J.J. 2014. "The Power of the Elite: The Officials of Hatshepsut's Regency and Coregency." In *Creativity and Innovation in the Reign of Hatshepsut: Papers from the Theban Workshop 2010*, edited by J.M. Galán, B.M. Bryan, and P.F. Dorman, 173–245. Chicago: Oriental Institute.

Smilgin, A. 2009. "Sandstone Sphinxes of Queen Hatshepsut from Deir el-Bahari: Preliminary Remarks." *PAM* 21: 255–60.

Smith, G.E. 1912. *The Royal Mummies*. Cairo: Institut français d'archéologie orientale.

Smith, R.S. 2020. *Two Sons from Egypt: The Story of Thutmose III and Moses*. n.p.: URLink Print & Media.

Spalinger, A.J. 2006. "Covetous Eyes South: The Background to Egypt's Dominion over Nubia by the Reign of Thutmose III." In *Thutmose III: A New Biography*, edited by E.H. Cline and D. O'Connor, 344–69. Ann Arbor: University of Michigan Press.

———. 2021. *The Books behind the Masks: Sources of Warfare Leadership in Ancient Egypt*. Leiden: Brill.

Staring, N. 2023. *The Saqqara Necropolis through the New Kingdom: Biography of an Ancient Egyptian Landscape*. Leiden: Brill.

Stupko-Lubczyńska, A. 2016. *Offering Scenes in the Chapel of Hatshepsut: Diachronic Development of Their Composition and Content*. Warsaw: IKŚiO PAN.

Szafrański, Z.E. 2007. "King (?) Neferure, Daughter of Kings Tuthmosis II and Hatshepsut." *E&T* 21: 139–50.

Tateka, F. 2017. "Military Expeditions of King Hatshepsut." In *Current Research in Egyptology 2016: Proceedings of the Seventeenth Annual Symposium: Jagiellonian University, Kraków 2016*, edited by J. Chyla, K. Rosińska-Balik, J. Debowska-Ludwin, and C. Walsh, 90–106. Oxford: Oxbow Books.

———. 2019a. "The Co-regency of Thutmose III and Amenhotep II Revisited." *JEA* 105: 43–57.

———. 2019b. "Hatshepsut's Punt Reliefs: Their Structure and Function." *JARCE* 55: 189–203.

———. 2019c. "The Secretary Bird of Deir el-Bahari: One More Piece to the Puzzle of the Location of the Land of Punt." *RdE* 69: 231–50.

———. 2022a. "'I Have to Put It on My Wall!': The Function of 'Historical' Reliefs in the Temple of Hatshepsut at Deir el-Bahari." In *Of Gods and Men: Research on the Egyptian Temple from the New Kingdom to the Graeco-Roman Period*, edited by A.I. Fernández Pichel, 35–79. Alcalá de Henares: Universidad de Alcalá.

———. 2022b. "An Intriguing Inscription from Hatshepsut's Punt Portico Mentioning a Royal Elephant Hunt." *Ä&L* 32: 373–91.

Thiers, C. 2020. *La chapelle-reposoir de barque de Philippe Arrhidée à Karnak*. Vol. 1, *Relevé épigraphique*. Cairo: Institut français d'archéologie orientale.

Thiers, C., and P. Zignani. 2013. "Le domaine du temple de Ptah à Karnak: premières données de terrain." *Cahiers de Karnak* 14: 493–513.

Thimes, J.L. 2008. "A Dental Observation." *Kmt* 19/3: 6–8.

Thomas, E. 1966. *The Royal Necropoleis of Thebes*. Vol. 1, *The Major Cemeteries*. Princeton, NJ: Privately printed.

Ullmann, M. 2002. *Die Häuser der Millionen von Jahren: eine Untersuchung zu Königskult und Tempeltypologie in Ägypten*. Wiesbaden: Harrassowitz.

Uphill, E.P. 1961. "A Joint *Sed*-festival of Thutmose III and Queen Hatshepsut." *JNES* 20: 248–51.

Valbelle, D. 2006. "Hatchepsout en Nubie." *BSFE* 167: 33-50.

———. 2014. "The Part of Hatshepsut in Some Architectural Programs of the Early Eighteenth Dynasty." In *Creativity and Innovation in the Reign of Hatshepsut: Papers from the Theban Workshop 2010*, edited by J.M. Galán, B.M. Bryan, and P.F. Dorman, 437–41. Chicago: Oriental Institute.

Valbelle, D., and C. Bonnet. 1996. *Le sanctuaire d'Hathor, maîtresse de la turquoise*. Paris: Picard.

Vandersleyen, C. 1995. *L'Égypte et la vallée du Nil*. Vol. 2, *De la fin de l'Ancien Empire à la fin du Nouvel Empire*. Paris: Presses Universitaires de France.

———. 2005. *Iahmès Sapaïr: fils de Séqénenré Djéhouty-Aa (17e dynastie et la statue du Musée du Louvre E 15682)*. Brussels: Editions Safran.

———. 2016. *L'Égypte au temps de Moïse: l'invasion des étrangers nomades: Keftiou, Hébreux, Philistins, etc.; l'Exode: le retour en scène des pharaons égyptiens*. Paris: L'Harmattan.

Van Siclen, C.C. 1980. "The Temple of Meniset at Thebes." *Serapis* 6: 183–207.

———. 1989. "New Data on the Date of the Defacement of Hatshepsut's Name and Image on the Chapelle Rouge." *GM* 107: 85–86.

———. 1995. "Queen Meryetre-Hatshepsut and the Edifice of Amenhotep II at Karnak." In *Seventh International Congress of Egyptologists, Cambridge, 3–9 September 1995. Abstracts of Papers*, edited by C.J. Eyre, 167–68. Oxford: Oxbow.

———. 1999. "New Kingdom Temples at Elkab." In *Gold of Praise: Studies on Ancient Egypt in Honor of Edward F. Wente*, edited by E. Teeter and J.A. Larson, 415–17. Chicago: Oriental Institute of the University of Chicago.

———. 2010. "The Third Stela of Kamose." In *The Second Intermediate Period (Thirteenth–Seventeenth Dynasties): Current Research, Future Prospects*, edited by M. Marée, 355–58. Leuven: Peeters.

Velikovsky, I. 1952. *Ages in Chaos*. Garden City, NY: Doubleday.

Vercoutter, J. 1952. "Tôd (1946–1949). Rapport succinct des fouilles." *BIFAO* 50: 69–87.

Virey, P. 1891. *Sept tombeaux thébains de la XVIIIe dynastie*. Paris: Ernest Leroux.

Wachsmann, S. 1987. *Aegeans in the Theban Tombs*. Leuven: Peeters.

Waddell, W.G. 1940. *Manetho*. Cambridge, MA: Harvard University Press; London: William Heinemann.

Wallet-Lebrun, C. 1982. "Notes sur le temple d'Amon-Rê à Karnak (I): L'emplacement insolite des obélisques d'Hatshepsout." *BIFAO* 82: 355–62.

———. 1994. "Contribution à l'étude de l'histoire de la construction à Karnak: la substitution du grès au calcaire comme matériau de construction dans le temple d'Amon-Rê." In *L'égyptologie et les Champollion: recueil d'études publié par Michel Dewachter et Alain Fouchard à l'occasion du Colloque international célébrant le bicentenaire de la naissance de Jean-François Champollion "De l'Égypte des Pharaons à celle de 1990, Hommage de Grenoble aux frères Champollion" (Université Pierre Mendès-France, Grenoble 2, 29 novembre–1er décembre 1990)*, edited by M. Dewachter and A. Fouchard, 223–56. Grenoble: Presses Universitaires de Grenoble.

Weeks, K.R., ed. 2001. *The Treasures of the Valley of the Kings: Tombs and Temples of the Theban West Bank in Luxor*. Cairo: American University in Cairo Press.

Weigall, A.E.P. 1906. "A Report on the

Excavation of the Funeral Temple of Thoutmosis III at Gurneh." *ASAE* 7: 121–41.

Wente, E.F., and J.E. Harris. 1992. "Royal Mummies of the Eighteenth Dynasty: A Biologic and Egyptological Approach." In *After Tut'ankhamūn: Research and Excavation in the Royal Necropolis at Thebes*, edited by C.N. Reeves, 2–20. London: Kegan Paul International.

Wente, E.F., and C.C. Van Siclen III. 1976. "A Chronology of the New Kingdom." In *Studies in Honor of George R. Hughes: January 12, 1977*, edited by J.H. Johnson and E.F. Wente, 217–61. Chicago: Oriental Institute.

Wilkinson, J.G. 1828. *Materia hieroglyphica: containing the Egyptian pantheon, and the succession of the pharaohs, from the earliest times to the conquest by Alexander, and other hieroglyphical subjects; with plates, and notes explanatory of the same.* Malta: Government Press.

———. 1830a. *Extracts from Several Hieroglyphical Subjects, found at Thebes and other parts of Egypt, with remarks on the same.* Malta: Government Press.

———. 1830b. *Topographical Survey of Thebes, Tapa, Thabe, or Diasopolis Magna*. London: [Royal Geographical Society].

———. 1835. *Topography of Thebes and General View of Egypt: being a short account of the principal objects worthy of notice in the valley of the Nile, to the second cataract and Wadee Samneh, with the Fyoom, oases, and eastern desert, from Sooez to Berenice; with remarks on the manners and customs of the ancient Egyptians and the productions of the country, &c, &c.* London: John Murray.

———. 1837. *Manners and Customs of the Ancient Egyptians*. 3 vols. London: John Murray.

Williams, J.S. 2012. *Moses and Hatshepsut*. n.p.: CreateSpace Independent Publishing Platform.

Williamson, J. 2022. "Power, Piety, and Gender in Context: Hatshepsut and Nefertiti." In *Women in Ancient Egypt: Revisiting Power, Agency, and Autonomy*, edited by M.F. Ayad, 121–45. Cairo: American University in Cairo Press.

Wilson, J.A. 1951. *The Burden of Egypt: An Interpretation of Ancient Egyptian Culture*. Chicago: University of Chicago Press.

Winlock, H.E. 1924. "The Tombs of the Kings of the Seventeenth Dynasty at Thebes." *JEA* 10: 217–77.

———. 1928. "The Egyptian Expedition 1925–1927: The Museum's Excavations at Thebes." *BMMA* 23/2: 3–58.

———. 1932. "The Egyptian Expedition 1930–1931: The Museum's Excavations at Thebes." *BMMA* 27/2: 4–37.

———. 1942. *Excavations at Deir el Baḥri 1911–1931*. New York: Macmillan.

Winnermann, J. 2023. "Divine Kingship and the Royal Ka." In *Ancient Egyptian Society: Challenging Assumptions, Exploring Approaches*, edited by D. Candelora, N. Ben-Marzouk, and K.M. Cooney, 40–48. London and New York: Routledge.

Wong, Jun Yi. 2023. "Reading the Erasures at Hatshepsut's Temple." *EgArch* 63: 9–13.

Zangani, F. 2022. "Was There Ever an Egyptian Empire in the Northern Levant? Debunking the Egyptological Myth of Dynasty 18." *JEgH* 15: 43–82.

Zivie, A.-P. 1984. "Un chancelier nommé Nehesy." *Mélanges Adolphe Gutbub*, 245–52. Montpellier: Université de Montpellier.

———. 2007. *The Lost Tombs of Saqqara*. n.p.: Ankhtawy.

Sources of Images

All images by author unless otherwise stated.

1.	Top right: Dyan Hilton; bottom: Emile Brugsch
5.	Howard Carter (EES)
6.	Naville 1895–1908: pl. cxlv
9.	Inset: Louvre Museum
10.	Winlock 1932: fig. 6
11.	Davis 2017: figs. 2, 5
12.	Dyan Hilton
13.	Oriental Museum, University of Durham
16.	Top: †Martin Davies; bottom: Caminos 1998a: pl. 38–40, 42
19.	De Morgan 1894: 41[181bis]
20.	Bottom: Dyan Hilton
22.	Naville 1895–1908: pl. xlvi–liv
23.	Naville 1895–1908: pl. lvi
24.	Author, with element from Champollion 1845: pl. cxcii[3]
25.	Gardiner and Peet 1917: pl. lviii[179]
26.	Lacau 1909: pl. ix
27.	Louvre E27135
28.	Left: Gardiner and Peet 1917: pl. 56[177]
30.	Upper: †Stephanie Roberts; lower: Naville 1895–1908: pl. cliv.
31.	Bottom: Dziobek 1994: pl. 9.
33.	Top: Naville 1895–1908: pl. lxix–lxxvi
34.	Naville 1895–1908: pl. lxxxv–vi
35.	Top: Habachi 1957: fig. 6
37.	Hayes 1957: pl. xi.

38. Lesley Hammam
39. Bottom: Nina Davies (MMA)
40. Bottom left: MMA; bottom right: Charles Wilkinson (MMA)
43. Dyan Hilton
47. Bottom left: Lesley Hammam
49. Bottom left: Gary Parks; bottom right: Dylan Bickerstaffe
51. Lepsius 1849–59: III, pl. 28[1a-b].
53. Top: Dyan Hilton
55. Right: Trustees of the British Museum
56. Lepsius 1849–59: vol. 3, pl. 38
57. Top: Radwan 1969: pl. viii[1]/Virey 1891: 368, fig. 4; middle: N. de G. Davies 1935: fig. 7
59. Salima Ikram
60. Dyan Hilton
64. Top right: adapted from Nelson 1913: map 1; bottom: Avram Graicer via Wikipedia
65. Bottom: †Martin Davies
66. Gardiner and Peet 1917: pl. lxiv[196, 198].
70. Bottom: Bill Petty
71. Top: Lesley Hammam
72. Bottom: adapted from Lepsius 1842: pl. i.
73. Bottom left: Lynne Cole
80. Top: †Martin Davies; upper middle: Institute for the Study of Ancient Cultures, Chicago; lower middle and bottom: Museo Egizio, Turin
81. Middle and bottom: Patricia Mason; inset: Lepsius 1849–59: vol. 3, pl. 59d
82. Left: MFA; right: Dyan Hilton
87. Adapted from Theban Mapping Project
88. Left: Salima Ikram; right: adapted from Carter 1917: pl. xx
89. Top: adapted from Carter 1917: pl. xxi
90. Adapted from Theban Mapping Project
91. Bottom: adapted from Theban Mapping Project; inset: Davis 1906: pl. ix
92. Bottom: †Martin Davies
94. Top: Theban Mapping Project
95d. Theban Foundation
97. Top: Lesley Hammam
98. Top: Lesley Hammam
100a. Maciej Jawornicki, courtesy Polish Centre for Mediterranean Archaeology, University of Warsaw
100b. Naville 1895–1908: pl. cviii–cx
100c. Naville 1895–1908: pl. cxv
102. Bottom left: Dyan Hilton
103. Naville 1896: frontispiece + 1895–1908: pl. cliii–clvi.
106. Theban Mapping Project
107. Top: Theban Mapping Project; bottom: Dyan Hilton
108a. †Martin Davies

108b–e. Theban Mapping Project
109. UCLA Coffins Project, © Egyptian Museum Cairo
110. Theban Mapping Project
113. Top: UCLA Coffins Project, © Egyptian Museum Cairo; bottom right: Maspero 1889: pl. xxiv
114. †Martin Davies
117. Trustees of the British Museum
119. Top left: Pococke 1743: pl. xxxv bottom left; bottom: *Description de l'Égypte, Ant.* 2: pl. 38–39
120. Wilkinson 1830b
121. Top: Lepsius 1842: pl. ii; bottom: Champollion 1845: pl. 149–50
122. Trustees of the British Museum
123. Top: Laborde and Linant 1830: pl. [viii]; bottom: Peet and Gardiner 1917: pl. xiv[44]
124. Antonio Béato
125. John Beasly Greene (1832–56), via J. Paul Getty Museum
126a,b,c. Lepsius 1849–59: vol. 3, pl. 25
127b. E. Brugsch and Maspero 1881: pl. 22
127c. E. Brugsch and Maspero 1881: pl. 23
127d. †Martin Davies
128. Top: Naville 1894: frontispiece; inset: Dūmichen 1871: vol. 2, pl. 17; bottom: EES
129. Left: EES
130. Loret 1898: pl. 2
136. Left: Dyan Hilton collection; center and right: Brunton 1925
135. Felix Bonfils

INDEX

Kings of Egypt are given in CAPITALS.
Alphanumerics in parentheses are those of an individual's tomb.